OUR HOUSE

Nature, Culture and Literature
02

General Editors:

Hubert van den Berg (University of Groningen)
Axel Goodbody (University of Bath)
Marcel Wissenburg (University of Nijmegen)

Advisory Board:

Jonathan Bate (University of Warwick)
Hartmut Böhme (Humboldt University, Berlin)
Heinrich Detering (University of Kiel)
Andrew Dobson (Open University)
Marius de Geus (Leiden University)
Terry Gifford (University of Leeds)
Demetri Kantarelis (Assumption College, Worcester MA)
Richard Kerridge (Bath Spa University College)
Michiel Korthals (Wageningen University)
Svend Erik Larsen (University of Aarhus)
Patrick Murphy (University of Central Florida)
Kate Rigby (Monash University)
Avner de-Shalit (Hebrew University Jerusalem)
Piers Stephens (University of Liverpool)
Nina Witoszek (University of Oslo)

Our House

The Representation of Domestic Space in Modern Culture

Edited by

Gerry Smyth and Jo Croft

Amsterdam - New York, NY 2006

Drawings by Rosa Barnard and Esther Smyth

Cover Design: Erick de Jong

The paper on which this book is printed meets the requirements of "ISO 9706:1994, Information and documentation - Paper for documents - Requirements for permanence".

ISBN-10: 90-420-1969-7
ISBN-13: 978-90-420-1969-0
©Editions Rodopi B.V., Amsterdam - New York, NY 2006
Printed in the Netherlands

CONTENTS

6

ACKNOWLEDGEMENTS

We would like to thank all the contributors for being so patient waiting for this volume to be produced. Our thanks also go to all the people who offered help and advice throughout this project: Nancy Duncan, Axel Goodbody, Wendy Hyde, Richard Kerridge, Nickianne Moody, Helen Rogers, Marieke Schilling, David Sorfa, Mike Storry, Ric Tyson, Roger Webster, and the members of the Department of English Literature and Cultural History at Liverpool John Moores University. Our thanks to Joe Moran and to Jeff Adams for help with the technical aspects of the MS. Finally, we thank all the friends, family and colleagues with whom we shared ideas about the representation of domestic space.

We dedicate this book to our families.

Jo Croft and Gerry Smyth

CONTRIBUTORS

Jeff Adams is a lecturer in Education in the Department of Educational Studies at Goldsmiths College, University of London. His research interests include documentary comics and graphic novels, contemporary art in education, web-based learning and the professional development of art teachers.

Shane Alcobia-Murphy is a lecturer at the School of Language and Literature at the University of Aberdeen. His main research interests lie in twentieth-century Irish writing and visual arts. He has published articles on Seamus Heaney, Brian Friel, Willie Doherty, Paul Muldoon and Medbh McGuckian. Two monographs - *Sympathetic Ink: Intertextual Relations in Northern Irish Poetry* (Liverpool University Press) and *Governing the Tongue: Essays on Northern Irish Culture* (Cambridge Scholars Press) - are forthcoming.

Joseph Boughey has been a Senior Lecturer in the School of the Built Environment at Liverpool John Moores University since 1990. His research interests include the history of British inland waterways history, the politics of landscape and heritage, environmental valuation and, increasingly, the relations between grief, loss and environments. He has been a widower since March 2002.

Scott Brewster is Lecturer in Twentieth-Century Literature and Culture at the University of Salford. He co-edited *Ireland in Proximity: History, Gender, Space* (1999) and *Inhuman Reflections: Thinking the Limits of the Human* (2000). He has written essays on Irish poetry and fiction, the Gothic, deconstruction and psychoanalysis. He is currently writing *Lyric* for the Routledge *Critical Idiom* series.

Peter Childs is Professor of Modern English Literature at the University of Gloucestershire. He has written extensively on twentieth-century fiction and has recently published a book on contemporary fiction with Palgrave.

Jo Croft is Senior Lecturer in English at Liverpool John Moores University. Her research interests include adolescence, children's literature and psychoanalysis.

Mari Hughes-Edwards is Senior Lecturer in English Literature at Edge Hill University College. Recent publications include an edited collection of essays on medieval women religious entitled *Anchorites, Wombs and Tombs* (University of Wales Press, 2005), articles on sexuality and space in the poetry of Lee Harwood, and also on medieval asceticism and the medieval body in pain. She is about to submit an extensive monograph on medieval anchoritism for publication in 2006 / 07.

Ruth McElroy is Senior Lecturer in Media and Cultural Studies at Liverpool John Moores University. Her research centres upon the imaginative purchase of home upon producers and consumers of literary and visual texts. She is currently working on a cultural history of DIY, as well as a comparative analysis of lifestyle television across Britain, Wales and the USA. She is the author of several journal articles and in August 2002, guest edited a special issue of the *European Journal of Cultural Studies*, entitled *Sexing the Nation: The Spaces of Belonging(s)*.

Joe Moran is Reader in Cultural History at Liverpool John Moores University. He is the author of *Star Authors: Literary Celebrity in America* (2000) and *Interdisciplinarity* (2002). He is currently writing a book for Routledge entitled *Reading the Everyday*. He lives in a redbrick, by-law terraced house, built in 1902.

Ron Moy is Senior Lecturer in Popular Music Studies at Liverpool John Moores University. His research interests include popular music genres and sonic architecture in the domestic environment.

Karen Sayer is Senior Lecturer in History at Leeds, Trinity and All Saints. She has published extensively on constructions of rurality as linked to gender. Her second monograph, *Country Cottages: A Cultural History*, was published in 2000 with Manchester University Press.

Gerry Smyth is Reader in Cultural History at Liverpool John Moores University. He has published widely on different aspects of Irish cultural history. His books include *The Novel and the Nation: Studies in the New Irish Fiction* (1997) and *Space and the Irish Cultural Imagination* (2002), and *Noisy Island: A Short History of Irish Popular Music* (2005).

Introduction:
Culture and Domestic Space

Gerry Smyth and Jo Croft

I

In one of those coincidences with which we are all familiar (but which no one – and certainly no 'professional' academic – likes to speak about too much), the editors of this book happened to move house within a two-week period of each other around about the end of April 2004. One consequence of this was that matters which had exercised them at an abstract theoretical level during the early stages of the editorial process for this book now began to impact upon their 'real' lives. Academic analysis of the 'meaning' of domestic space suddenly became a little ... well, academic, as the various physical, emotional and administrative ordeals which are part and parcel of moving house in contemporary Britain came (so to speak) home to roost with a vengeance.

What were the chances of two people moving house during a period in which they were editing a book about houses? Pretty good, it seems. In Britain, we live and breathe houses: we talk about them all the time; we watch television programmes about them; we read magazines about them; we spend large amounts of money buying and doing them up; some of us even self-consciously try to ignore them, thereby confirming the absolute centrality of the house to the culture at large. Once you start looking – as we did when we began thinking seriously about the scope of this collection – images of the house appear everywhere, bearing upon contemporary life in a great variety of ways.

For scholars working in the general area of the humanities, writing about the meaning of domestic space is not the same as writing about the development of the novel, or the evolution of classic cinematic narrative, or the emergence of a modernist avant-garde in the fine arts.

These issues touch our lives (and the lives of our intended readers – students, colleagues, or whomever) at various points; we like them, we're interested in them, we can become 'experts' to a greater or lesser degree with regard to their histories and their characteristics. No matter the extent to which they bear upon our lives, however, such issues are generally removed from our day-to-day experience of the world. The relationship between Cathy and Heathcliff can tell us a good deal about gender discourses in the mid-nineteenth century, and it would be an interesting and useful exercise to track the progress of such discourses into the present. Some might even like to consider their own relationships in the light of these fictional characters (although we would not recommend this).

The house, though, is something else again. Everyone in our reading constituency will have had experience of 'the house' – the latter being a handy catch-all term for any constructed place of dwelling in which people conduct the multitude of activities encompassed by the verb 'to live'. We may or may not wish to die for love; none of us may feel as centred or as capable as a Hollywood hero; some may even wish to stop making sense in conventional bourgeois terms. All of us, however, know what it is to step over a threshold separating 'outside' from 'inside'; most of us will be aware that 'stuff' – paint, furniture and ornaments, for example – can change the atmosphere of a house in certain ways; many will have felt conflicting emotions in relation to the building or buildings in which they grew up. Put simply, the house is an absolutely fundamental part of our lives.

The current British vogue for all things to do with the house should be placed in the context of post-war changes in the meaning and function of domestic space within society at large (Langhamer 2005). Whilst acknowledging this, however, it behoves us to recognize that there is something primordial about the house – something elemental hovering just below surface concerns with changing usage patterns and gender roles and socio-economic factors. Houses function as a particular form of 'the built environment' – a form that has existed since the first hominid lashed two ferns together with a third to provide some basic shelter from the elements. No doubt our far distant ancestors used natural physical features (trees and caves, for example) to avoid certain weather conditions (rain or sun, for example) since time immemorial, and as a species we have continued to do so throughout our history in certain circumstances. But by modifying the natural environment for such specific ends that ur-architect (let's call him Al) took a leap forward for the species as significant in its way as the evolution of the prehensile thumb, the control of fire, or the ability to speak.

Although protection from the elements would remain its primary function, it could not have been too long before the dwelling (in however basic or temporary a form) became an arena for more complex human practices. At this point, someone (let's call her Anna) must have given a thought as to the best use of the available materials in the construction of a suitable edifice, as well as to the best use of the available space to reflect the desires and the fears of the occupants. Thus was born the idea of the house as something *in excess* of its primary function as artificial shelter – as a place, in fact, which expressed something of the identity of the builder or owner or occupier, as well as something of the culture of the society in which it was built.

The history of the house is the history of the dialectic that emerges between these two impulses: shelter and identity, Al and Anna. As befitting his 'hard' masculine disciplinary status, the former connotes a science, a history, a sociology and a philosophy of architecture. This is a discourse with which the essays in this book do not, for the most part, pretend to engage. The latter, however, connotes a dimension of human experience which as it turns out has always haunted the humanities, but which has been systematically disregarded or trivialised – not by the cultural agents themselves but by the critical community that services cultural discourse. This is a key point: even a cursory glance over any of the fields engaged by the contributors to this volume reveals a deep pre-occupation on the part of artists and cultural agents with the question of dwelling and with the impact of the house upon human experience. Critics, however, have by and large been reluctant to expend their valuable time and energy on anything so quotidian as 'a house', unless it is an obviously 'important' or 'glamorous' prospect such as Howards End or Satis House or Brideshead or Wuthering Heights itself. It would seem as if the very ubiquity of domestic space as a feature within so many art forms has militated against its serious critical engagement.

II
The scholarly consideration of domestic space represents a Pandora's Box of theories, methodologies, disciplines, institutions and interven-

tions – a veritable industry, in fact, which the present editors weren't *quite* totally ignorant of when setting out upon this project.[1] The genesis of our present interest in house and home, however, lies in a chance encounter with *The Poetics of Space* by Gaston Bachelard during a library browsing session. With its conjoining of the humanistic and the scientific, the soft and the hard, the intriguing title alone was enough to draw the attention of anyone with an interdisciplinary curiosity. Each of the main terms, in fact, contains ambivalent traces of both scientific and humanistic discourses. 'Poetics' alludes etymologically to 'poetry' – a word and a concept that has regularly been identified as a 'blue sky' discipline in institutional terms; at the same time, 'poetics' appears to promise a 'scientific' formalism which has traditionally been cast against effete humanist responses to the cultural text. 'Space' is likewise overlain with an assortment of disciplinary resonances – as reflected, for example, in the term's invocation by the great range of geographical and architectural subdisciplines. All in all, as a phrase 'the poetics of space' retains a potential significance for just about everybody with an academic interest in domestic space. It should come as no surprise that, given the range of those disciplinary interests, the book has exasperated just as many as it has charmed since its first publication.

As part of our concern to ensure the volume's thematic consistency, we directed all the contributors towards Bachelard's classic work. As the essays came in, however, it became increasingly clear that the invitation to 'engage' had been robustly enjoined, and that Bachelard himself had not done so well out of the various encounters. That is, of course, entirely as it should be; as a reflection of the democratic ideal which forms the historical basis of this particular critical genre, *Our House* comprises a series of 'essays' (from the French 'to try') on a delimited issue – in this case: domestic space. How individuals approach that issue, and what they make of it, was (beyond adhering to certain scholarly standards) up to them. It came as little surprise, therefore, to encounter a wide range of responses to Bachelard's work; and thus, while some researchers discovered a well of ideas leading to all sorts of insights and possibilities, others found ahistorical blindspots and oversights and insupportable claims. Perhaps the main point that emerges from the essays collected here is the socio-political specificity of Bachelard's model of domestic space,

and the dangers of extrapolating general theories from singular phenomena.

If Bachelard is the great modern philosopher of 'the house', Martin
Heidegger performs a similar function with regard to the related concept of 'the home', and he was the second figure with whose work we
invited contributors to engage. Heidegger enjoys (if that's the term) a
reputation as a thinker of intimidating depth and complexity, and it
would be a brave editor indeed who tried to summarise the thought of
this imposing figure in a few paragraphs. Here, it's enough to signal
that Heidegger's philosophical concerns with the nature of being, consciousness and reality led him towards an interest in space and place –
more specifically, to an interest in 'the house' as both physical location ('dwelling', signifying a building) and concept ('dwelling', signifying home) wherein these concerns became manifest. Put as simply
as possible, Heidegger argued that consciousness (and the culture produced in specific historical moments of consciousness) is caught between opposing tendencies towards home, or being 'homed', and
homelessness. The former represents a condition in which humankind
is at one with itself, balanced between the earth and the sky, between
physicality and spirituality; 'homelessness', on the other hand, describes the alienation of that balance, an estrangement of body and
spirit brought on by (amongst other things) the species' energy for
technological evolution. Heidegger's suspicion that modern consciousness was particularly susceptible to alienation, to existential
homelessness, led him to espouse a romantic attachment to home and
homeland which flirted dangerously with the principal political philosophy of his own time and place: fascism. Nonetheless, his conviction that authentic art must needs be grounded in the actual or metaphorical space of 'the home' has proved enduringly influential.

Variations on the thought of both Heidegger and Bachelard (and
indeed of many other figures) pop up throughout the essays in this
volume. Indeed, reading with a mind sensitised to the imagery of domestic space, it becomes increasingly apparent how thoroughly such
imagery has penetrated modern consciousness and culture – how frequently it features as a metaphor in a variety of philosophical and aesthetic systems, and how ubiquitous it is as an element within narrative,
irrespective of derivation or context. The idea of the house, as we
averred at the outset, is every-where; and not only in popular culture
(that myriad of British reality television programmes that emerged

during the 1990s, for example) but as one of our most fundamental responses to the situation in which we find ourselves: self-aware organisms dependent upon some form of shelter to ensure survival.

A corollary of this is the realisation that *all* cultural space – indoors and outdoors, built and 'natural' – is a function to a greater or lesser degree of the human response to its own evolving condition. Space, as J. Hillis Miller puts it, is made meaningful 'by the living that takes place within it. This transforms it both materially, as by names, or spiritually, as by the ascription of some collective value to this or that spot' (1995: 21). This is not to subscribe to some form of philosophical idealism, however, as if space possessed no material reality outwith the human imagination. Rather, the space *enables* the response, which in turn *creates* the space – as Hillis Miller goes on to say: 'Causer and caused, first and second, change places in a perpetually reversing metalepsis' (21). Put in the terms introduced above, Al and Anna appear to be locked together in an embrace which is always part struggle and part support – at once both a fight and a dance – for even as they vie for dominance, there is an implicit realisation that the one cannot exist without the other.

Space, then, is the discursive arena wherein the battle for subjectivity has been played out in a great variety of discourses (nature versus nurture, fear versus desire, will versus fate, and so on) since time immemorial. And to return to our original point – the one which was the motivation for *Our House* – within the 'space' of space, so to speak, it's our conviction that the house represents a peculiarly privileged location for the enactment of the human drama.

III

From *Exodus* to Evergreen Terrace, from Pemberley to Poe, the slightest glance reveals both the ubiquity and the centrality of the house as an image within human culture. The fact is that modern cultural history is saturated with representations of domestic space; and before launching into the collection proper it might be worthwhile taking a moment to remind ourselves of some of the forms taken by such representations, as well as the range of concerns and issues which tend to underpin them.

Charles Dickens's *Great Expectations* (1861) provides as good an example as one could find of the centrality of domestic space to the canon of world literature. The novel has traditionally been characterised as a proto-modernist *bildungsroman*: the hero Pip wishes to be a 'gentleman', and the narrative tracks the development of his character in relation to the various contemporary discourses vying to define that term. The text could just as easily be defined, however, as Pip's search for a 'home' amongst all the houses he encounters throughout the narrative. In this sense it's ironic that the closest he will come to feeling 'at home' is in the forge which adjoins the wooden house where he lives with his shrewish sister and her 'gentle' husband, the blacksmith Joe Gargery. The house itself is a place of physical pain and emotional restraint, offering nothing of the nurture (beyond accommodation and sustenance) traditionally associated with the domestic dwelling. The forge, on the other hand, though not a 'house' in any accepted sense of the term *is* a place of sanctuary where Pip and Joe, although lacking blood ties, 'forge' a bond of love and commitment that Pip will spend the remainder of the novel coming to understand.

Pip's quest to become a gentleman is triggered in the first instance by his contact with Satis House – the crumbling pile occupied by Miss Havisham and her protégée Estella. Satis joins a long list of famous houses (both before and since) which have featured in a variety of national literary traditions (many of them alluded to above and throughout the remainder of this volume). Miss Havisham is an anomaly: a living ghost, her emotional life permanently frozen at that precise moment (her wedding morning) when her public 'life' ended so spectacularly. She 'haunts' Satis, refusing to allow time to perform its natural function, and poisoning Estella's mind against those emotions – hope, love, empathy – which invest the domestic stage with so much of its resonance and power. Satis is truly a 'house of horror' – not in the supernatural sense that would in aftertimes come to dominate representations of the gothic mansion, but in the desperately human sense in which all our aspirations appear doomed to end in disappointment, regret and madness.

Opposed to the emotionally bankrupt space of Satis House (and paralleling the forge as a positive representation of domestic architecture) is the suburban London house occupied by one of Pip's friends, Mr Wemmick (a solicitor's clerk) and his 'aged parent'. Pip describes his first visit to the neighbourhood and to the edifice itself:

> It appeared to be a collection of back lanes, ditches, and little gardens, and to present the aspect of a rather dull retirement. Wemmick's house was a little wooden cottage in the midst of plots of garden, and the top of it was cut out and

painted like a battery mounted with guns.
  'My own doing,' said Wemmick. 'Looks pretty; don't it?'
  I highly commended it. I think it was the smallest house I ever saw; with the
queerest gothic windows (by far the greater part of them sham), and a gothic door,
almost too small to get in at.
  'That's a real flagstaff, you see,' said Wemmick, 'and on Sundays I run up a
real flag. Then look here. After I have crossed this bridge, I hoist it up, so – and
cut off the communication.'
  The bridge was a plank, and it crossed a chasm about four feet wide and two
deep. But it was very pleasant to see the pride with which he hoisted it up, and
made it fast; smiling as he did so, with a relish, and not merely mechanically.
  'At nine o'clock every night, Greenwich time,' said Wemmick, 'the gun fires.
There he is, you see! And when you hear him go, I think you'll say he's a Stinger'
(Dickens 1974: 199).

The eccentric lengths to which Wemmick has gone in an effort to
maintain the border between the house in Walworth where he lives
and the outside world (including the city office in Little Britain Street
where he works) is indicative of the enduring significance of the built
environment in relation to identity. Despite his father's age and various infirmities, despite its architectural limitations, Wemmick's Walworth house is a place of life and love – everything, in fact, which
Satis House is not. It offers Pip (and the reader) a crucial reminder of
the complex interplay that subsists between material space and the
experience of home – an understanding that his insistent pursuit of
gentlemanliness has caused him to lose.

We alluded above to the 'house of horror': the enduring vogue for
house-based ghost stories. As an example from the 'popular' end of
the cultural spectrum, we find that the image of the haunted house
forms a recurring motif within the genre of the horror film – as borne
out, for example, in the plethora of horror franchises which have
emerged in recent years: *Amityville, Evil Dead, Candyman, Last
Summer, Jeepers Creepers, Scream, Jason, Chucky, Freddy*, and so
on. This genre draws intertextually on various landmark texts in which
domestic interiors of one sort or another form the indispensable backdrop for the developing horror – even in the relatively modern period
consider films such as *Psycho* (1960), *The Exorcist* (1973), *Straw
Dogs* (1973), and *The Texas Chainsaw Massacre* (1974) (films which
in some cases have gone on to achieve franchise status themselves).

Of course, this is not to deny the prevalence of the outdoors (most
usually, the woods) as another favorite locus for popular horror – witness one of the most successful efforts of recent times: *The Blair*

Witch Project (1999). 'Outdoors' horror, if it may be so termed, draws on the threat of exposure to the unknown, the absence of a solid, familiar built environment (with its traces of benign human endeavour) as sanctuary against malign forces. With 'indoors' horror, those forces (supernatural or not) have entered the dwelling, infiltrating both the safe, recognisable spaces of childhood (the bedroom, the kitchen) as well as those spaces (the cellar, the attic, the locked room) about which we always had ambivalent feelings anyway. Indoors horror plays with the received idea of the house as sanctuary, subverting the archetype bequeathed to us by history. Just as night inheres within the idea of day, however, so darkness inheres within the idea of light; so, also, the horror narrative has always relied on a complex economy of exoticism and banality – the proximity, indeed, the domesticity, of malign forces: the bogeyman beneath the bed, the uncanny trace of otherness within the familiar. We find variations on this economy (and of the underlying indoors / outdoors dialectic) in many of the classic western folk tales – including *Little Red Riding Hood*, *Hansel and Gretel*, *Snow White and the Seven Dwarfs* – tales which frequently serve as prototypes for modern cinematic horror.

The Others (Amenábar 2001) provides a good example of a modern horror film in which the house figures prominently. The action is set in a large gothic mansion on Jersey in 1945, where Grace (played by Hollywood A-lister Nicole Kidman) is waiting with two young children for her husband to return from the war. Conveniently enough, the house has to be kept in perpetual darkness owing to a rare disease which makes the boy and girl susceptible to sunlight. The stress caused by having to keep rooms constantly locked with curtains perpetually drawn, added to the fear over her husband's fate and her own unreconstructed Catholicism, is clearly telling on Grace, as the film's opening live action shot of her screaming herself awake make clear. The house itself, we soon see, is a classic gothic pile, complete with turrets, roman arches, portrait-bedecked corridors, and angular stairways leading to ominously locked rooms.

The plot commences with Grace taking on a new set of servants, having been abandoned, apparently, by the previous crew. Ghostly goings-on ensue; the daughter reports the presence of other people in the house – the 'others' of the title, as we are led to believe; the servants act suspiciously, dropping cryptic hints about the history of the building and the previous occupants; the house itself, meanwhile, is shrouded in a dense fog which only contributes to the pervading air of menace and gloom. The film eventually 'twists' on the revelation that the characters with whom we have been invited to identify from the outset – mother, children, servants – are in fact ghosts whose afterlife existence is symbiotically enmeshed with the fate of the house wherein they lived. The husband (played by Christopher Eccleston) 'visits' his old home but cannot remain there, his spirit-trace being drawn back to the place where he lost his life during the war. Grace and her children claim the domestic space as their own, and the film ends with the family gazing from a window at the potential buyers they have frightened away, and repeating the classic owner-occupier mantra: 'This house is ours, this house is ours, this house is ours'.

The Others is a populist meditation on the persistence of the past into the present, and on the ineluctable, symbiotic relationship between human experience and domestic architecture. In structural terms, it is indebted in roughly equal measures to *The Sixth Sense* (1999) – an extremely successful film in which the apparently 'live' protagonist turned out to be dead all along – and to *The Innocents* (1961), a film based on the Henry James novella *The Turn of the Screw* (1898). In wider cultural terms, *The Others* rehearses a familiar narrative trope in which the house figures not as a mere neutral setting for the developing action, but as a proactive force in and of itself, trailing a host of associations and values from deep within the psychic history of the human species.

IV

Our House is a multi-disciplinary colloquy on the state of domestic space at the present time, comprising a study of the way in which the house has been represented in a number of selected texts from a variety of media (including fiction, poetry, television and music) and in a variety of scholarly disciplines (including literary criticism, media and cultural studies, history and architecture). Each contributor has observed the brief to engage with the practical, theoretical and disciplinary issues raised in this introduction. If the volume offers a backwards glance at some of the ways in which the house came to occupy the place it does in contemporary culture, however, it is also a message from the present to the future. *Our House* reveals, in other words, some of the fears and desires at large at the present time in relation to the fundamental issue of domestic architecture.

The collection opens with a chapter that goes to the heart of the matter: what is the relationship between the 'felicitous space' of Bachelardian memory and the practical space that house-dwellers are obliged to negotiate on a day-to-day basis? Joe Moran suspects that the meanings attributed to domestic space are as much a matter of marketing and management as of personal memory. The modern representation of the house as an evocative, nostalgic site is, he argues, achieved only through a highly developed process of media organisation – one that is itself acutely sensitive to the wider economic and political systems abroad in any society during any given period. It is precisely this process that cultural texts such as Rachel Whiteread's *House* (1993) help to expose. This contributor suggests that the real power of domestic space lies not in the bourgeois promise of a return to some mythical lost domain, but in its offer of a location wherein the dialectical nature of modern life – public / private; romantic / banal; past / present; etc. – may be both realised and interrogated.

As mentioned in Section I above, the house connotes an extra-academic status which renders it different from most other scholarly subjects – put simply, domestic space impacts upon the lives of everybody (including the researcher) in ways, and to a degree, that other phenomena do not. This means that there is always going to be a strong autobiographical impulse attending the analysis of the house, and this is something we see emerging in many of the essays in this collection. Gerry Smyth broaches the relationship between textual and personal space in his discussion of *The Wind in the Willows*, showing how issues which are raised *in* the text – for example, the ambivalent nature of domestic space in contexts of socio-political crisis – are replicated in terms of the reading subject's changing relationship *with* the text – for example, the different meanings attributable to the text as a function of the subject's changing location and status.

'The Life of a Country Cottage' is another contribution rooted firmly in the researcher's own experience. In her description of a lost family home, Karen Sayer deploys a combination of oral testimony and material objects to reveal how the meaning of domestic space emerges from a complex interweaving of memory and everyday usage. As with the other autobiographical pieces here, the personal narrative is underpinned by a rigorous theoretical narrative. Drawing on Doreen Massey's concept of 'space-time', Karen Sayer suggests that it is necessary to regard the special role afforded the house in western culture as an effect of specific temporal-spatial negotiations which are themselves answerable to recognisable socio-political developments. Space is not 'outside' time, but exists in dialectical relationship with it; the meaning of a place is always in part an effect of a temporal shift (one which the observing subject is always obliged to negotiate) from past to present. It is the provisional nature of 'space-time' – its intricate enmeshing of spatial and temporal categories – that accounts for the ambivalence which characterises our attitude towards the house and its function as *the* elemental human space.

Even a cursory familiarity should be sufficient to reveal the absolute centrality of the house to any consideration of Art History. From cave daubing to Rachel Whiteread, artists working in various media have always embraced the practical and philosophical challenges of domestic space, attempting to understand amongst other things the ambivalent role it plays in relation to the evolution of the species. Jeff Adams touches upon this during the course of his examination of the representation of domestic space in the neglected form of the graphic novel. In the crisis situations which constitute the setting for each of his chosen texts (to which contexts, he suggests, the graphic novel is particularly well suited), the contributor finds domestic space to be a recurring and crucial motif, but one which answers better to the theories and methodologies of self-consciously politicised intellectuals such as Edward Said and Michel Foucault rather than the relentlessly abstract phenomenology of Gaston Bachelard.

Adams' discussion of Palestine provides an example of space assuming super-sensitive connotations in contexts of heightened political and / or social tension. Another region which has been obliged to endure a situation of "great hatred, little room" is Northern Ireland. In the first of two essays in this collection on contemporary Irish culture, Scott Brewster considers the ambivalent representation of house and home in the poetry of Seamus Heaney and Tom Paulin. As with many of the contributors to this volume, Brewster discovers a fundamental tension between an archetypal resonance (identifiable with reference to Bachelard and Heidegger) informing the representation of domestic space in Northern Irish culture, and the invocation of house and home in terms of specific historical discourses, such as (in this particular case) religion, politics, language and class. Traditionally, this tension has contributed to the general context of misunderstanding and suspicion underpinning 'the Troubles', leaving the contributor to speculate on the role and representation of domestic space in a 'peaceful' Northern Ireland.

As Scott Brewster demonstrates, the case of Ireland provides an opportunity to study the representation of domestic space in the context of a dynamic confrontation between discourses of tradition and modernity. Spiralling property costs, allied to attempts to modify ages-old political culture, have combined to elevate the issue of (the) dwelling to the top of the island's cultural agenda. In an essay which draws together many of the concerns of Adams and Brewster, Shane Alcobia-Murphy traces a socio-political provenance for the different representations of domestic space currently abroad in the Republic of Ireland and Northern Ireland. With special reference to visual media, the author compares the way in which images of house and home have been informed by broader cultural imperatives connected with the advent of rapid economic growth in the South, and the ongoing 'Peace Process' in the North.

In his essay on the relationship between sound and domestic space, Ron Moy draws an important distinction between active 'listening' and passive 'hearing': the former, he suggests, describes a relationship between consumer and text that emerged as a response to the particular discursive context of the 1960s and 1970s (what he terms 'the Hi-fi generation') – one in which popular music and the technology available to reproduce it were adapted to each other; the latter, on the other hand, is the characteristic response of a postmodern culture in which the social sound ratio comprises a much less focused, much more dispersed set of practices. The slightest familiarity with life in the contemporary West is enough to convince that we are in fact much more likely to 'hear' music in the new millennium than to 'listen' to it. While arguing for a re-orientation of contemporary audience engagement back towards a more active listening, this contribution also reveals the extent to which the house itself has adapted to the new regime, becoming a place that *enables*, but at the same time a place that is *enabled by*, the changing role of sound in the contemporary world.

The sociology of domestic space is also something that concerns Ruth McElroy in her essay on the history of home improvement and the rise of do-it-yourself. With reference to the popular BBC programme *Changing Rooms* the author characterises the vogue for home make-over as a phenomenon clearly overdetermined by issues of class and gender: Al and Anna are in the building, so to speak, and are en-

gaging with a range of established discourses which 'help' us to organise the ways in which we think about and experience domestic
space. Home improvement also functions, however, as an element of a
wider cultural phenomenon – what the author refers to as the 'aestheticization of everyday life'. Paradoxically, the complex dynamic of
private and public space negotiated in British television's huge housing schedule is one of the principal media through which the public
learn to be private, while at the same time it offers an arena (the
house) and a practice (DIY) in which the individual subject may come
to a sense of their identity.

Although it's not a systematic part of his analysis, Bachelard's thesis regarding the poetics of space depends in large part on an age conceit in which the child is parent to the adult – that's to say, in which
the preoccupations of childhood and adolescence determine the role
domestic space plays in the imagination of the mature subject, or the
many imaginative writers he quotes throughout his book, or indeed the
author himself. Jo Croft's contribution to *Our House* engages with this
element in Bachelard's work, in so far as she offers an analysis of the
ways in the teenager's status as a liminal quasi-subject is encapsulated
in fictional and semi-autobiographical depictions of the adolescent
bedroom. The bedroom is indeed a place of dreaming and play, the
author suggests, but in ways which challenge the established definitions of those terms, as well as the unformulated psychology which
informs Bachelard's influential study.

Each of the contributors to this volume is obliged to confront at
some level or other an inherent ambivalence informing the idea of the
house – its function, in other words, as a site of peace and sanctuary,
on the one hand, and of danger and incarceration, on the other. Because of its prevalence as a more or less universal human space,
moreover, the ambivalence underpinning the concept of the dwelling
comes to inform some of the most potent, and at the same time the
most contradictory, of social discourses. One such discourse is gender.
In an essay exploring the correlation between gender and domestic
space as represented in three contemporary novels, Peter Childs shows
how each of these discourses is symbiotically linked with the other so
that what emerges in each text is an image of the house as a site in
which female identity is always on the point of formation and yet also
always on the point of dissolution.

The question of gender and domestic space is also the chief focus of Marie Hughes-Edwards' essay on the poetry of Carol Anne Duffy. In an analysis of Duffy's use of different poetic forms (specifically, the dramatic monologue and the autobiographical poem), Hughes Edwards reveals how the poet uses the image of the house to confront the challenges of modern life, especially as experienced by women. The house, it emerges, is the principal arena wherein the most intense of human emotions – both negative and positive – are articulated; the house, in this respect, simply *is* society, *is* history, *is* life itself in all its contradictions and confusions of pain and sorrow, joy and fulfilment. As with all the essays in this volume, the message here is that any honest endeavour to express and / or understand the human condition must involve a consideration of domestic space, for it is there – in our use of, and attitudes towards, the house – that the human subject is constantly constructed and deconstructed.

The volume ends with another autobiographical intervention: Joseph Boughey's meditation on the complex relations between writing, memory and grief. In an incredibly courageous effort, this contributor considers the ways in which his own response to domestic space has been modified by the death of a beloved spouse whose life was intimately enmeshed with that space. The "poetics of grief" is revealed as the dauntingly difficult prospect one always suspected it might be – one of the key experiences which we humans are bound to encounter at some point during our lives. Given their centrality to life, it is perhaps unsurprising that concepts such as death, grief and loss should resonate so strongly in relation to the essential human space which is the domestic dwelling. Indeed, this essay helps to expose the fact that lurking behind all the contributions collected here is a key human preoccupation with the potential loss of home, as well as a recognition of the always already provisional nature of sanctuary in any of its metaphysical or phenomenological forms.

The focus of the essays in *Our House* is not 'ecological' in the narrow sense, in as much as the contributions do not appear to be oriented in the first instance towards issues of natural environment, biodiversity, sustain-able resources, etc. The book *does* reflect developments in ecocriticism over the past decade, however, a period which has witnessed an initial (and entirely understandable) concern with the status of wilderness or 'natural' landscapes slowly learning to accommodate interest in the status of various urban and constructed environments.

The focus upon the house in this volume may be seen as an articulation of more general concerns with space and identity, with the ongoing relationship between 'natural' and 'cultural' environments (such as we may conceive them), and with the adaptation of new environmentalist discourses to long-established discourses of social justice.

Notes

1. See David Morley, *Home Territories: Media, Mobility and Identity* (2000) for a good introduction to many of the theoretical and methodological concerns raised by the contemplation of 'house' and 'home'.

Houses, Habit and Memory

Joe Moran

ABSTRACT
With particular reference to public policy and the housing market in post-Second World War Britain, this chapter examines the relationship between houses and memory. It critiques Gaston Bachelard's association of the house with an eternalised "poetics of space", arguing that questions of memory and desire need to be connected to history, economics and politics. Bachelard's house of dream-memory, locked securely into the earth by the thickness of its load-bearing walls and the depth of its foundations, conveys the possibility of return to a pure point of origin. But no such reassuring meanings are conveyed by dilapidated high-rises, derelict houses and the rubble and empty spaces left by demolished slums. The capacity of the house to represent what Bachelard calls "felicitous space" is thus partly a question of how successfully time and memory are managed. The association of the house with nostalgia has become inseparable from a marketing process in which the culturally and economically advantaged use their homes to convey the effects of 'period' and 'heritage'. Above all, though, houses owe their evocative power to the fact that they connect these wider discourses of wealth, taste, class and nostalgia with the routine and unnoticed activities of everyday life.

Introduction

Rachel Whiteread's now demolished sculpture, *House* (1993), a concrete cast of the interior of a mid-terraced house in London's East End, remains a powerful, although ambiguous, statement about the relationship between memory and domestic space. Bow Council made the original house available to Whiteread because, in a story which will be familiar to local authorities across Britain, a single tenant had resisted being moved into modernised accommodation and defiantly remained *in situ* long after all the other houses on his street had been demolished. As the last surviving 'house' in a former row of nearly identical, late-nineteenth-century by-law terraces, Whiteread's sculpture was as much about absence and forgetting as it was about recovery and remembrance. Several commentators, including Whiteread herself, focused on the disturbing way in which her sculpture opened up the intimate areas of the house to public scrutiny (Lingwood 1995: 23; Morley 2001: 28). But what was made visible seemed fairly mundane and impersonal: the indentations left by light switches, old plug sockets and door latches, soot-blackened fireplaces, party walls, exposed joist ends slightly rotten from damp. The banality of these commonplace phenomena raised questions about the very possibility of memory within the repetition and sameness of the everyday. Taking its cue from Whiteread's sculpture, this essay is about how houses retain and convey memories of the most routine elements of our lives, and about the complex relation between these memories and broader narratives of heritage, taste and class. While grounded in the specific context of public policy and the housing market in post-Second World War Britain, it also explores more general issues about memory and material culture in the modern world.

The Poetics of Houses
Gaston Bachelard's *The Poetics of Space* (1958) remains the seminal exploration of the relationship between houses and memory. For Bachelard, the house is essentially a place of tranquillity, solitude and contemplation, which allows us to "dream in peace" (1994: 6). He is interested in the house on two levels: firstly, as an actual building, made of solid materials such as bricks, slate and timber, whose permanence gives us the reassuring sense that memories can be nurtured and recovered, excavated from a containable past; and secondly, as an imaginary entity, which reduces the experience of inhabiting to its concentrated, ideal essence. Bachelard argues that "inhabited space transcends geometrical space", and that a house which is worked on by the poetic imagination is distinct from the Cartesian, three-dimensional space mapped out by the builder or surveyor (1994: 47, xxxvi). This "oneiric house" is a kind of "synthesis of immemorial and recollected" (1994: 17, 5) in that it conjures up distant autobiographical memories of the house in which we were born, and (in an echo of the Jungian collective unconscious) the shared, timeless past of humanity.

Despite Bachelard's insistence that this imaginary house is a cultural universal, it is clearly reminiscent of the actual houses of a specific historical tradition, and more particularly of the kind of house in which he was raised in rural Champagne at the end of the nineteenth century. The house described in *The Poetics of Space* is a permanent structure which allows us to put down roots in our own "corner of the world" (1994: 4) and satisfy essential human needs for intimacy and solitude. In this sense, it seems to refer to a particular kind of Euro-American settlement, made of brick or stone, with a rectangular structure which allows it to be divided into separate rooms connected by stairs and hallways. Bachelard suggests that the layering and subdivisions of this kind of house allow its collective unconscious to intersect with private languages and personal affinities. In its separate floors, secret rooms and secluded alcoves, memories can be clearly differentiated and classified: "Thanks to the house, a great many of our memories are housed, and if the house is a bit elaborate, if it has a cellar and a garret, nooks and corridors, our memories have refuges that are all the more clearly delineated" (1994: 8).

In this sense, the oneiric house could only belong to a particular moment in Western modernity. The houses of pre-industrial Europe were multifunctional spaces which brought together a wide variety of people (extended family, apprentices, domestic help) and activities (work, leisure, care of the sick) (Muthesius 1982: 39). As Witold Rybczynski has shown, the ideals of privacy and comfort which we now associate automatically with the house only began to emerge in the democratic society of seventeenth-century Holland, spreading rapidly to the rest of Europe. During this period, the house was divided into rooms with different functions, and boundaries between public and private became more fixed (1988: 51-75). The house also became an increasingly gendered space as it was re-imagined as a private, womanly haven, away from the burdens of male professional work. Bachelard's description of the home as maternal and womblike, and his ecstatic description of housework as a potentially life-enhancing activity, shows how much he has internalised these historically recent distinctions (1994: 67).

Bachelard's dreamhouse has a more specific context: his antipathy to twentieth-century urbanism and modernist architecture. Le Corbusier and his followers had famously attacked the "cult of the house" in Western culture, with its "sickening spirit" and "conglomeration of useless and disparate objects" (1946: 18, 22). They argued that the traditional gabled house was mired in the past: its small rooms and cluttered interiors trapped not only dust but memories, making it a kind of private museum to the insular preoccupations of the middle classes, a place in which people gathered together "gloomily and secretly like wretched animals" (1946: 18). As an antidote to these claustrophobic and class-ridden refuges from the outside world, modernist buildings aimed to provide transparent environments opened up to light and space, with their undivided interiors, clean lines and floor-to-ceiling windows. They also proudly announced their modernity in their use of mass-produced materials and new technologies. Preferring to stop time (through weather-proofing) rather than manage it (through traditional weatherings such as pitched roofs, sills, copings and downpipes), they imagined a building as "a finality that manifests itself upon the completion of a construction", and its afterlife as purely detraction and deterioration (Mostafavi and Leatherbarrow 1997: 36, 82).

Bachelard's unwillingness to describe houses specifically in *The Poetics of Space* means that many of his cultural reference points need to be inferred. But this apparent description of the system-built tower blocks of the Parisian suburbs shows his antagonism towards the modern movement:

> In Paris, there are no houses, and the inhabitants of the big city live in superimposed boxes […] The number of the street and the floor give the location of our "conventional hole," but our abode has neither space around it nor verticality inside it. [The buildings] have no roots and, what is quite unthinkable for a dreamer of houses, sky-scrapers have no cellars. From the street to the roof, the rooms pile up one on top of the other, while the tent of a horizonless sky encloses the entire city (1994: 26-7).

For Bachelard, the varied topography of a house allows it to accommodate and distinguish between particular memories and psychological states. Attics and cellars are especially important because we can retreat into these blank, functionless, rarely visited places and experience states of abstraction and reverie. Modernist buildings, though, are less likely to have attics (because of their preference for flat roofs) and cellars (because of their common use of slab-on grade, pouring concrete onto the ground for an instant foundation). In the high-rise, the necessary verticality of a building is reduced to a mere visual spectacle which is not experienced by the inhabitant, since "elevators do away with the heroism of stair climbing" (1994: 27).

Bachelard's ideal house is yet more specific in that it has "space around it", its ultimate embodiment being the thatched cottage or hermit's hut first encountered as a distant glimmer of light on a dark night (1994: 31). For Bachelard, the problem with the townhouse is that we cannot experience dreams of shelter and protection within it, because we are

> no longer aware of the storms of the outside universe. Occasionally the wind blows a tile from the roof and kills a passer-by in the street. But this roof crime is only aimed at the belated passer-by [...] In our houses set close against one another, we are less afraid (1994: 27).

Bachelard's disregard for the unfortunate pedestrian is telling, because it suggests that his oneiric house represents a retreat not only from the harsh elements but from the social sphere – after all, intimate space is "space that is not open to just anybody" (1994: 78). In effect, he turns a potentially political critique of the planned housing built for the working classes in the postwar period into an implicit championing of private property over the "house on streets where we have only lived as transients" (1994: 43).

The Politics of Memory

Bachelard's discussion of the house shows that the poetics of space are always unavoidably linked to a politics, whether this is explicitly acknowledged or not. The key question, then, is how the nebulous entities of memory, desire and the imagination intersect with the material culture of houses, a process that is crucially connected to history and economics.

In post-Second World War Britain, houses have been of huge symbolic and cultural importance, largely because of a dramatic shift towards owner-occupation, from 26 per cent of houses in 1945 to 70 per cent in 2001 (Burnett 1986: 282; *Social Trends* 2002: 166). The increase in homeownership has been the result of a number of factors, including the growing strength of lending institutions such as building societies and the introduction of tax incentives for mortgage holders. A policy of encouraging private ownership which was initially associated with the Tories – Anthony Eden's espousal in 1946 of a "nationwide property-owning democracy" (Short 1982: 118) – gradually became a cross-party consensus in the 1960s and 1970s. A Government White Paper in 1971 announced that home ownership "satisfies a deep and natural desire on the part of the householder to have independent control of the house that shelters him and his [*sic*] family" (Short 1982: 119). The encouragement of this "natural" desire (which does not seem to be felt so keenly in other European countries, such as France and Germany, where the rental sector is still strong) has also created a moral economy in which owning a house, particularly in a 'nice' area, indicates prosperity, stability and civic responsibility.

The house's signification of durability for middle-class mortgage-holders has been almost inversely proportional to the transience it has represented for less fortunate participants in the housing market. The great slum clearances of the postwar period provide an obvious example of this. 1.3 million houses in traditional working-class communities were demolished between 1955 and 1975, and three million people were rehoused, with little popular participation in the decision-making process (Dunleavy 1981: 1). Postwar architects and planners shared an optimistic belief that substandard housing could be swept away and replaced by innovative modern buildings and communal open spaces. As Anthony Vidler argues, though, "this housecleaning operation produced its own ghosts, the nostalgic shadows of all the 'houses' now condemned to history or the demolition site" (1992: 64). The high-rises and new housing estates to which the working classes were moved, often against their wishes, deprived them of the strong collective experiences and memories associated with the densely-packed terraces (Young and Wilmott 1962: 198).

The development of an unfettered private housing market, which was accelerated in the Thatcher years as the encouragement of home-ownership became a firm policy objective, has exacerbated this problem of the division between durable and ephemeral houses. The Thatcher government's deregulation of the financial system created favourable conditions for borrowing and encouraged massive speculation in the housing market. Most notoriously, the 1980 Housing Act gave millions of council house tenants the right to buy their houses, often in desirable locations and at huge discounts ranging from 33 to 50 per cent, partly in the expectation that these new homeowners would be more likely to vote Tory.

In this uncontrolled marketplace, the key factor was, as the Estate Agent's mantra put it, 'location location location'. An inevitable process of self-selection and zoning produced massive variations in house prices, which have risen spectacularly in certain areas and gone into freefall in others. Within these latter areas, building societies and banks are increasingly reluctant to give mortgages (so-called 'red-lining'), and housing is more likely to be in the form of council houses, housing association flats and cheap, privately rented accommodation. Here the definition of a 'slum' is clearly culturally detemined, the by-product of a broader social and economic process. In the deprived areas of major British cities, for example, there are often whole streets of boarded-up or bricked-up terraced houses, only a mile or so from expensive and well-maintained properties that were built in the same period and are structurally identical.

As Walter Benjamin has argued, the afterlife of material artefacts, once they have ceased to be useful as commodities, opens them up to concealed histories and involuntary memories. In particular, the ruination of objects in capitalist society exposes the inevitability of decay within a system that presents itself as an endlessly replenishing cycle of the modish and up-to-date (1999: 112, 203, 207). Benjamin would probably have recognized this quality in the remaining high-rise flats of Britain's inner cities, with their vandalized lifts, graffitied walls and stained, blistered concrete. When yesterday's state-of-the-art is revealed as today's quintessence of the unpopular and unfashionable, it is a visible reminder of what is normally overlooked in the comforting repetition and sameness of everyday life: the inevitability of aging and death.

Houses convey this inevitability for precisely the same reason that they represent continuity and permanence: they often outlive us, and will probably have already housed people who are now dead. As Freud notes in his essay on 'the uncanny', the *unheimlich* is crucially related to the *heimlich*, in that it leads us back to what is "known of old and long familiar", and which "ought to have remained secret and hidden but has come to light" (1985: 340, 345). For Freud, one of the ways in which the uncanny represents the return of the repressed is that it confronts us with the reality of death as something utterly familiar but also unthinkable (1985: 364). What is missing from Freud's account, though, is how and why certain houses convey this haunted quality.

When we examine houses as social artefacts, we can see that they communicate different kinds of memory and nostalgia depending on their relative reserves of cultural and economic capital. Coined by a Swiss doctor in 1688 to refer to an apparently lethal kind of homesickness suffered by itinerant Swiss soldiers missing the Alpine air, the word 'nostalgia' is closely associated with ideas of home: it comes from the Greek words *nostos* ('to return home') and *algia* ('longing'). This dual root, though, suggests an ambivalence at the heart of the term itself. It can represent both the desire to return to a stable and secure point, and a recognition that such desire is always painfully deferred because past experience is unrecoverable (Boym 2001: xiii, 3). Bachelard's house of dream-memory, locked securely into the earth by the thickness of its load-bearing walls and the depth of its foundations, conveys the possibility of return to a pure point of origin. Clearly, no such reassuring meanings are conveyed by dilapidated high-rises, derelict houses and the rubble and empty spaces left by demolished 'slums'. But the unsettling nostalgia evoked by these decaying environments is rarely channelled into a critique of the system. As Patrick Dunleavy argues, the primary 'lesson' learnt from the rapid and visible decline of the high-rises has been that planned, social housing is uniformly bad (1981: 2). Used as an argument for an unrestrained free market, this has exacerbated the problem of a system which allows the relatively privileged to retreat from deteriorating social spaces into privatised housing.

In her Bachelardian reading of the relationship between houses and desire, Marjorie Garber writes that one of the great dreams of the house-hunter is to find "the Cinderella house – or the Beast that becomes a beauty when looked upon with the eye of love [...] a neglected, falling-down property that needs to be nursed back to health and beauty – to be, in short, Understood" (2001: 12). Garber examines what she sees as an erotically charged housing market in which real estate is a form of "yuppie pornography" (2001: 3), and the process of viewing and making an offer on a house resembles the semiotics of dating and courtship. The structural dynamics of the housing market, though, will always force buyers into hard calculations, so that properties are only bought as sound financial investments with the guarantee of a high mark-up when they are eventually sold on. For this reason, the Cinderella house could never exist in the sink estate; Prince Charming does not pass that way.

Houses and Heritage

The capacity of the house to represent what Bachelard calls "felicitous space" (1994: xxxv) is thus partly a question of how successfully time and memory are managed, which is also about the unequal distribution of power, status and money. In a classic text outlining a theory of rubbish, Michael Thompson traced this process by examining the power struggle between two groups in Islington in the mid-1960s: the middle-class "knockers-through" and the working-class, rent-controlled sitting tenants. Prior to this period, Islington was a down-at-heel North London suburb, its once grand Regency houses split into poorly-maintained, multi-occupation tenements. This situation was now being complicated, though, by the arrival of a "frontier middle class" (1979: 43) which was buying up slum properties and transforming them into attractive period dwellings. In a process of gentrification which was later to be duplicated in other areas of London, this class was attracted to Islington by its relatively low house prices.

In keeping with his concern with the politics rather than the poetics of space, Thompson focused not on the Bachelardian enclosures of the house but on its negotiable borders, particularly its doors and windows. Looking at the houses in one Islington square from the outside, he saw that members of the frontier middle class were making them look older by fitting pseudo-Georgian, panelled front doors, restoring the fanlights and adding brass knockers and letter-plates. Through their enlarged windows, it was possible to see that they had knocked their dividing walls through and laid down hardwood floors. The working-class tenants, meanwhile, were covering their original panelled doors with hardboard, painting them in cheerful colours, installing plastic bell pushes, and hiding the insides of their houses behind net curtains (1979: 42-3). Thompson argues that this anthropological case study demonstrates the permeability and crossover between three main categories of material culture: the transient (the usual status of commodities, which enter the market at their highest value and then gradually decline in worth), the durable (the role assumed by 'period' houses and antiques) and rubbish (things which have no value, such as slum houses, car wrecks or obsolete fashion items) (1979: 9-11).

For Thompson, the house is the ultimate example of a commodity that can actually appreciate in value as it gets older if it has been lovingly restored or happens to be located in a gentrifying area (1979: 36). While the 'knockers-through' are successfully transforming their houses from rubbish into durable objects, the working-class tenants are unsuccessfully attempting to prevent their houses shifting from transient objects into rubbish. The greater knowledge of the middle classes about the housing market, and in particular about which areas are 'on the up,' gives them the "power to make things durable" (1979: 52). Anyone familiar with the current demographic of Islington, now one of the most expensive and desirable places to live in the capital, will know who won this particular battle. Thompson's account is of a concerted effort by the culturally and economically advantaged to translate the lived quality of houses into socially valuable forms.

It is useful to read Thompson's account alongside the work of critics such as Stewart Brand and Christopher Alexander who have sought to redress what they see as an imbalance in architecture and urban planning by dealing with the relationship of buildings to time and memory. Like Bachelard, these critics prefer improvised, vernacular building styles to those of centralised planners and developers. They criticise a modernist universalism which reduces human experience to abstractions and concepts, and which, by celebrating its contemporaneity and progressiveness, avoids dealing with the gradual depredations of time (Brand 1997; Alexander 1979). In particular, they attack what Brand calls "magazine architecture" (1997: 52) which is overly concerned with visual spectacle at the expense of the lived aspects of the built environment. Both Brand and Alexander argue that certain building styles and materials inspire feelings of belonging in humans, while others do not. Brick and timber, for example, have the grain and texture to allow them to weather and improve with age, so creating a sense of gradual, organic change and "accumulated human investment" (Brand 1997: 10); other materials, such as untreated concrete, a porous substance which ages badly as it absorbs rainwater and pollution, only convey feelings of discontinuity and impermanence (Brand 1997: 125-6).

These arguments can be countered in two ways. First, Brand and Alexander assume that the aesthetics of buildings, and their concomitant ability to convey the passing of time and the persistence of memory, can be measured by absolute, unchanging criteria. As various critics of the heritage industry have shown, the aesthetic or nostalgic value attached to particular objects from the past is often socially determined and historically variable (Lowenthal 1985; Samuel 1994). In Britain, for example, the reviled high-rises of the 1950s and 1960s have started to be regarded more affectionately by architectural critics and property developers, as some of them have become listed buildings or have been converted into luxury flats.

Second, their historical account of the decline of vernacular into quantity building is too simplistic: specialist builders, architects and planners have been involved in housebuilding for centuries, and neo-traditionalist forms have survived within centralized planning and mass-produced systems. The modernist revolution in British architecture was always incomplete, incorporating social housing in urban areas (but not usually new towns and suburbs) and a relatively small number of private houses and commercial buildings. High-rise flats were built primarily as homes for the displaced working classes; the more prosperous almost always preferred to live in vernacular-style semi-detacheds or older, refurbished houses.

As part of his examination of heritage culture in Britain, Raphael Samuel has discussed the recent development of 'neo-vernacular' building styles, the "return to brick" as a construction material, and the trend for "retrofitting" in interior design (1994: 51-82). He interprets these developments as a response to the creative possibilities unleashed by the property boom and DIY revolution of the 1980s, and a reaction against the conspicuously modern formica surfaces, streamlined kitchens and gee-whizz gadgetry of the 1950s and 1960s. When read against Thompson's account, though, the retro elements of contemporary design could be seen as a filtering down of the specialised knowledge of the savvy middle classes, and their traditional ability to "make things durable". As one example of this, Samuel notes that the panelled Georgian door, Thompson's marker of gentrification in Islington in the 1960s, became the most common way for the new owners of ex-council houses to mark their upward mobility in the 1980s (1994: 72).

The 'country kitchen' look, associated with furniture and design stores such as Habitat and Heals in the 1960s, is another instance of the long-standing ability of the professional classes to use the house as a way of negotiating modernity, combining the comforts of mass consumption with older ideals of homeliness and craftsmanship. This type of kitchen combined all mod cons and bright, contemporary colours with nostalgic signifiers such as untreated wood, quarry tiles and earthenware. The country kitchen allowed the suburban middle classes to embrace a comfortable version of the below-stairs lifestyle of the servants they would have employed in a previous era. For Peter Halley, who identifies a similar trend in the US in the preference of WASPs for colonial furniture, this nostalgia for the everyday life of the past functions as "a signifier for the identity of a powerful class" which no longer has to assert its pre-eminence so forcefully and can embrace simple lifestyles through choice rather than obligation. It therefore reflects "the desire of that class both to hide its existence with an anti-iconography and to claim its connection to an earlier industrial materiality whose reality it has effectively usurped" (1997: 191).

A similar process can be identified today in the marketing and selling of houses, as an increasingly cut-throat business conceals its baser aspects by appealing to the simplicity and authenticity of the past. The most desirable properties are often renovated 'lodges' and 'cottages', and new builds make themselves look older with cottagey styles and historical detailing. As Samuel puts it: "The more nomadic business becomes [...] the more it affects a homespun look, recycling old trade names, refurbishing old properties, and laying claim to the production of classics." The international style of neo-vernacular architecture, which uses standard construction processes, prefabricated technologies and universal materials imported from centralized production lines, is thus "passed off as homegrown and indigenous" (1994: 78). The association of the house with nostalgia has become inseparable from a marketing process in which memories are self-consciously stage-managed in order to convey the effects of 'period' and 'heritage'. No wonder the rural retreat that Bachelard idealizes in *The Poetics of Space* is now one of the most valuable commodities on the property market, particularly in the expanding area of second homes for rich urbanites.

Habit and Memory
The memories associated with houses would not be so compelling and enduring, however, if they were simply a result of the preferred meanings of the heritage industry intruding on domestic space. Houses owe their evocative power to the fact that they connect these wider discourses of wealth, taste, class and nostalgia with the unstated force of habit and custom. Houses are, above all, spaces for everyday, routine activities. While they sometimes evoke specific events from the past – the wine stain on a carpet from a party, the notches on a wall that measure the stages of a child's growth – these sorts of memories are likely to be drowned out by the traces of mundane experiences which are unattachable to an event or individual.

Theorists of everyday life have tended, in various ways, to empha-
size its invisibility, its capacity to conceal itself in the unnoticed elements of people's lives. Michel de Certeau argues that this invisibility
allows room for "microinventions" which can provide a space "between the symmetrical errors of archaistic nostalgia and frenetic over-
modernization" (de Certeau *et al.* 1998: 213). Often seen as deadening
and stifling, habit can actually free experience from the controlled
meanings of manufactured retro-chic or trend-setting design. Unlike
the show home or the carefully arranged tableaux of the interior design catalogue, the lived-in house blends into the background, moulds
itself seamlessly around our bodies, gestures, activities and thoughts.
These cumulative remnants of habitual experience are what is so conspicuously absent from the impenetrable concrete facade of
Whiteread's *House*: the indentations of bodies on upholstery, the wear
and tear of well-trodden carpets and stairs, the build-up of hair and
dust in hard-to-reach corners. For de Certeau, the evidence of these
generic, unspecific experiences points to a notion of memory as "a
sort of anti-museum [which is] not localizable" (1984: 108).

As Pierre Nora argues, though, our modern understanding of memory primarily emphasises its use as a symbolic way of recovering the
linear, irreversible time of modernity, and of formulating sequential
narratives of individual identity (1996: 1-20). This can be linked to the
increasing importance in the post-Renaissance Western world of stan-
dardized clock time, and of the notion of a "disengaged, particular
self, whose identity is constituted in memory" (Taylor 1989: 288). The
idea of childhood has become symbolically significant in the modern
era partly because it expresses this sense of interiority and historicity
within the individual self (Steedman 1995: 4).

One of the more useful insights of Bachelard's work is its
questioning of this conventional linkage of time, memory and identity.
Bachelard sees our memories as an effect not of the "sentimental re-
percussions" of childhood (1994: xxiii) but of our everyday interaction with matter and space. He suggests that memory is not a wholly
interiorised experience in which we seek to retrieve the lost time of
the past, but a practical activity involving the substances and sensa-
tions of the physical world. Memory is "motionless": it "does not record concrete duration, in the Bergsonian sense of the word" but needs
to be "fixed in space". The unconscious, instead of being the location

of repressed memories of the foundational experiences of childhood, simply "abides" (1994: 9).

In this sense, Bachelard's work recalls pre-modern ideas of the memory palace or theatre that date back to late antiquity. In the ancient art of mnemonics, first identified by Cicero and widely practised up to the Renaissance period, memory had a fundamentally spatial quality. The memoriser created vivid mental images and then placed them within familiar *loci memoriae*, or memory places, such as the rooms of a house, the placings at a dining table or the different parts of a theatre (Yates 1984). Bachelard similarly suggests that the concreteness of the physical environment provides an important fixing agent for memory. The house we were born in exists "over and beyond our memories" because it is "physically inscribed in us". It is experienced not in autobiographical reflection but in the actual creak of a staircase tread or the feel of a doorknob: "Habit is too worn a word to express this passionate liaison of our bodies […] with an unforgettable house" (1994: 15).

Why, though, does Bachelard seem reluctant to use the word 'habit' to describe our relationship to the house? It is partly because he persists in associating houses with the "primary function of inhabiting" (1994: 4), a kind of organic and timeless connection with the earth and universe. An important insight into the ordinariness of memory, its embeddedness in daily experience, is lost. It is interesting that Bachelard seems to use the term 'inhabit' as the opposite of 'habit,' even though these words share the same etymological root. Both words derive from the Latin *habitus*, the past participle of the verb *habere*, 'to have', which was also used reflexively for 'to be'. *Habitus* thus referred to both "what one has" and "how one is": it meant outward appearance or demeanour as well as mental constitution or character. Pierre Bourdieu, significantly, uses the term 'habitus' as a way of connecting individual thought and agency to more structural forces, defining it as a system of internalised dispositions which are the product of one's material circumstances, background and class position (1990: 53).

In both these senses, the house is the space of habit: it brings together the social expectations and imposed routines of modernity with the intimate texture and detail of individual lives. As Henri Lefebvre argues, everyday life in the modern world exhibits powerful tendencies towards standardisation and recurrence (1984: 18). Houses form part of this process in the sense that they are increasingly colonised by new technologies and patterns of consumption, physical and cultural constraints which expect us to behave in certain repetitive and predictable ways. But habits are more than merely social compulsions: the slower, cyclical rhythms of daily life can also create a comforting sense of continuity in a society characterised by rapid change.

As Mary Douglas points out, habits are not simply disembodied, meaningless experiences but memories, ways in which the house can function as "an organization of space over time" (1993: 268). The memory of sunlight and darkness, for example, makes us respond by fitting lamps, curtains and blinds in the house; the memory of summer and winter makes us respond with patios, air-conditioning, double-glazing and central heating. The entire contents of a house are a visual and material prompt to memory: we remember that beds are for sleeping in, that chairs are for sitting in, that stairs are for climbing up and down. Joëlle Bahloul stresses the significance of such "embodied memory" (1996: 113) in her ethnographic study of several Jewish and Muslim families who lived in a huge, multi-roomed house in Colonial Algeria between 1937 and 1962. Now uprooted to France, Bahloul's informants use the architecture of the house to structure their memories, which are "lodged in the monotonous repetition of the necessary acts of concrete experience" (1996: 29). In their memories of these everyday activities, time is imprecise and boundless:

> It is as if, when dealing with time, memory sought to cancel it out, to locate the past in eternity, to give it a dimension of the absolute. Domestic memory does not count time: time is an intangible dimension of remembrance of the domestic space. This remembrance flows like a river that never runs dry, re-creating a world in which objects and gestures are endlessly repeated without interruption (1996: 102).

Unlike Bachelard, Bahloul argues that this apparent timelessness means that domestic memories have an unquestioned truth status that allows them to convey culturally specific meanings. Her informants therefore use these recollections as a way of articulating their feelings about kinship obligations, social hierarchies, gender codes and, above all, the experience of diaspora. For Bahloul, habits are powerfully evocative precisely because these cultural meanings interact with the personal signatures of individuals and families, their particular ways of interacting with the physical environment which are invested with feelings of security, well-being and belonging.

Conclusion
Our extraordinary emotional and cultural investment in houses has often been explained in terms of their capacity to evoke nostalgia. For Bachelard, the house promises "far distant voyages into a world that is no more" (1994: 143), returning us to early childhood or our primeval origins. In this chapter, though, I have suggested that our attachment to houses in Western culture has more to do with the mundane and ongoing activities of daily life than with an idealised past. It is true that houses provide us with a sense that the past can be preserved within the stable confines of their solid walls. But the house is not fixed forever by its site and structure: it is also an evolving entity of layered residues and accretions, responsive to the subtle modifications of habitual experience. As Brand puts it: "The house and its occupants mold to each other twenty-four hours a day, and the building accumulates the record of that intimacy" (1997: 7). In a sense, the house reflects the dual status of everyday life, which combines the concrete and textural with the contingent and ephemeral. Of course, the very invisibility of memory within the house makes its cultural meanings all the more potent. We overlook the fact that the buildings to which we have formed such an apparently organic, indissoluble bond are the product of particular circumstances, and connote specific meanings about wealth, class and cultural distinction. As the zoning of residential areas demonstrates, the inherent competitiveness and inequalities of the housing market mean that our feelings of homeliness are achieved at the expense of the most deprived and excluded sections of society. This is what Lefebvre means when he argues that "a revolution takes place only when people can no longer lead their everyday lives" (1984: 32). As the main arena for the obscured practices of everyday life, the house comes to seem a space for poetics, not politics. For this reason alone, it will remain a significant cultural battleground.

'You understand what domestic architecture ought to be, you do': Finding Home in *The Wind in the Willows*

Gerry Smyth

ABSTRACT

This essay offers an analysis of the classic children's novel The Wind in the Willows *(1908) by English writer Kenneth Grahame in two aspects of its engagement with domestic space. The first concerns the representation of house and home within the text itself, and discusses how this representation is linked both to Grahame's biography and to the wider politico-cultural condition in which he was living and writing. The second concerns the ability of fiction to assume a quasi-architectural presence in the perception of the reading subject, and examines the manner in which* The Wind in the Willows *became a sort of reading 'home' (with all the ambivalent values and associations that such a concept implies) for the author of the essay. The contribution concludes by suggesting a link between the image of home as represented in the text and that assumed by the text itself in the perception of the reading subject.*

Introduction

The vast amount of critical literature produced on the subjects of house and home is evidence of the fact that they are concepts possessed of the ability to function on a number of different cognitive levels. In this essay I want to consider a number of such levels as they relate to an analysis of Kenneth Grahame's celebrated children's novel *The Wind in the Willows* (1908). These levels of engagement are categorically distinct but, as I shall go on to argue, are also and at the same time indissolubly interdependent. In many ways, in fact, the principal interest of such an analysis lies in catching the resonances that lie (as here) between literary critical, socio-historical, biographical, autobiographical and philosophical discourses.

The first level of engagement is concerned with the text itself and the ways in which the various characters experience and negotiate concepts of home, especially as these concepts are manifested in the built environment known as 'the house'. Indeed, at the level of plot alone, *The Wind in the Willows* is clearly all about houses – the Rat's "cosy quarters [...] Toad's beautiful hall [...] Badger's great house"[1] and Mole's humble underground dwelling – owning them, leaving them, caring for them, and ultimately fighting for them. At a deeper level, however, we may discern an anxious engagement with the concept of 'home' as a place of nurture and safety on the one hand, but one of restriction and limitation, on the other. This contradictory response to the idea of house and home may be linked on one level to Grahame's own biography which, in common with many of the writers from what one critic called "The Golden Age of Children's Literature" (Carpenter 1985), was not the straightforward ideal prescribed in contemporary ideology. More tellingly, however, I believe it's a reflection of the fragile politico-cultural formation in which, as a subject of the world's most successful modern empire, he lived and worked.

Meaning is never created in a cultural void, of course. My own experience as a reader of *The Wind in the Willows* has been coloured by particular circumstances, both in the moment of initial encounter and subsequently. As a second level of analysis, therefore, I want to track my own changing response to Grahame's novel, describing first of all what occurred when this middle-class English classic (encoding, as remarked above, very particular models of house and home) was consumed sixty years later in a working-class Irish "reading formation" (Bennett 1983) possessed of very different experiences of domestic architecture and a very different understanding of what it meant to belong and what it felt like to be excluded.

In the second part of the essay I want to consider the ways in which fictional narratives assume both geographical and architectural dimensions in the consciousness of the reading subject. Specifically, I shall suggest that *The Wind in the Willows* began to function as a sort of narrative home for me, a notional place that in time accumulated its own contradictory resonances in my spatial apprehension of the world. As an exile from class, country and childhood, 'home' has become a deeply ambivalent concept for me to engage – familiar and ever-present in some respects, uncanny and always already lost in others. In the final analysis, the essay may achieve nothing more than a proof of the suspicion that a personal response to my fictional 'home' as embodied in Grahame's text, therefore, is symbiotically enmeshed with a professional apprehension of house and home as abstract theoretical concepts.

Finding Home

Kenneth Grahame's best-known work has been a phenomenon of world publishing since its first appearance in 1908. With countless imprints and republications, the tale of the four friends and their various adventures has (in the marketing parlance) captured the imagination of generations of people: not only in England, in which country the book is set – *The Wind in the Willows* is one of a select number of stories to enjoy transnational appeal; and not only for children – the text possesses the rare ability to continue to resonate for mature readers who might be expected to have outgrown its childish charms.

In the second part of this essay I consider how a text changes in relation to the altered circumstances (including most crucially the age and the background) of the reading subject. Before that, however, I want to revisit the story in relation to certain aspects of the author's own experience, and the experience of the society in which he lived and worked. *The Wind in the Willows* appeared in that period between the end of the Boer War and the beginning of the First World War – a period which in retrospect has been seen as somewhat of a golden age of English life, the last late stirring of an older world before the destruction wrought by the first great modern military conflict. In reality, Edwardian England was (as ever) anxious, uncertain, frantically attempting to modernise in economic and military terms while at the same time desperate to hold on to what centuries of ideological accretion had determined to be the core constituents of English identity.

On one level, *The Wind in the Willows* may be read as an allegory of the conflict between tradition and modernity at a key stage in modern British history.[2] The class basis of the conflict with which the text closes has, for example, been noted more or less since its first publication: various conservative elements (landed gentry, old aristocracy and bourgeoisie) combine to quell the discontented lower orders as represented by the weasels, stoats and ferrets. Behind such class conflict, however, lie deeper anxieties concerning Britain's imperial status and the status of those subjects (specifically, English men) charged with the task of winning and holding the empire. Deeper still, underpinning and informing all these issues, lies a concern with space and place – specifically, with calibrating the meaning of the contemporary world as a function of that most fundamental of human concerns: domestic dwelling.

In a letter to a friend, the young Kenneth Grahame described a recurrent dream in which he experienced

> a gradual awakening to consciousness on a certain little room, very dear and familiar [...] always the same feeling of a home-coming, of the world shut out, of the ideal encasement. On the shelves were a few books – a very few – but just the editions I had sighed for, the editions which refuse to turn up, or which poverty glowers at on alien shelves. On the walls were a print or two, a woodcut, an etching – not many [...] All was modest – Oh, so very modest! But all was my very own, and, what was more, everything in the room was exactly right (quoted in Carpenter 1985: 117).

For the critic Humphrey Carpenter, this intriguing report encapsulates one pole of Grahame's personality: 'the Home-lover'. Carpenter is referring here to a familiar cultural trope in which the notion of 'home' (often associated with a sentimentalised representation of the childhood house) functions as an implicit balance to a discourse of travel (frequently troped as 'wanderlust' or 'adventure') which, always present to some extent, begins to make itself felt with the coming to maturity of the subject. In some intellectual traditions, the dialectic thus formed (home-lover / adventurer) is understood to be fundamental to the modern human condition. In this respect, it's interesting to note the extent to which Grahame's dream accords with the description of a similar apprehension encountered early in Gaston Bachelard's *The Poetics of Space*:

> If we give their function of shelter for dreams to all of these places of retreat, we may say [...] that there exists for each one of us an oneiric house, a house of dream-memory, that is lost in the shadow of a beyond of the real past. I called this oneiric house the crypt of the house that we were born in. Here we find ourselves at a pivotal point around which reciprocal interpretation of dreams through thought and thought through dreams, keep turning [...] In order to sense, across the years, our attachment for the house we were born in, dream is more powerful than thought [...] And so, beyond all the positive values of protection, the house we were born in becomes imbued with dream values which remain after the house has gone (1994: 15-17).

The parallels are striking and suggestive; but more interesting, perhaps, are the discrepancies between theory and experience. Grahame's dream-room represents not the surfacing of 'values' associated with the house of childhood, but rather the eruption of unfulfilled desires – the books he never owned, the peace he never knew, the home he never had. This reading is clearly supported by a knowledge of Grahame's early life which (as described in Peter Green's definitive biography), although far from the ideal of a settled childhood in the bosom of a nuclear family, was not the disaster which his circumstances might have warranted. His alcoholic father decamped for France soon after the death of Grahame's mother, leaving four children in the care of their maternal grandmother. Thereafter the future author of *The Wind in the Willows* experienced many geographical and architectural resettlements before coming to maturity and taking responsibility for his own domestic arrangements. There can be no doubt that Grahame did possess a 'home-loving' dimension to his personality, for it clearly emerged in his work; this dimension, however, was animated (in Bachelard's terms) as much by 'thought' as by 'dream' – by a conscious desire to realise a cultural ideal rather than an unconscious retrieval of a lost childhood space.

If Grahame was on one level merely compensating for the childhood he never experienced, however, he did so in a way that revealed the contradictions underlying the ideal to which he aspired. Looking again at the description of his dream room, it's interesting to note that it is *already* riven to some degree by competing desires and fears. The womb-like properties of the room are clearly in evidence – the feeling of absolute safety, of a secure anchorage against the cares of the world – and this constitutes the invocation of 'nature' as a discourse within both the dream and the description. The world is excluded, "shut out", precisely *because* it is a place where "everything" can never be "exactly right". That (as so much Victorian literature attests) is a condition reserved only for childhood and dreams. At the same time, the space described is in some senses already a cultural one – a built environment (encompassing shelves and walls, and presumably a roof and door) in which are housed a range of materially preferred objects. Culture is also present in the allusions to the social context of poverty, and to the taste that prescribes the superiority of certain "editions". What, after all, do these prints and woodcuts and books represent – what do they *stand for* and what do they *depict*? The answer is: the world – the real world *outside* the room upon whose exclusion depends the natural feelings of homecoming and of things being "exactly right".

Culture and nature inhere within the same narrative, in other words, a narrative in which neither home nor travel has priority over the other – in which, in fact, these concepts depend upon each other for their coherence *as* concepts. This, in turn, makes the spatial narratives within which such concepts are invoked profoundly ambivalent – something which may be observed in the representation of house and home in *The Wind in the Willows*. Each of the four main characters in the text is identified with a particular kind of dwelling, and has a particular kind of relationship with that dwelling.[3] The text begins with the Mole hard at work in his modest little underground house, beavering (!) away on home maintenance in a manner that has become almost hysterically fashionable a century or so later. But in an act familiar to generations of DIY victims, he suddenly takes a different perspective and abandons his work to go, literally, in search of pastures new.

Thus the beginning may be regarded as the key moment in the text, the event which *enables* everything that comes after. This is the point at which the responsibilities of home-ownership and building maintenance – essentially adult responsibilities – are neglected in favour of more trivial pursuits. Mole's desertion of his home represents a turning away from adulthood, and this in turn may be read as an embodiment of one entire strand of so-called 'children's literature' – which on closer inspection turns out to be not *for* or *about* children at all, but for adults who, under pressure from their responsibilities, hypostasise a particular model of childhood wherein such responsibilities may be, at least temporarily, abrogated.[4] And thus it is with Mole who, soon after leaving home, encounters Rat with whom he becomes involved in a life defined principally by the irresponsible activity of "messing about in boats" (4). The life lived by the two friends represents the lost Eden, the "secret garden" of childhood, worshipped by so many of the late Victorian and Edwardian children's authors.

Rat's bijou riverside residence appears to provide the perfect base for "messing about in boats". We soon learn, however, that this is to some extent *already* a fallen world, a world under pressure from the forces of change, and this reminds us of Raymond Williams' comment that the defining characteristic of the organic community is that it is always already lost (1979: 252). In response to Mole's naïve question regarding the solitude of his life by the river, the Rat replies:

You're new to it, and of course you don't know. The bank is so crowded nowadays that many people are moving away altogether. O no, it isn't what it used to be, at all. Otters, kingfishers, dabchicks, moorhens, all of them about all day and always wanting you to *do* something – as if a fellow had no business of his own to attend to! (5).

In such passages we begin to catch a glimpse of the forces of change that are threatening both the riverbank and the nation that it symbolises. For if on one level Grahame was clearly dramatising a range of personal anxieties and desires, on another we observe that he came to maturity during one of the most active and successful periods in British imperial history, at a time, that is, when issues of home and belonging, safety and danger, travel and dwelling, were being redefined in relation to a very specific politico-economic mission. In Britain itself, industrialisation had precipitated new patterns in homebuilding, dwelling and ownership, all of which impacted significantly upon the bourgeois imagination. One of the distinguishing characteristics of the modern world which the late Victorian commentators (Arnold, Ruskin, Kingsley and Forster, to name but a few) could hear creeping out of the great industrial centres was its encouragement to working-class people to cluster together in new kinds of buildings and in new kinds of communities. In this way the proletarian house became one of the great repositories of bourgeois angst regarding both the moral and the physical health of the nation.

The nervousness engendered by the re-organisation of Britain's social fabric contrasted with the ostensible confidence resulting from the nation's status as motherland to the world's most successful modern empire. Yet this latter consciousness also brought its anxieties and doubts. For if on the one hand the empire offered male characters an arena wherein they could realise their identities *qua* British (or more often than not simply 'English') men in relation to a variety of exotic others, on the other it seemed that the turn to empire represented an abrogation of the responsibilities of home and a concomitant embrace of perpetual childhood. Thus, whereas Hardy's Jude Fawley (1896) *stayed* and lost himself amongst the contradictions besetting late-Victorian England, Stevenson's Jim Hawkins (1883) *departed* and found himself amongst the swamps and woods of the treasure island. Jude is obliged to become a man before he has finished being a child. Even as Jim *becomes* a man, however, he *remains* a child, both in terms of the text wherein he is represented (he will always be the teenage cabin boy in *Treasure Island*) and in terms of his representation as a model of English masculinity.[5]

Mole's initial rejection of home is compounded by his enthusiasm for the open road (Chapter Two) and his reckless adventure in the Wild Wood (Chapter Three). Wild oats thus well and truly sown, he thereafter displays a marked domestic inclination as well as a keen sense of responsibility, something reflected in his close association with Badger. Both Toad and Rat, on the other hand, are overcome at various points throughout the story by strong impulses to leave, to realise themselves in relation to exotic landscapes and unfamiliar peoples. Whereas Toad's rejection of home serves to confirm his immaturity in relation to the other characters (a lack of responsibility towards his name and his property) the temptation of Rat figures much more ambivalently. Throughout the chapter entitled 'Wayfarers All', Rat perceives the narrowness of his life on the riverbank with an increasing sense of dissatisfaction. Through the narratives of the Sea Rat and the migratory swallows, Grahame depicts the departure from home as an exotic adventure, full of colour and excitement. The appeal, it appears, lies in a denial of routine, a rejection of the humdrum repetitions that constitute life at home, and a *realisation* of the self through encounter, danger, achievement – all those staples, in fact, of the high imperial adventure story. That the Mole is obliged to physically prevent his friend from leaving at the end of 'Wayfarers All' is a clear indication of the seriousness of the situation; but Grahame reveals that the more significant assault in this instance has been upon Rat's 'true' identity, for as they grapple Mole finds himself staring not into "his friend's eyes, but the eyes of some other animal!" (105).

Moving up the social scale, we find the dwellings of Badger and Toad are likewise implicated in both Grahame's personal psycho-drama and in England's domestic response to its imperial status. Although different in many obvious ways, Badger and Toad nonetheless share a relatively privileged social standing in the community, such a position being dialectically linked to the dwellings they inhabit. The description of Badger's underground home as a "safe anchorage" (36) carries echoes of Grahame's dream room; in this regard we should note that subterranean dwellings represent an especially intimate way of inhabiting the landscape – a way of being present even when appearing to be absent. Adapted as it is from an ancient human settlement, Badger's home represents the stability and durability of English rural life; as such, it functions as a conservative rejoinder to the onset of rapid, remorseless change precipitated by the great social, cultural and political revolutions of the nineteenth century. Above all, home for Badger represents "security [...] peace and tranquillity" (42); and when Mole heartily acquiesces, Badger grants a telling compliment: "You understand what domestic architecture ought to be, you do".

In some key respects, Badger is clearly a representation of the responsible father figure which his creator never knew, and this is reflected in his ambivalent status within the text; for if we are invited to acknowledge his sense of duty and the high respect in which he is held by all parties, at the same time his humourless, bullying presence appears faintly ridiculous when set against the Toad's subversive laughter. Badger plays the bluff, rough squire to Toad's feckless son-of-the-big-house; and it is here, beneath Grahame's comic depiction of the latter, that we may observe the anxiety with which issues of property and class were regarded in the wake of the industrial revolution, and the nervousness attendant upon Britain's precarious role as first among imperial equals in the years leading up to the First World War.

Toad is without doubt the most memorable of the four main characters, and this is principally because he possesses material resources the others do not, and is willing to jeopardise those resources in spectacularly comic ways. Put simply, his personal wealth allows the Toad to work in large colourful gestures, and to make large colourful blunders, and this makes good reading in a way that the gestures and blunders of those with less to lose do not. At the same time, as a member of the landed gentry Toad represents one important cornerstone of English society, which in turn supports and informs the British imperial project abroad; while he may be mocked for comic purposes, the narrative works to restore the order which Toad, in spite of himself, symbolises.

That order is embodied in the house Toad inherits from his illustrious father. Like Badger's home, Toad Hall plays an important regulatory role within the local community, representing power, privilege, wealth and influence. In Toad's case, however, these factors derive not from the personal prestige of the owner (for Toad is clearly a figure of fun amongst all and sundry) but from the ostentatious power embodied in the edifice itself; as Toad himself remarks, his ancestral pile is the "[finest] house on the whole river [or] anywhere else, for that matter" (14). It's entirely fitting, then, that the social revolution

attempted by the Wild Wooders should take the form of an expropria-
tion of Toad Hall. It's likewise appropriate that the house itself should
constitute both the prize for which, and the arena wherein, the battle
between order and anarchy takes place.

The heroes are aided in their endeavour by a secret passage enabling them to emerge right in the heart of Toad Hall. This secret
knowledge symbolises an organic connection between dwelling and
identity – Badger simply *knows* who belongs where. His thorough
command of the architecture contrasts with the disdain for decorum
demonstrated by the weasels who, we are informed, "[lie] in bed half
the day, and breakfast at all hours, and the place in such a mess [...]
it's not fit to be seen" (127). Even so, given the size of the threat and
the numbers of the enemy, it's surprising just how quickly victory is
achieved. The characters' faith in their own abilities is matched by the
author's conviction that nature will assert itself and order will prevail,
regardless of the odds or the situation. Such faith and such conviction
were to disappear forever from the world by the Christmas of 1914. In
the meantime, Grahame achieves classic ideological closure, resolving
in narrative what could not be resolved in reality, and temporarily re-
lieving anxieties that continue to plague English national consciousness to the present day.

Grahame took aspects of the prevailing political climate, of his
own personal experience, and of a deeply embedded species response
to the phenomenon of dwelling, and orchestrated them into an enduringly successful narrative. The 'home-lover' is encapsulated in 'The
Piper at the Gates of Dawn', the chapter in which Grahame gives
clearest expression to a conviction (one he shared with many Victorian and Edwardian writers) regarding the mystical that inheres within
the domestic. The 'adventurer' is encapsulated in 'Wayfarers All', the
chapter in which the author gives vent to a suspicion that Pan may
indeed be dead, and that such magic as remains in the world may be
encountered only by forsaking the domestic.

Grahame can only ever provide the raw materials from which
meaning is produced, however; he cannot guarantee that a single intended meaning will subsist over the potentially endless range of reading contexts within which the text will be invoked. Reading, in fact, is
always a discursive event in itself – always, that is to say, the result of
negotiation between *a* meaning intended by the author and *a* meaning
produced by the reader in response to their specific location in time

and space. Sometimes, the discrepancy between the ideal reader encoded in the text and the actual reader who productively activates the text can produce anomalous, yet deeply compelling, responses. It's just one such response that I wish to describe in the second part of this essay.

Leaving Home

I first encountered *The Wind in the Willows* in or around July 1970 when approaching the age of nine. One of Dublin County Council's mobile libraries was a regular visitor to our small estate throughout that summer, and I would take time off from the usual holiday activities – playing football, or messing about in boats on the River Dodder which ran close by – to climb the van steps and enter its cool, book-lined interior. On the first occasion, the young librarian directed me to the children's section at the back of the truck, while the driver looked on suspiciously. On a later visit I found a large hardback edition of Grahame's novel, although why that volume and not some other should have been chosen on this particular occasion escapes me. Of such unfathomable chances are life-long obsessions made.

Although typical in every other way of the contemporary Irish working-class milieu to which we belonged, our household was unusual in the depth of the family's passion for books. Both grandfathers enjoyed reputations as 'readers'; the paternal one was especially well regarded in the local community, being an educated Protestant who had voluntarily come down in the world so as to marry his Catholic sweetheart (who turned out to be far from 'sweet') at the end of the nineteenth century. A respect for the printed word descended to my generation, although at the time my siblings and I were ignorant of both its provenance and its implications; reading was just something we did and did a lot, something that our peers – otherwise similar in more or less every other respect – did not do so much or did not do at all.

By the time I first encountered *The Wind in the Willows* I had been engaged in self-directed reading for a number of years. Graduating from the ubiquitous *Peter and Jane* school series, the first book I read for pleasure was *Shadow the Sheepdog* by Enid Blyton. From that I moved on to other Blyton texts – the Secret Seven, the Famous Five, as well as selected titles from an elder sister's library of Mallory Towers and St Clare's volumes. All these books were consumed with that

intensity of identification and that obliviousness to 'the real world'
which are recurring characteristics of reading children. None made the
impression, however, that Grahame's novel did. I re-read it continu-
ously for the remainder of that year, and returned to it at frequent periods throughout the next decade or so. Sometimes I had time only for
favourite chapters; occasionally I would indulge myself by settling
down in some secluded place to consume the entire text at one four- or
five-hour sitting. But why? Why should this "heady evocation of the
English pastoral dream" (Wullschläger 2001: 161) resonate so
strongly with a late twentieth-century Irish boy?

   One answer must be the text's ability to create a world alternative
to the 'real' one outside the text. As Francis Spufford writes:

> The books you read as a child brought you sights you hadn't seen yourself, scents
> you hadn't smelled, sounds you hadn't heard. They introduced you to people you
> hadn't met, and helped you to sample ways of being that would never have oc-
> curred to you. And the result was, if not an "intellectual rational being", then
> somebody who was enriched by the knowledge that their own particular life only
> occupied one little space in a much bigger world of possibilities (2002: 10).

Growing up in Dublin in the 1960s and 1970s, I experienced *The
Wind in the Willows* in a cultural and political milieu which was
deeply inimical to the one in which the text had been produced, the
one which its ideal reader would inhabit. The political revolution of
1916-1922 (in which the state that would become the Republic of Ireland was established) was accompanied (and to a significant degree
precipitated) by a cultural revolution that had been underway since the
late eighteenth century. This revolution in thought, word and deed was
dedicated to the rediscovery (its critics would say 'invention') and
subsequent celebration of a unique Irish identity defined in large part
over and against the Englishness which had been the dominant cultural force throughout the Atlantic archipelago for nigh on a millennium (Smyth 1998). Life in the Republic had been liberalising
throughout the 1960s, but by modern European standards the place
was still a provincial backwater, dominated by an ultra-conservative
Catholic clergy and by a political culture still in thrall to values and
practices with roots in the nineteenth century. The commencement of
'the Troubles' in Northern Ireland towards the end of the 1960s, and
their escalation into something akin to a full-scale revolution during

the early years of the 1970s, appeared to confirm the entire island's benighted status.

As a working-class Irish child I was fully implicated in this milieu, trapped like the rest of my generation by discourses of nationality and class into which, through no choice of my own, I had been born. It was not that it was such a bad environment; it was the fact that its limits had been determined by unaccountable forces, removed in time and space from the child's purview. Its everyday culture, powerful and attractive though it could be, seemed insular and dull when set against the colourful outside world which filtered in from time to time through a variety of unofficial channels. One important connection to the outside world was provided by British television that, through a broadcasting anomaly, was available all along the eastern Irish seaboard. Thus it was that *Top of the Pops* and *Dr Who*, *Coronation Street* and *Play for Today*, became the cultural staples of a generation growing increasingly frustrated with the long shadow of the past that appeared to lie over modern Ireland.

I participated in this cultural rebellion, finding solace from the dissatisfactions of the present first of all in Blyton and *The Beano*, later in British and American pop music. In the early months of 1977 my world, like that of the rest of my generation, was turned upside by The Sex Pistols and The Clash. Besides being propelled forward into a new and exciting future, however, I was also drawn (via the family penchant for reading) backwards into a world very different from the one into which I had been socialised, a world, in fact, more or less diametrically opposed – in terms of its values, its language and its general cultural atmosphere – to post-revolutionary Ireland.

Fiction, I have suggested, can remove the child from one social and cultural environment to another – therein, indeed, lies perhaps its chief appeal; the environment described by Grahame in *The Wind in the Willows* was powerfully attractive for a young mind in search of colour, romance, and a model of identity radically *other* to the one with which he was so familiar. In terms of language, for example, commentators justly celebrate the richness of the Hiberno-English dialect that I grew up speaking. For me, however, it was the language of the kitchen and the schoolyard, and it faded before the linguistic richness of the riverbankers, who spoke in such perfectly formed sentences and who employed those comic locutions so unselfconsciously.

In *The Child that Books Built*, Francis Spufford employs a number of spatial images to describe the development of his early reading practices: the forest, the island, the town and the hole. These spaces function at times as metaphors – as when, for example, he likens the infant's developing brain to a primeval wood; at other times, the spaces are deployed much more literally – as when he tracks the influence of post-glacial forest upon the development of folk narrative (2002: 23-63). There is one space, however, so absolutely fundamental in its relevance to human evolution that it comes as a real surprise when Spufford does not engage with it at length: the house. For it seems to me that fiction functions at a number of levels to recreate the relationships that humans have with houses; and this certainly helps to account, in a number of important respects, for my changing relationship with *The Wind in the Willows* over the years since first encountering it.

Let me try to describe what I mean by this: Science and philosophy (and latterly, although much more modestly, literary criticism) have suggested that we all inhabit a number of different realities. While some of these realities are susceptible to material analysis (in terms of their physical properties, economics and politics, for example), others are less amenable to empirical description – worlds in which memory, atmosphere and dreams reign. One of the worlds we all inhabit, however, is the world of fiction. By this I do not mean solely the written word (although that is a significant source); I mean the world of memories and impressions and prejudices and beliefs that is constructed by our encounter with all the narratives we encounter in all the representational media to which we are exposed throughout our lives. In some senses, the reading subject is reborn into the house of fiction every time he she engages with narrative. This is a world that is akin to our own, but nevertheless different, a world populated by subjects similar to us, but again recognisably 'other' at the same time. This is a world that possesses its own morality, its own logic, its own reality; most significantly for present purposes, it's a world in which architecture and geography function according to the internal logic of the reading subject's fictional reality.

What I would like to suggest is that certain texts can come to represent 'home' within the world of fiction that we all, to a greater or lesser extent, inhabit; and this 'home' – like those in the 'real' world – is capable of creating contradictory feelings in the home-dwelling subject: feelings of security and belonging, certainly, but also feelings of restriction and resentment.[6] What I would further like to suggest is that for a variety of reasons – some of which are describable (in the terms I have attempted above), some of which are ultimately inscrutable – *The Wind in the Willows* came to function at an early stage in my reading career as a sort of home, the still, secure point of my imaginary world of fiction. While this is clearly a metaphor on one level, on another it is equally clear that my feelings in relation to the text were cognitively the same as those towards the actual edifice in which I slept and ate and read – feelings of familiarity, belonging, proprietorship and security. The fact is that I *lived* in *The Wind in the Willows* in the same way that I *lived* in that small south Dublin house; coming home to one (house) provided an opportunity to come home to the other (text).

As Rat discovers in 'Wayfarers All', however, the thing about home is that at some point the feelings of familiarity and safety can give way to feelings of restriction and resentment. As part of their bid to achieve full and independent subjectivity, children are obliged to negotiate a traumatic re-orientation of space as they approach puberty – especially the key space of the home which dominates their early imagination. This was especially the case in a deeply patriarchal country such as twentieth-century Ireland, in which the mother's domestic role was instituted by law, and where the male child's formative experiences were dominated by a model of feminine domesticity. As a consequence, Irish adult masculinity characteristically involved a simultaneous rejection of, and nostalgia for, the childhood home. This pattern, in fact, forms the basis of a recurring theme within modern Irish cultural discourse: the hero puts away childish things with initial alacrity, only for some narrative crisis to prompt a wistful realisation of the power of feminine domesticity that has been left behind, followed by either an attempt to re-institute the childhood home in a new form with a new 'mother', or a stoical admission on the part of the lone hero that home is lost and gone forever.[7]

Approaching adolescence, my own home-within-fiction began to come under pressure. School friends began to talk about *The Odessa File* and *The Day of the Jackal* (both by British thriller writer Frederick Forsyth who was co-incidentally at the time resident in Ireland for tax purposes) and similar 'grown-up' books. These boys took obvious pride in the size and the difficulty (or hardness) of their reading material, as if there was a direct correlation between these factors and the adult male identity of which they were so assiduously in pursuit. I recall reading and hating both books, bored by the unfamiliar allusions, the tortuous plotting and the lack of dialogue, and threatened by the thought that I *ought* to be enjoying them. I spent the summer of 1973 reading Agatha Christie whodunnits. Although seldom guessing the identity of the murderer, these novels fed a lasting anglophilia that I have had to learn to accommodate in later life with some decidedly anti-English sympathies. From these flirtations I returned to *The Wind in the Willows* as to the maternal bosom, happy to be back again amongst the pages, paragraphs, sentences and even the individual words which I knew so intimately – happy, in a word, to be home.

Such a relationship could not be sustained indefinitely, however; just as the adolescent subject has to prepare to leave home by exploring spaces outwith the domestic realm, so I submitted to 'wanderlust' by beginning to explore the fictional world beyond *The Wind in the Willows*. While still in this transitional stage, I had the fortune to encounter two competitors of immense power and attraction: *Pride and Prejudice* and *The Lord of the Rings*. In Longbourn and Middle Earth, these texts depicted 'realities' every bit as compelling as the Riverbank, while also broaching issues – politics, sexuality, morality – too subtly embedded in *The Wind in the Willows* to be of much use at that stage in my critical career. The encounters between Darcy and Lizzie, or between any of the huge cast of characters in Tolkein's epic, pointed towards new experiences, new languages – in short, new and more complex ways of being in the world. Later I perceived the ideological limitations of both texts, and the way both worked to naturalise certain privileged notions of reality. All this notwithstanding, *Pride and Prejudice* and *The Lord of the Rings* materially altered the map of my fictional world more than anything I have read since. In the meantime, the re-visitations to Grahame's world grew fewer and fewer, the colours faded and the pleasure waned. It was time to leave home.

Conclusion

In one of the most effective passages in *The Wind in the Willows*, Mole and Rat are returning from a day's outing when the former smells his old underground home, the one he abandoned in the opening pages of the story as he rushed off in search of adventure above ground. The power of Mole's feeling for the abandoned dwelling is only just overcome by the power of his friendship for Rat, although when the latter learns the situation he insists that they return to find Mole's pre-Riverbank abode. Mole is initially mortified by the condition of his old home, but Rat brings him around by degrees to an appreciative estimation of its worth. The stoical conclusion to the chapter is typical of the tenor of the book as a whole:

> [Mole] saw clearly how plain and simple – how narrow, even – it all was; but clearly, too, how much it all meant to him, and the special value of some anchorage in one's existence. He did not at all want to abandon the new life and its splendid spaces, to turn his back on sun and air and all they offered him, and creep home and stay there; the upper world was all too strong, it called to him still, even down there, and he knew he must return to the larger stage. But it was good to think he had this to come back to, this place which was all his own, these things which were so glad to see him again and could always be counted upon for the same simple welcome (58).

Here, the irresistible force of adventure meets the immovable object of the home. I would suggest that insofar as Mole, sensible fellow that he is, manages to reach an accommodation between these two forces in his life, this passage becomes central to Grahame's vision, as well as to an entire tradition of English culture. When occasionally I come across *The Wind in the Willows* – in critical works, in reading lists, in the houses of friends with children, on video or on television – I feel like Mole encountering a place which used to offer a secure and familiar "anchorage" on the world but which has been abandoned for a "new life". Given the trajectory of this essay, the issue I then – now – have to face is the extent to which the resolution of competing desires achieved by Mole is available to me.

In this essay I have suggested that I experienced the same predicament in relation to *The Wind in the Willows* as may be discerned throughout the text itself. The characters have to negotiate a range of moral and emotional dilemmas in relation to the geography and the architecture of the Riverbank – all variations on the central dilemma of whether to leave in search of adventure or to stay and fully inhabit a 'natural' environment. These dilemmas can themselves be linked to Grahame's own experience as an 'abandoned' child, as a semi-reluctant banker and a somewhat more reluctant husband and father. The narrative may also be regarded as a reflection of the general political climate of the age in which it was conceived, especially the decade of the 1890s which, as well as being the high point of British imperial activity, was also the happiest period of Grahame's life. There may initially appear to be a great distance between the concerns of the Riverbank and those of the empire, but it's clear that they are in fact animated by the same matrix of desires and anxieties.

I first read *The Wind in the Willows* in a very different social, cultural and political context to the one in which it was written. Yet my relationship *with* the text came to mirror the spatial relationships described *in* the text – the desire for home cast against the desire to realise the self by leaving home. The anxious closure achieved *in* the narrative is likewise similar to the uneasy accommodation I have reached *with* the text. Grahame's novel will always constitute 'home' within my fictional world. It waits, a secure anchorage, while I sport up here in the sunshine, still messing about in boats – happy to have left it behind, but glad that it's still there.

Notes

1. Grahame 1999: 50. All future references will be incorporated within the main body of the essay.

2. Although they are related in many key aspects, this is the quality in which Grahame's later story most resembles Jerome K. Jerome's *Three Men in a Boat* (1889), in which text, amid all the facetiousness, there remains a deep anxiety regarding "that fretful haste, that vehement striving, that is every day becoming more and more the bane of nineteenth-century life" (1984: 151).

3. As Jackie Wullschläger notes: "[We] remember Alice or Peter Pan for what they say or do, but Mole and Toad and Rat are unimaginable without the context of the river bank; and river, wild wood and Toad Hall are characters as vivid as the animals" (2001: 163).

4. This is the central thesis of one of the most influential modern studies of children's literature, Jacqueline Rose's *The Case of Peter Pan, or, The Impossibility of Children's Fiction* (1984).

5. As Wullschläger points out, however, Grahame and Hardy are similar insofar as "[both] were engaged by the rural myth [...] and both pit the majesty and timelessness of rural traditions against a 'modernist' enemy who would destroy them" (2001: 167).

6. Compare this central point with the one made by Milan Kundera in relation to the emigrant Russian composer Igor Stravinsky: "[The] start of his journey through the history of music coincides roughly with the moment when his native country ceases to exist for him; having understood that no country could replace it, he finds his only

homeland in music; this is not just a nice lyrical conceit of mine, I think it in an absolutely concrete way: his only homeland, his only home, was music, all of music by all musicians, the very history of music; there he decided to establish himself, to take root, to live; there he ultimately found his only compatriots, his only intimates, his only neighbors" (1995: 96-7).

7. A classic case in point is provided in Seamus Deane's semi-autobiographical novel *Reading in the Dark* (1996), a text which, given its obsession with memory, reading and domestic space (as explored in Smyth 2001: 130-58) in an Irish cultural context, is of clear relevance to the concerns of this essay.

The Life of a Country Cottage

Karen Sayer

ABSTRACT

Using oral testimony and material culture, this chapter interweaves theories of space with spatial memory in order to explore the ways in which the physcial traces of 'home' might, in Penelope Lively's words, "bear witness to" the past and thereby allow us to reconstruct the layout and use of an ordinary home. Descriptions of objects and their placement and use, it is argued, constitute a 'folkhistory' wherein the past is accessed through the present and remains real. The chapter in part therefore constitutes the story of a Site over the last hundred years. In telling this story it becomes clear that the construction of 'home' is complex, and involves a dialogue between past and present.

Introduction: A House Unlocked

The house as I knew it exists now only in the mind. In my head, I can still move easily and vividly around it. The furnishings are precise and clear, the sounds and smells are as they ever were. I can walk through the front door into the vestibule, and thence into the hall [...] This mansion in the mind, with its many rooms, each complete with furnishings [...] seems to me an eerie personal reflection of those imaginary constructions of another age, the mnemonic devices of the classical and medieval art of memory [...] the system whereby the sequence of an oratorical argument was retained by means of the creation of an imaginary mansion, within which the orator moved from room to room, each space serving as a stage in the argument [...] In the same way, I can move around my memory house and focus upon different objects. The house itself becomes a prompt – a system of reference, an assemblage of coded signs. Its contents conjure up a story; they are not the stations of an oratorical argument, but signifiers for the century (Lively 2001: ix-x).

Black Boy House sits alongside the A146 on a crossroads near the Norfolk-Suffolk border. It was once a public house called 'The Black Boy', a name derived from Royalist sympathies, but most recently signified by the picture of a black boy standing next to a palm tree. It is now a private home from which a driving school has been run for the last forty or so years, with a small service station attached. A little further up the road, on the pub's land there are two cottages. Abutting and partly enveloping this property, a neighbour's bungalow and ½ acre plot front onto the byway that intersects with the main road. All in all, the location qualifies to be described as "the middle of nowhere".

This triangular site existed long before the present buildings were erected (the eighteenth century in the case of Black Boy House, with later additions; in the 1890s in the case of the cottages). Over time the site has changed very little, bar the loss of some trees (mainly oaks and elms, characteristic of the area), some variation in use, and a shift in the relative importance of the roads. Where the byway once linked the site and the parish to a religious order a few miles to the East and as far as the River Waveny in the West, the A146 now carries the bulk of the traffic North to Norwich and South to the coast. This is quite typical; in the history of building, of 'Site, Skin, Structure, Services, Space plan and Stuff', Stewart Brand (following Duffy) has shown, it is the Site that will always last longest (Brand 1994: 12-16). Like many rural settings, however, Black Boy Cottage also demonstrates the "paradox of apparent isolation co-existing with real access to the outside world" (Caunce 2003: 335), as we shall see. It is this ongoing flow of communication – wherein monks, farmers, merchants and visitors, and latterly servicemen, holidaymakers and articulated trucks hastening to just-in-time destinations, all see an opportunity to stop – that has created and continues to create the Site, wearing away at the space, eroding it and making room.

Today, my parents dwell here. Over the period of their residence (some seventy years) so memories have condensed; so the place has yielded to them, preserving and gathering meanings; so the things, the 'Stuff', of their lives has gathered together and has become 'home'. Meanwhile, the spatial limits of their lives have expanded. My mother (the focus for this research) was born in one of the cottages; the spaces of her life have encompassed her mother's family in Grinstead Green, Essex (for three and a half years from the age of eight to twelve), getting work three miles away in Beccles when she was fourteen, and holidays abroad (Europe, North Africa and the United States of America) with my father. She has always 'lived' here, however. My father was born in London. He moved to the pub with his parents and brother in the 1930s as a boy, when his father became the tenant. My father travelled abroad before he married my mother, first to Newcastle, then Longmore, Halifax, and Egypt, as a young solider and Royal Engineer during the latter part of the Second World War, while his working life took him to Bedfordshire, until he set up on his own. As yet, these spatial limits have not contracted, though they may be expected to with increased age (Massey 1996: 75).

Entering these homes (Black Boy House still lived in, still a dwelling place, the cottages decaying and empty), seeing and hearing tell of their fittings, fixtures and functions, a wealth of ordinary stories are disclosed. It is these stories on which this chapter focuses, and which make it a "folkhistory" (McRae 1994: 218). As such it belongs to that tradition of reflective life writing rooted in Carolyn Steedman's *Landscape for a Good Woman* (1986), but also encompassing Penelope Lively's *A House Unlocked* (2001) and Julie Myerson's *Home: The Story of Everyone Who Ever Lived in Our House* (2004). If we are to understand 'home', to read that space as it is lived, to understand the human encounter with intimate space, to recognise that "thanks to the house, a great many of our memories are housed", then we must value this history, this "theatre of the past that is constituted by memory" (Bachelard 1994: 8). Memory, moreover – even its discrepancies – always remains "true" (Yow 1994: 23-5). So, in recognising that "space contains time", and in order "to go beyond history", we must ask:

> Was the room a large one? Was the garret cluttered up? Was the nook warm? How was it lighted? How, too, in these fragments of space, did the human being achieve silence? How did he [sic] relish the very special silence of the various retreats of solitary daydreaming? (Bachelard 1994: 9).

Bachelard's questions take us beyond memory to daydream, as "to localize memory in time is merely a matter for the biographer and only corresponds to a sort of external history". He therefore aims at "ridding history of its conjunctive temporal tissue"; to grasp at "a knowledge of intimacy, localization in the spaces of our intimacy is more urgent than determination of dates" (1994: 9). This takes us to those narratives of the past that rely on "naught but capricious memory to transmit [...] atmosphere, texture, character" (McRae 1994: 219) to the realm of anecdote where the contents of history are detached from external events, from distant dates and dry facts;

"whereas *history*, concerned with precision and rational interpretation, is *intellectual* in its apprehension of events, folkhistory relies on an intuitive, impressionistic organization of the same material" (McRae 1994: 221, original emphases). Folkhistory tells the story of 'synchronistic time', where the past becomes part of the immediacy of the intimate present. Here, the past is made to make sense in the narrator's own terms and remains real; "it is another way of knowing" (McRae 1994: 219-21). This is the past as it is lived, not as it is written. It is only in this way that we can begin to access the constantly shifting, experiential spaces of the past, the ways in which people have lived in their homes.

Over the last hundred years, the cottages have undergone considerable change at the level of Skin, Services, Space plan and Stuff. Where the Structure of a home undergoes little alteration, the interior is normally constantly modified to suit the residents' needs (Brand 1994: 13). Indeed, as Caffyn has observed, most workers' housing, urban and rural, if it hasn't decayed, has been transformed or destroyed (1986: 1). This means that there is normally very little material evidence left of the ways in which "the occupier of a vernacular dwelling expressed his (or more likely her) decorative wishes and turned a house into a home" (Brunskill 1992: 120). Wall paintings, hangings and mouldings are the first things to go during modernisation, while wallpaper and paint are probably more subject to fashion than any other aspect of interior design (Brunskill 1992: 121). Though vernacular buildings like these cottages do survive, they have therefore been 'interpreted' and 'reinterpreted' by each generation that has lived in them. This is how people dwell. In this particular case, the cottages are now relatively decayed, and their Stuff in part dispersed. Nonetheless, much of the Stuff remains accessible, and, as Penelope Lively found in *A House Unlocked*, "from each object there [spins] a shining thread of reference" (2001: xi). Using oral testimony and the material culture of one of the cottages, this chapter therefore interweaves theories of space with descriptive spatial memory to explore the ways in which the material traces of 'home' might, in Lively's words, "bear witness to" the past (2001: xi), and allow us to reconstruct the layout and use of domestic space (Lawrence 1987: 29-30).

Structure, Services and Occupation
A 'house' is always much more than its physical embodiment, more

than its built form and aesthetic. Material descriptions, as R.J. Lawrence (following Levi-Strauss and others) has argued, can provide the detail but can never explain why it was built in a given manner, why *those* materials were used in *that* way (1987: 19, 25-9). Buildings, he therefore observes, "ought to be defined in relation to their own tradition: here tradition is not just a repertoire of historical building forms, but the ways in which they have been used and regarded by people in specific social, cultural, geographical and historical contexts" (1987: 31). This is to recognise that vernacular buildings like the cottages in question are experienced both physically and symbolically, and that the meanings attached to them may (and their uses will) change over time.

Of Brand's six 'S's 'Structure' – the "foundation and load-bearing elements" – is the second most durable component, with a life of "30 to 300 years" (1994: 13). Built at the end of the nineteenth century, the cottage that my mother was born in has lasted just over a century so far – though it has been unoccupied since about 1973 or '74. Built as one of a pair, in machine-made brick, roofed in slate, it consists of a two-up, two-down Structure, with attached scullery and outbuildings, plus a brick-built toilet down the garden path. Otherwise almost identical to its partner, it also has an annex built onto one side, an element included in the original building plan and designed as a shop. There is a small front garden, fenced with iron railings and land set aside for a larger garden to the side and rear. Set back about eight or nine meters from the road, its windows now rattle to the roar of passing juggernauts (indeed, passing traffic may be heard throughout the interview with my mother that I taped there). Although in style it is more like a terrace than the thatched, rose-covered image that the word 'cottage' might suggest, Black Boy Cottage is in fact typical of single-household speculative properties built in the late nineteenth century.

The context for the build was the housing shortage that existed throughout rural Norfolk during this period, which reformers suggested would lead to widespread moral and physical decay. The subject was discussed at length in numerous Parliamentary reports. Responding to this, there were any number of prize essays and advice books published on the construction of labourers' cottages – texts tending to focus (at least in the case of agriculturalists) on issues of outlay and return as much as on the well-being of the poor. As Ralph

Neville-Grenville MP put it in the *Journal of the Bath and West of England Society* (1873):

> From the pages of our own 'Journal,' from those of the 'Journal of the Royal Agricultural Society', or from the numerous publications by societies, by architects, and by others who have turned their attention to the subject of labourer's cottages, plans can be selected suited to all circumstances and situations, or which, with a little care and attention, can be adapted to them.
>
>   The great question to be solved is how can they be erected more cheaply than the sum hitherto paid for them – in other words, at an expenditure for which there would be a fair return in the shape of rent (1873: 196).

Uninterested in the mores of social reformers (beyond the decision to separate the sexes at night), most cottage builders therefore focused on workable common custom and cost. Given their layout and use of modern standardised materials, the cottages in question seem to employ the old Board of Agriculture's two-bedroom standard, an 'off the peg' basic design, coupled with a vernacular 'low-road' approach to adaptation (Brand 1994) and an interest in profit. By the 1890s, new methodologies and technologies had transformed the production of all buildings, rural and urban; the Black Boy's cottages belonged to the same set of economic, use, aesthetic and exchange values as other new builds of the time (Lawrence 1987: 42-9).

The same factors shaped the cottage's 'Services'. Water was obtained from rainwater butts at the back of the buildings and from a well at the pub. There was no mains gas, though a gas supply pipe ran (and still runs) down the main road. Therefore candles, plus oil, kerosene, and paraffin lamps lit both the cottages and the shop. This was typical of the area; two of the shop's staple items were candles and paraffin. Fireplaces, plus the kitchen ranges, later supplemented by portable paraffin stoves, provided heat. Beds were warmed through with stone hot-water bottles. There was no mains sewage disposal, just soak-aways. Water and then electricity were only laid on in 1953, even though a neighbouring farm had an electrical supply before this – the brewery refused to pay for a connection to the grid. As tenants, the occupants had no power to effect change at this level, and the cottages were never connected to the main sewer.

Built and maintained cheaply by the brewery (it is rumoured that the builder was never paid), the cottages in question were clearly designed to provide a shop near to other local services – the blacksmith's and the pub – plus additional labourers' housing at a good rate of return. It's not known what the rent was, but a Mr and Mrs Claxton and their daughter were the first to move into the cottage attached to the shop. Mr Claxton was a cobbler and his daughter later married a Mr Lawn who also made and repaired shoes. The Lawns were relatively well-to-do. They had a horse and trap or pony cart, which, as Mr Lawn obtained his leather from Bungay (a market town about five miles away), could be seen in part as a business expense, but also signified that these were people who at least aspired to some social standing in their community. They also had a live-in servant: the woman who was to become my grandmother. When Mrs Lawn died, my future grandmother married her employer, for the sake of propriety, and took over the running of the shop. When he in his turn passed away, she continued to live at the cottage and to manage the shop. A few years later, my grandmother married the man who would become my grandfather: an agricultural labourer who had been living and working nearby. My mother's family continued to run the shop together until 1947. They then went on living in the cottage until first my grandmother and then my grandfather died. My mother lived at the cottages until the 1950s (except for the period that she spent with her cousins in Essex), first as a child at the shop, and then as a young married woman in the cottage attached to her father's.

Touring Stuff

> If we return to the old home as to a nest, it is because memories are dreams, because the home of other days has become a great image of lost intimacy (Bachelard 1994: 100).

A modern visitor to Black Boy House would find many objects that once stood in the cottage. In fact, it appears as if it is entirely possible to re-construct the living space of the home that my mother grew up in, through her memory, without her ever needing to set foot in the house itself. It is as if the larger house contains the smaller, though only through the plane of imagination and representation. As Pearce observes:

> The past survives in three ways: as objects or material culture; as physical landscape [...] and as narratives [...] To these should be added a further dimension, that of individual memory [...] this memory forms itself as images of objects and places, linked with physical remembrances like heat and cold and with remem-

bered emotions, to construct narratives similar to those which have external form
(1994: 28).

Meanwhile, as Lawrence argues, "the relationship between habitat and
resident is dynamic or changeable and it includes factors which may
remain unresolved over a relatively long period of time [while] a
building can have many meanings at a specific time, and / or through
its history" (1987: 51). Black Boy House, for example, has two bathrooms, two sets of stairs and even two kitchens. First of all, rooms
were added for drovers to stay in overnight; later, these were converted into bedrooms, and then into living rooms. For a while in the
1970s the whole building was split into two dwellings, one for us, one
for my paternal grandparents. At the same time, the Stuff from the
cottage has moved, and has acquired additional meanings and uses.

There is, for instance, an oak chest of drawers (a simple piece of
furniture made up of three long and two short drawers) which now sits
in what is now known as 'the club room'. This 'room' is a long low
structure running alongside the byroad, a room attached to the main
body of the house via a lobby, which was once used for dances and
club meetings. The Club Room now houses some of my father's collection of Second World War Stuff and is used for parish meetings.
The chest of drawers, which once stood in my mother's bedroom, with
a large old bible and two wooden tea chests on top, and which used to
contain underwear and jumpers, now has gaskets, headlights and other
car parts in it for use in vehicle restoration. Meanwhile, the two tea
caddies – one with brass fittings, one with a moulded lid – which
"came from the old people my mum used to look after before she was
married" are now upstairs, as is the bible.[1] There is a mirror that used
to stand "on my mum's dressing table in the same room", the stand of
which "used to have a hair tidy handing from one of the knobs, and
brush, hand mirror, and either side a china candlestick, china tray with
three little china bowls with roses, or a floral design on them". Where
the chest of drawers has been adapted for storage and now sits 'exposed' in a public space, the more intimate items that were once displayed with it have remained in the realm of the private (if unused)
spare bedrooms.

Each room at Black Boy House seems to have a trace of the cottage in it, a material trace of the past. In the kitchen (originally the
pub's cellar, filled in when it closed), there is my grandmother's roll-
ing pin (adapted long ago by her from a wooden towel rail) which

"goes back to when mum used to look after the old couple." In the front room (the pub's lounge) there is a wooden ornament of a rabbit (possibly a hare) standing by a tree stump, which "was always in the cottage", also a small china bird pepper pot, which was given to my mum when she was six by her aunt who had got it on a day trip somewhere. It had been kept as a great treasure by my mother in her cupboard in the cottage, alongside her books, games and "keepsakes". There is a small homemade wooden doll's house on the landing. One bathroom has an ornate wooden and marble washstand in it that belonged to Mr and Mrs Lawn before my grandmother arrived. Today it still functions as a high status piece as this is the guests' bathroom. But the room with most pieces in it is that now known as the 'Rayburn Room'. Once the public bar, this room has since been used as a sitting room, and then had a Rayburn installed (later removed). The most 'low-road' of the living rooms at Black Boy House (the other having a faint air of 'parlour' about it) the Rayburn Room has somehow become the setting for most of the cottage's Stuff.

Near the door to the old 'snug', there is a grandfather clock that used to stand in the corner of the cottage's front room; it used to belong to "the old people that mum came there in the first place to look after. Just a cottage grandfather clock with painted face, and calendar dial, made in Norwich". Near it there is also a wooden armchair. Across the room, a four-shelf wooden bookcase hangs on the wall; on the adjoining wall a stuffed kingfisher; by the clock a Kean's mustard tin used as a button box; in the fireplace a small set of hand bellows; on a shelf a glass flycatcher; on the floor a small wooden stool with E. M. carved into the top – "made by my mother's father who was a carpenter for one of my mother's sisters" (Elleen May). A large pestle and mortar that used to be kept in a cupboard in the cottage's front room is also here; a yellow, green and pink embossed cup and saucer; and the 'chiffonier' – a relatively small, and moderately ornate mahogany (veneer) sideboard that was my grandmother's highest status piece, and in which she kept her most important, prized possessions.

The chiffonier stood in the "downstairs front room", almost opposite the fireplace. Inside was a set of Victorian china – twelve cups and saucers, a sugar bowl, cream jug and tea pot: the best tea set – in white, with lilac classical floral relief, also another teapot (a wedding present) and a set of six small glass cups, what were called the "custard cups", used for trifles at birthday teas. Each of these objects is in the Rayburn room – indeed, the tea set is still in the chiffonier. Today the chiffonier carries a light burden of family photos and cards in amongst its ornaments, a pile of randomly collected correspondence, but it always used to have letters and papers in its drawers, while on top there were a pair of brass candlesticks (they are still on it) and (as now) a small, rectangular black paper-maché coin box, with little painted flowers on its lid, plus the wooden rabbit / hare now in the other room. Beside these were a silver plated teapot, cream jug and sugar bowl, a china model of a fireplace (now in the front room) and a wooden biscuit barrel with silver shield (now in a bedroom). Currently a large black china teapot, which used to be kept in a cupboard in the front room with glass bowls "and things, for making trifle", stands on top and was once used at large family parties. My mother's birthday party typically attracted around twelve people, although a family event could draw twenty people.

We tend to suppose that the countryside is populated by people who have not moved very far, just as we tend to suppose that cottages are thatched and have roses around the door. My mother's mother grew up near Colchester, however. Beginning as a girl in service, she moved to Beccles with her employer in about 1918 before taking a job in the village rectory and finally joining the Lawns. Her sister, also in service, moved to a village nearby. What might be less obvious are the geographical distances implicated in creating this particular home. Four objects in this story have, so far, gone unmentioned: two amateur watercolours in an upstairs corridor of women picking tea, plus a 'Kukri' or ceremonial knife from India and a Royal Staffordshire tea-pot, 'Home Series' from New Zealand in the Rayburn Room. My mother's father – one of eight children (four boys, four girls) – was born in India. He was raised on a tea plantation (managed by his parents) by an English father and Indian (perhaps Nepalese) mother. My mother tells me that he went to college in India, this education being interrupted when he joined the army during the First World War. When it had finished he found that his place had not been kept open, so in about 1920 he travelled to the UK. Taking whatever jobs he could get, he became a farm labourer and began living in a converted railway carriage about a half a mile from the shop. The Kukri – which has beading on the sheath and a carved handle – used to hang in the living room. His sister gave it to my grandfather when she visited from India – she later emigrated to Australia. One of his brothers, who sent the teapot as a wedding present, moved to New Zealand. Back in India, my great-grandparents' new bungalow was named after my mother. These are the lived interconnections, the experiences of border-crossing and flow that went to make up empire, captured at home.

Doors

> How concrete everything becomes in the world of the spirit when an object, a mere door, can give images of hesitation, temptation, desire, security, welcome and respect. If one were to give an account of all the doors one has closed and opened, of all the doors one would like to re-open, one would have to tell the story of one's entire life (Bachelard 1994: 224).

My mother detailed almost a complete inventory of the fixtures and fittings of Black Boy House during the research for this chapter. Indeed, although many items have acquired new places and uses, many of the smaller things have returned to the furnishings that they originally stood on; the larger items like the clock and the chiffonier once more in juxtaposition, despite the passage of at least thirty years. Each piece had its own 'home'. Moreover, for my mother each object still has its place in the cottage. Through memory she can walk into her old first home, the home into which she was born, and locate each and every article. In this way, the two houses talk to each other, the smaller still living with the larger, while the objects continue to tell their own story. Through the dialogue her old home is re-presented, re-made.

Today, though, the actual cottage from which this Stuff came might best be described as a heterotopian space (Foucault 1986) rather than a home, displaced somehow from the 'real' world, existing mostly in memory yet containing memory, a site of transgression and crisis. Uninhabited, it stands with its partner unseen by the cars and lorries that rattle the windows, the recourse of thieves who visit at night to take furniture and, more recently, pieces of 'architectural salvage' such as cast-iron fireplaces and floor tiles. This despite the fact that rural crime statistics for the period 1983 to 2001 show that "less than 3% of people living in rural areas became victims of burglary and a similar proportion were victims of violent crime in 1999, compared to almost 5% for both crimes in non-rural areas" (Aust and Simmons 2002: 1, 11).

Boarded against the ravages of time as well as burglary, consider-able effort is now required to gain access. These cottages have a dou-ble life; they remain concrete, actual places, but they have also be-come sites of nostalgia. My mother's old home must be entered by the shop door. When my father opened it, for the purposes of this study, heavy black sheets of spider web hanging from walls and ceiling met him in addition to plywood panels, bolts and ordinary locks. Secured as they are against intruders (especially the cottage attached to the shop), they seem to exist just to be kept safe. These are houses that no longer function as homes; they have no life, except as sites of crime and in the imagination. They have become, for my father at least "a Bluebeard chamber" of the present, "that should not [be] opened, even half-way […] or capable of opening half-way" (Bachelard 1994: 224). According to Andrew Bush, home

> can be about the sense of permanence we come to know through habit: an article of clothing repeatedly worn, a favourite turn of phrase, a melody of which we are fond, or the many visits to see a friend. Home is about the familiar, about gravity, about falling back into the self after being dispersed and overextended in the world (quoted in Brand 1997: 158).

However, what the cottage shows is that old homes can also be simul-taneously emptied of familiarity, can become closed to families and communities as people lose the relationship they once had with such spaces.

The Shop
Entering the old shop today, you come first of all to what looks like a whitewashed passageway; dirt and soot cover the walls, and sand (the sand that the floor tiles had been bedded down on) serves as the floor. Bits of blanketed furniture moulder at the far end; the way is partly blocked by the remains of old bags of concrete, now set. The place smells of mothballs (stored here since the building was shut up, but disturbed by intruders) and the sound of passing traffic makes the road feel much too close. Once there was a bell over the door – rescued and kept down at the old pub – to call the proprietor. To the left, unseen, is what was the counter, now boarded-up. Customers would have stood here, "front of house" (Lawson 2001: 152-3): customers who came to gossip and chat as well as to shop. Finally, as you round the corner at the far end, you can peer behind to see the fixtures and fittings, the

place where goods were kept, money taken: the site of behind the scenes action. The shop's large window – its frame decorated simply with little classical details – is now obscured with ply, its bedraggled white curtains covered in cobwebs. The counter is hidden by the large rusting tins that were used to store honey after it closed, and the wooden drawers at the back are empty and broken. With all these signs, this backstage space reveals itself as a place of old commerce.

Here the people before my mother's mother sold "everything from sheets to shovels", but she remembered the preserved peel first, kept in the shop's fitments in large lumps and "cut up at Christmas time to go into cakes, and special candied sugar, stuff like that". Indeed, throughout this testimony the objects, smells and moments recalled first, and referred to with greatest warmth, were those connected with sweetness. This is the value of testimony: it reveals levels of thinking that run deeper than the conscious, and it is subjective:

> its subjectivity is at once inescapable and crucial to an understanding of the meanings we give our past and present. This is the great task of qualitative research […] to reveal the meanings of lived experience (Yow 1994: 25).

The things that came back from childhood with greatest immediacy – memories of cakes and candied sugar, for example – were the things that unconsciously made a 'happy home'.

Next there was string, and in the counter two big drawers full of bags "that mum used to weigh out sweets", and tobacco wrapped up in little packets. Cigarettes were kept loose on the shelf behind. Bread was ordered and delivered twice a week; a vinegar cask was used "to sell vinegar by the pint". There were cornflakes, "everything you could think of really". My mother used phrases like this a number of times; another was "all things to do with the shop" – for her it is obvious what a village shop carried, but I had to ask if my grandmother sold hardware because there was no memory in my mind to draw upon.

With the material evidence and my mother's testimony, it becomes clear that the shop was essentially a small grocer's. By the 1930s it sold mostly foodstuffs, although out the back my grandfather (indicative of the gendered nature of this sort of work) often measured out and sold paraffin at the end of the day. The merchandise sold in the shop was typical of the kinds of goods stocked by small country stores at this time throughout the UK. Account books kept by a village grocer in Somerset over the same period, for instance, record sales of bread, butter, bacon, pork, cheese, eggs, flour, potatoes, pepper, sugar, currants, nuts, sweets, tobacco, calico, black treacle, spirit, blacking, cocoa, coffee, candles, mustard. Its biggest sales in the late nineteenth century were of bread, bacon, butter and cheese (P POOL AC1/3 & 4), whereas by the 1950s the records suggest that there were more takings from cheese, washing supplies – Persil, starch, blue, Lifebuoy soap – cigarettes and matches, biscuits and sweets, tea and coffee, bread and butter (P POOL AC1/5 & 6). Over time the stock changed with more small 'luxury' items being added and the shopkeeper registering the sale of more branded goods. The books also show how trade was organised: regular customers had an account at the store, and settled up monthly. In line with the shift towards little luxuries, one woman by 1950 regularly purchased '2 Polos; ½ biscuits; ¼ tea; 3 oz cheese; 4 cig' and another 'coffee; matches; sugar; tea; biscuits' (P POOL AC1/5). My mother's father put a stop to people buying on account – more of an informal system of 'tick' than a regularised practice in the shop near the Black Boy – but, as in the West (P POOL AC1/3 to 6), trade gradually declined. Although my mother says the shop was successful, being the only one for some miles, it had to shut in 1947 after wartime rationing "put the skids under it".

The Cottage
Moving through the door at the end of this passageway (which was out of bounds to customers) you finally pass into the cottage proper. Spatially there are thus clearly defined, physically determined, zones – of 'public' trade and domestic 'privacy' – between shop and house. The transition from one to the other is rapid, however; someone entering the shop and being shown into the house would have walked almost straight into the intimate space of the living room / kitchen. The shop entrance was a figurative, as much as a physical, barrier; the garden path and doorway linked to the wider community, rather than processionals. The shop was a space where people stood and talked, but in this way what might be read as the more 'public' space of the front room is bypassed, even though the cottage proper is laid out according to the conventions of its time in regard to division by "status, role, and […] perceived needs of the home's occupants and visitors" (Walker 2002: 824; Lawrence 1987: 90, 104-5). This allowed the shopkeeper's family (in this case, always my grandmother) to move quickly be-

tween shop and home as required – remember the bell over the door to call them – and thereby to combine such domestic tasks as needed to be done throughout the day with running the business. In this way, two forms of work were combined. In terms of significance, this door first and foremost links home to shop, not shop to house – a clear example of the multifaceted meanings of space.

Going through this door into the house, the next door (on the right) leads into the pantry. This walk-in area has a small window that looks into the old shoe shop; its once whitewashed walls are now blackened, and three wooden shelves on which stand a few bottles, jars and a cup run its length. At the far end is a cupboard, described by my mother as "a very very early type sort of 'Easy Work' cabinet, that's really just two plywood cupboards one on top of the other. In the bottom half mum used to keep saucepans, in the top half she used to have cakes and sugar and you know all the usual household type things". In the corner there used to be a pail of drinking water, "with a particular jug hanging above it, in fact the pail is still there", "because, you realise, there was no water laid on, there was no tap water, and water was drawn from the well down at the Black Boy". On the shelves "were the usual things, cups and saucers," and "on the little tiny windowsill was everything, there was … Oh egg cups. Why that sticks in my memory I don't know".

After the pantry comes a short hallway "where we used to hang all the coats", and a door to the under stairs cupboard (a "general purpose cupboard") where the ironing boards, brooms, dusters and shoe polish were kept. Through this transitional space is the private domain of "the living room" giving access left into "the front room" (facing West onto the main road). This latter space has the front door leading to the outside (although it was practically never used). Alternatively, you can turn right, going past a door that leads up onto the stairs, and through into the scullery, which has a door in it leading to the back yard and a path to the toilet – an earth closet, which had to be emptied once a week into a "great big pit" that was gradually filled up. In urban and suburban environs, waste "that has been mediated by the human body is ejected from the entire domestic arena via drains" (Alexander 2002: 866), but in the country it stays put.

In the living room / kitchen, the hanging oak bookcase that is now in the Rayburn Room at Black Boy House was in the alcove to the left of the fireplace. On the wall there is the 'shadow' of two small pic-

tures: pictures of Alice and Nelly, my grandmother's sisters. In the
centre hung a clock. In the other alcove there was a shelf and at the
bottom a chair. On the mantelpiece there were ornaments, "two little
glass vases of a sort of goldy colour, also two slippers that matched
with them, also gold" and a perpetual calendar. The fireplace was an
open fire, the Rayburn that is there now was installed in the late forties
/ early fifties, "which was a great improvement; much more use could
be made of the fire". As well as a guard on which towels and things
hung, the old fire had trivets on the bars in front of it on which a kettle
always stood; there was "always a kettle on to make a nice cup of
tea". In the centre was a work table, "just a deal table", and a chair
that was "dad's chair" in which he read the paper. At one time "mum
had a paraffin cooker [...] a three-burner cooker, and that stood
against the wall", which had the facility to have an oven on top for
baking. The floor was made of floor bricks and on top of these were
stretches of coconut matting and 'piece' rugs made of pegged rag in
random patterns. This room (clearly gendered: "father" had his special
chair) was a collective space used for a range of activities: leisure (the
paper), play (children), meals and housework (Lawrence 1987: 73).
Meanwhile, the scullery, more restricted in use, contained pails, a
copper, a fire and a wall oven which was "the main source of mum's
baking".

   Baking was done once a week on a Friday, when the smell of it
would pervade the whole house: "she was a great dab hand at making
cakes, she used to make some lovely fruit cakes in the oven". This
was the way housework was customarily organised (Schwartz Cowan
1989; Chamberlain 1975; Thompson 1979; Romines 1992). Indeed,
every big household task had its day: Monday for washing – involving
my grandmother getting up at half past six in the morning to get the
fire lit under the copper; Tuesday for ironing and shopping – the shop
shut at one o'clock on Tuesdays allowing my grandmother to go into
Beccles; and Friday for baking. Baths were had on Saturdays in the
'bungalow bath' in front of the fire, the water heated like that for the
wash in the copper. Washing up was done on the table in the living
room, the water thrown down the drain in the back yard that connected to a 'soak away' and ditch at the bottom of the garden. On
Sundays, there was a roast to cook – arranged around going to morning service at the Anglican Church half a mile away.

The role of the good housewife was to ensure that everything was in its place, and to regulate the home for her family. My mother's testimony records this work, and a reading of it quickly reveals the conventionally gendered divisions of home life during her childhood. As Romines has observed, in the nineteenth century the woman of the house was meant to manage effortlessly a variety of day-to-day unpaid tasks that, because they were repetitive, circular, or "ordinary women's work", were generally deemed unworthy of attention (1992: 131). This practice clearly continued well into the twentieth century. "What these women do", she argues, "is essential yet impermanent and invisible [...] The culture consumes the products of the house-keeper's labor; the fact and the process of that labor are suppressed" (1992: 6). Yet, domestic work preserved the order of the house as 'home', preventing a gradual descent into decay, into Nature. To adapt Ortner (1974), it transformed the Natural order, making it safe for Culture. In this way, "the domestic world of ordinary life holds as much significance as the world of extraordinary adventure", which is how women writers have generated value out of domestic life (Mezei and Briganti 2002: 843; Romines 1992). In this case housework and shop work were interwoven, from eight o'clock in the morning when the shop opened until six o'clock in the evening when it closed. My grandmother never had any paid help in the shop or the home; my grandfather went out to work, though he started doing the books after he married (he was trained as a bookkeeper).

Unlike the living room / kitchen, the front room (also known as "the best room") was not recollected at first as a place of visible work; it was remembered, rather, as a space of comfort: "in the winter time to keep more warm, and I used to always get quite excited because I'd think 'oh well it won't be far before Christmas now', because we used to more or less move into this room [...] to keep away from the drafts coming in possibly from the shop." "Nice thick curtains" used to hang over the door and at the windows and "mother always had a lamp" on an oval table in the centre of the room. Looking left from the door into this room, the grandfather clock stood in the corner at an angle, there was "a space", then the chiffonier (in a much higher status here than it is now) and above it, on the wall, three large pictures of "my mum's three brothers that were in the First World War" (all killed in action) enlarged from smaller copies. There was a little table "that mum had either a pot of flowers or a vase of flowers on" in the corner, then the

front door. Under the window there was a "settee" – described as having no arms and a bolster at one end, a chaise longue perhaps – while
above this "on the window sill was pots of geraniums, always geraniums" one red, one white, one "sandy-pink-coloured". Either side of
the alcove there were waist high cupboards, on which stood a bowl of
fruit, and "things you were working on". The left-hand cupboard contained glass bowls, the right hand cupboard was "given over" to my
mother as a toy cupboard. The fireplace was an open fire, on the mantelpiece there was a small clock in the centre and a small "secondary"
paraffin lamp. On the hearth was a fender which held fire irons.
Above that there was a mirror, now revealed by its shadow on the
wall. Opposite the window there was a piano.

    Furnishings and objects together like this constitute what Chevalier
has designated "an entity", while the formality of the décor

> shows that there is a recognizable system [...] The basic pieces of furniture char-
> acterize the room and embody the *home*. This home is framed by culture: objects
> more or less similar are displayed differently in order to satisfy cultural require-
> ments regarding the organization of space (2002: 849, original emphasis).

Though most of the objects here were mass-produced and handed
down, my mother's family used them to express their own cultural and
individual identity. They made the material of their lives their own.
When remembered these objects still carried traces of their personal
history – the higher status pieces that my grandmother acquired when
she married Mr Lawn were referred to throughout the interview as
"mother's". Meanwhile, even though the front door was never used,
the flowers at the window helped create an additional symbolic
threshold between private family space and the world outside (Lawrence 1987: 73).

    It was this symbolism that clearly took precedence in my mother's
memory: a clear indication of their significance in the multi-layered
meanings of 'home'. It was only much later, when asked about the
floor, that work reappeared. The front room – now just sand, like the
shop – was once paved with red ceramic floor tiles, nine inches by
nine inches, always scrubbed, the colour varying, until covered by
'red cardinal' for ease of maintenance by grandfather. There were just
two bought rugs over these, not many as it made the floor easier to
clean.

My mother couldn't easily climb upstairs on this visit to see the two bedrooms – one at the front that used to be her parents' room, and one at the back that used to be hers. In fact, when her mother was a servant to the Lawn family, the back bedroom would have been hers. There are still some old bedsteads, and a piece of furniture at the back, the walls painted cream, cobwebs over the frieze of autumn leaves and white ceiling. In the front room there is a gold-framed picture of a child on the mantle piece, a glass bottle, a tin of talc, and above it on the wall a black-framed photo of a family group. The walls are painted pink, the frieze of leaves falling off in parts, the space above and the ceiling painted white. There are more bedsteads, a box of pictures, some old suitcases and bags. The shallow closet is papered in flowers, the floor covered in traces of patterned lino.

Incomers

This then is a fairly commonplace working home of the 1920s to '40s, and it is worth describing in detail because such ordinary homes (especially rural homes) have rarely survived; the use of their spaces and what they contained are now barely known. It can also be seen from this record how a home's standing within a community could shift. While the status of each cottage remained relatively inferior to that of the pub, it nonetheless flexed with the social standing of its occupants. A child's room at the back of a house could become a servant's room and then go back to being a child's room; a housekeeper could become a shopkeeper. The objects that used to belong in these rooms have in turn moved, yet have often retained the same relative status. The chiffonier that had pride of place in my grandmother's home (and which still holds the best tea-set within it), for instance, has moved to a less elevated position within the old pub. In placing these objects within her home, my mother has worked with meanings they already embodied, but has also un- and re-made them.

Susan M. Pearce has written: "[the] need to decipher gives us the chance to bring out both what is in the object and what is in ourselves; it is a dynamic, complex movement which unfolds as time passes, and in the act of interpretative imagination we give form to ourselves" (1994: 27). Thus, a curator in a museum will use scholarly knowledge to help him her appreciate the object at hand, but while selecting that object for display, he she will also give it a rhetorical twist, a twist that would rest on persuasion and may not succeed (1994: 27). Similarly, what we can see here is that a householder will have affective knowledge of the objects in their home, memories of their meaning and use, but each time they make a choice about the position of those objects – a decision to keep this but get rid of that – they too become engaged in a rhetorical act. This act draws on memory and therefore on historical context, without necessarily drawing on simple facts or dates. What the material culture and memories of the cottage and 'Black Boy House' reveal is a complex, interwoven history at work, a history of dialogue and border-crossing through which 'home' is constructed and re-constructed – a history, in fact, which reads across the grain.

The connections made between dominant British culture and the countryside have, for example, predominantly been understood in such a way as to recreate a singularly white, male, middle-class story of rural life. Hence Philo states:

> There remains a danger of portraying British rural people [...] as all being 'Mr Averages', as being men in employment, earning enough to live, white and probably English, straight and somehow without sexuality, able in body and sound in mind, and devoid of any other quirks of (say) religious belief or political affiliation (1992: 200).

While whiteness has rarely been treated as an ethnic signifier, the representational boundaries between ethnicities and places have converged. Thus "for white people the 'inner city' has become a coded term for the imagined deviance of people of colour", while "'ethnicity' is seen as being 'out of place' in the countryside, reflecting the Otherness of people of colour" (Angyeman and Spooner 1997: 199). In this way, because the countryside has come to be seen as a white space, 'race' has slipped out of sight there while racism is perceived as a singularly urban problem:

> In the white imagination people of colour are confined to towns and cities, representing an urban, 'alien' environment, and the white landscape or rurality is aligned with 'nativeness' and the absence of evil or danger. The ethnic associations of the countryside are naturalised as an absence intruded upon by people of colour (Angyeman and Spooner 1997: 199).

This leaves little room for the presence of Anglo-Indian memories such as those possessed by my grandfather and mother. This act of imagination, therefore, requires effort to effect. Estate agents, Deborah Phillips argues, have aimed to preserve the "traditional character" (whiteness) of the countryside and have "associated black minorities with the inner city" (in Derounian 1993: 70).

As Martin Mayerfield Bell observes in his ethnographic analysis of the small Hampshire village of Childerley, there are also many ways of seeing the rural, even amongst those who live in the country. He found that moneyed incomers, for instance, have an elaborate and highly discriminating aesthetic language for describing the land as landscape; ordinary villagers on the other hand were less critical about the visual qualities of what they could see, but valued the land as place (1994: 166-70). He goes on to suggest that what ordinary Childerley-ans

> see around the village is still very important to them. But instead of putting mental pictures around village views, villagers like Ted Spencer (who has lived in Childerley since he was nine) speak of village places more as where things have happened – as sites of story and memory (1994: 170).

In the case of the home explored in this chapter, the past and the present remain in dialogue, so that objects retain 'story and memory', in the same way. It is through these objects and the material culture of home that the history, a *folkhistory*, of family is accessed, including family living at a vast continental distance from the narrator, and the history of lived relations in a community – in this case a rural community from the early twentieth century.

Massey notes that in academic study as well as wider culture "there has been a continuation of the tendency to identify 'places' as necessarily sites of nostalgia, of the opting-out from Progress and History". This, she believes, is related to a specific conceptualisation of 'place' as "bounded, as in various ways a site of authenticity, as singular, fixed and unproblematic in its identity" (1994: 4). This attitude relies on seeing space as itself something that is fixed and immutable, separate from time which is about change. Massey prefers to see space as "space-time ... formed out of social interrelations at all scales"; 'place' then becomes "a particular moment in those networks of social relations and understandings" (1994: 4). Those relationships may extend beyond the bounds of the place itself and the wider social relations of the world:

> Such a view of place challenges any possibility of claims to internal histories or to timeless identities [...] the particularity of any place is, in these terms, constructed

not by placing boundaries around it and defining its identity through counter-
position to the other which lies beyond, but precisely (in part) through the specificity of the mix of links and interconnections *to* that 'beyond' (1994: 5, original
emphasis).

Therefore, although in English the word 'country' is derived from
contrada / contrate (Latin), meaning "that which lies opposite", it is
not enough simply to set City against Country. Or rather, as Maclean,
Landry and Ward have put it: "While country and city may continue
to describe concrete and specific geographical places, they do so as
relational constructs within the social production of space, with its
movements of capital, labour and commodities" (1999: 4). And at
least in part it has been through the attempt to establish the urban and
rural as fixed, immutable and unconnected, that the cross-cutting experiences of class and gender have been elided, and whiteness established.

To understand the history of a 'home', we must therefore look at
descriptions of its objects and the stories and memories attached to
them: to English tea sets (birthdays and Christmas celebrations, sweets
and nice thick curtains), to pictures of women picking tea (father's
family and first 'home', where there is a bungalow named after me)
and to a teapot from New Zealand (my uncle, visitors, tea parties). In
this case, what might be dismissed as the simple 'nostalgia' associated
with 'place' leads to memories of the complexities of running a
household and a shop, of border-crossing and migration. This is perti-
nent not just to our understanding of the home, but also to the way in
which we write histories of the home, and to the way we re-present the
past as a whole.

Notes

1. The visit and interview that form the basis of this research were carried out in
May 2003.

Labouring at Leisure:
Aspects of Lifestyle and the Rise of Home Improvement

Ruth McElroy

ABSTRACT

Barely can British viewers turn on the television today without encountering scenes of domestic transformation, whether in the form of contemporary conduct guides to dress and health, or as manuals on how to do-it-yourself. This essay explores home improvement as a material cultural practice with a history, one that is often distinctly national in character. The history of home improvement entails substantial shifts both in patterns of housing and in ideas about dwelling during the course of the twentieth century. The rise of do-it-yourself (DIY) provides us with an example of how houses are made homes through the interaction individuals and families have with material objects, social structures and aesthetic paradigms. DIY's fashioning of domestic space is seen to operate as a gendered and classed phenomenon, but it also the case that in current televisual formations, home improvement has come to operate within a wider aestheticization of everyday life. This is never clearer than in television house shows, ranging from the makeover format of the BBC's Changing Rooms *to the more acquisitional narrative of Channel 4 and Channel Five's property shows such as* Location, Location, Location. *In their dramatisation of taste, style and location, these formats provide representations of home and inhabitation that extend beyond the domestic to the national home. Offering the audience new forms of intimacy, these shows mediate the fantasies, anxieties and rhythms of individual homes with the wider nations of which we are a part.*

Introduction

The sun rose up from behind the concrete of the block of flats opposite, beaming straight into their faces. Davie Galloway was so surprised by its sneaky dazzle, he nearly dropped the table he was struggling to carry. It was hot enough already in the new flat and Davie felt like a strange exotic plant wilting in an overheated greenhouse. It was they windaes, they were huge, and they sucked in the sun, he thought, as he put the table down and looked out at the scheme below him.

Davie felt like a newly crowned emperor surveying his fiefdom. the new buildings were impressive all right; they fairly gleamed when the light hit those sparkling wee stains embedded in the cladding. Bright, clean, airy and warm, that was what was needed. He remembered the chilly, dark tenement in Gorgie; covered with soot and grime for generations when the city had earned its 'Auld Reekie' nickname […] All that had gone, and about time too. This was the way to live!

For Davie Galloway, it was the big windows that exemplified all that was good about these new slum-clearance places. He turned to his wife, who was polishing the skirtings […] Susan rose slowly, respectful of the cramp which had been set-tling into her legs. She was sweating as she stamped one numbed, tingling foot, in order to get the circulation back into it. Beads of moisture gathered on her fore-head. – It's too hot, she complained.

Davie briskly shook his head. – Naw, take it while ye can get it. This is Scot-land, it's no gauny last. Taking in a deep breath, Davie picked up the table, re-commencing his arduous struggle towards the kitchen. It was a tricky bugger: a smart new Formica-topped job which seemed to constantly shift its weight and spill all over the place […]

Ah tel ye ah'd gie ye a hadn wi that Davie, yir gaunny huv nae fingers and a broken table the wey things are gaun, Susan warned him. She shook her head slowly, looking over to the crib. – Surprised ye dinnae wake her.

Picking up her discomfort, Davie said, – Ye dinnae really like that table, dae ye?

Susan Galloway shook her head again. She looked past the new kitchen table, and at the new three-piece suite, the new coffee table and new carpets which had mysteriously arrived the previous day when she'd been out at her work in the whisky bonds. (Welsh 2002: 3-4)

This is the opening of Irvine Welsh's novel, *Glue,* and it captures very well the sense of promise, excitement, social change and real labour that is at the heart of the story of home improvement in the twentieth century. It is a story about our relationship to things – new things of-ten, like the formica table and massive windows that lighten and cook the human inhabitants of these high-rise dwellings. It is a story of our relationships with one another and of how our domestic relationships are mediated through objects, buildings and new technologies in the context of significant social change. It exemplifies how we shape our space and boundaries through our tools and objects of everyday life. And too, it is a story of how home as a social, as well as geographical, location entails a negotiation with time, with the past lives of cities and communities, as well as the past lives of the house and its inhabi-tants. As Paul Oliver argues, dwellings "outlast lineages, change hands, are sold, re-occupied, remodelled and adapted, their survival to the present being a record of responsiveness to altering life-styles and societies in change" (1987: 10).

Houses become homes in part through our material re-shaping of them. Homes are fascinating sites for the investigation of material culture because they hold within them other things and spaces which together create a matrix of material, psychological and social relations that form the most routine elements of our everyday lives. Furthermore, few of us can conceptualise or shape our homes without reference to the place of their and our location. Home is always embedded in another map of spatialised meaning. Our homes are always somewhere, linked to others on our street or perhaps against those on the other side of town. Home holds together both a conception of place and a conception of social togetherness even as home is made meaningful partly by the privacy and distinction of its own rhythms, fabric and shape. Such distinctions may be all the more important once housing becomes increasingly standardised, such that not only the interiors but also the exteriors of housing – on high-rise blocks, streets and estates – become increasingly identical across the national, and even international landscape. New forms of housing pose new challenges to our inhabitations; the move for Davie and Susan from the tenements to the modernist high-rise blocks entails new skills of dwelling at height and new techniques for controlling and shaping the light that glares through the vast, revealing windows. In such domestic negotiations with material objects, we can witness both a social and deeply personal experience of what Michel de Certeau describes as the art of 'making do'. Born of necessity and executed with creativity, the arts of making do are for de Certeau "combined with ritual practices, habits and routines out of which the shape of everyday life emerges" (Dant 1999: 72). Such routines may be most visible to inhabitants at the moment of their disruption (through moving house, for example) or when 'making do' becomes a more deliberate act of design such as that entailed in home improvement.

This essay traces some of the key characteristics of home improvement as it develops during the course of the twentieth century and up to the contemporary phenomenon of televisual house shows. Although DIY may often be experienced as a personal activity, bank holiday Homebase deals and queues at B&Q tell us that this is indeed a social phenomenon, one that is both expressive and constructive of social relations. Home improvement in this essay thus entails consideration not only of DIY and its attendant literature, but of how home improvement functions as a place-based shaping of our sense of belonging to one another, to our milieu and to the nations in which our houses are located. The rise of lifestyle television has helped to establish home ownership as a hallmark of British national character even in the midst of rising house prices; in this way, screen representations of home act as forms of "banal nationalism" (of which more later), offering both intimate inclusion and judgmental exclusion to the viewers at home.

Home Improvement: Building, Design and Social Change
The twentieth century was a century of mass home improvement, not only in terms of private attempts at home decoration or remodelling, but in terms of public, large scale improvements to the nation's homes. As much policy as private project, home improvement often came on the heels of destruction, especially of course, after the Second World War, but also in the clearances of city slums to which Davie himself refers in the opening quotation of this essay. The construction of the new entailed the destruction of the old – a relationship of destruction and creation that is an important element in the consumer cycle of home improvement and DIY.

The first half of the twentieth century witnessed a substantial shift in patterns of inhabitation, not least of which was the increase on both sides of the Atlantic of owner-occupation, a trend that grew steadily during the second half of the century and into the twenty-first. Before the First World War, approximately 10-20% of occupants owned their home; by 1938 it was 32% (Roger 1995: 380). In the USA, "between 1890 and 1930 the number of privately owned homes grew from 3 million to more than 30 million" (Gelber 1997: 68). In Britain between 1981 and 2003, the number of owner-occupied dwellings increased by 44%, such that in 2003-4, 70% of dwellings were owner-occupied (*Social Trends* 2005: 137). Whilst owner-occupation alone cannot be seen as the cause of the rise in home improvement, fewer home improvements are likely to be made when the property and the value of the labour expended are not owned but rented.

A key element enabling the dramatic change in housing was financial. In the UK, for example, the period of the late 1920s to the late 1930s witnessed year-on-year increases in the number of mortgage advances, so that "between 1928 and 1938 the number of private individuals who turned to mortgage companies for housing finance increased from 500,000 to 1.5 million" (Roger 1995: 381). This was due both to the decreasing costs of borrowing and the rise, for those in work, of disposable incomes. In the UK, during the 1950s, just under two and a half million new houses were built, two-thirds of them by local councils. As in the inter-war period, new building often entailed slum clearances and large-scale demolition leading to the kinds of up-rootings to new schemes that Davie describes in the opening of *Glue*.

One of the striking things in Welsh's description of the new flat is the difference between Davie and Susan's response to it. Whilst Davie sees the acquisition of central heating and big windows as signs of the good life, Susan – busy on her knees cleaning the skirting boards, the epitome of working-class respectability – finds the space impractical; she worries about the costs of the new goods and Davie's all-too-conspicuous consumption. Alongside the promise held by the modern flat lie the gendered realties of home work and continuing labour. As Marianne Gullestad argues:

> Home decoration and home improvement are […] part of the construction and re-construction of social groups. Simultaneously the home is both highly gendered and highly shared as a cultural symbol and a focus of attention for women and men (1995: 322).

For Susan, the heat of the home makes her inhabitation of it uncomfortable. Such concerns with the practicality of house design were from the start a key element in home improvement. Home improvement – as the re-shaping of private domestic dwelling space –was tied to house building and to house design. Consequently, as a sphere of material culture and of consumption, it brought together quite different kinds social agents. These included design professionals and architects; manufacturers of mass-produced modern tools and materials, advertisers, journalists and editors of the increasing popular magazines, as well as, of course, the home owner and DIY-er, who could variously be called upon as citizen, mechanic, family member and increasingly, as imaginative and creative agent of transformation and change. The relations between these agents were not necessarily positive, and their expectations of domestic design were often quite different. Judy Attfield (1995) has shown how the women who lived in the new housing of Harlow during the 1950s, for example, struggled to mould the modernist aesthetic of the designers to the realities and cultural values of working-class life. As with Susan above, windows were often a key site for transformation and adaptation, with many of the Harlow women disliking the front-facing kitchen windows that placed them and the still quite bare landscape of the new town on display. In this regard, home improvement could be said to begin at the point at which we find ourselves dwelling in houses fashioned by the social and aesthetic values of those unlike ourselves, an experience that is common to most of us at some point in our lives.

The homes occupied immediately before and after the war were designed by people who were, more often than not, professionals. The burgeoning pre-made plans for owner-occupied houses (especially before the war) adumbrated the enduring paradox of mass-produced goods: on the one hand, the primacy of individuality and the personal identity and accomplishment of the new homeowner; on the other, mass production and its economies of scale, as well as the desire to maintain the professionalism of the architect. Some companies and manuals sought to negotiate this by offering customers the opportunity for minor changes and customised plans, other stressed the individuality of the architect who had 'authentically' as it were, tried and tested these plans. Time and again, manuals insist that neither the plans nor the advice on how to design and repair the home can replace the professional. For example, in a repair and maintenance manual of 1949 – after many men and women had gained a range of skills though the war effort – some home improvement experts were telling their readers that "repair jobs which require special knowledge and skill should be done only by a qualified person" (Phelan 1949: 1). It is here too that we see a crossover of discourses and impulses towards change, including, for example, shifts in the naming and usage of rooms. Such changes are indicative of wider cultural shifts in ideas of public and private space even within the domestic space of the home. In a 1945 special issue of *Better Homes & Gardens* on 'Remodelling Your Home', for example, the editorial exclaims:

> [Few] men are driving a horse and buggy today, and few women are wearing floor-length skirts. Yet more than half the families in America are living in houses as out of pace with modern life as buggies and bustles (Normile 1945: 96)

In telling their readership to "remodel the interior of your house", the magazine pointed to specific rooms and fittings that needed to be changed: "Many of these old houses had double parlours which convert into a modern living-room quite easily, once the dividing arch and fretwork are removed". If this advice (to knock down walls and open up the living space of the home) is familiar to us today from the countless house programmes on television, it is an echo of an earlier time when people had been told to do the same thing.

Between the turn of the century and the 1920s, we see the decline of the parlour and the bedchamber in house design, and the rise of the living room and bedroom. The significance of the latter is still in evidence, with a shift from one to two-bedroom flats and an increase in the percentage of four-bedroom houses being built by private enterprise in Britain today. This shift points to both higher expectations of individual space within households and an increasing slippage between domestic and work zones, epitomised by the growth of the home study. In her study of parlour making and middle-class identity in the USA, Katherine Grier points out the irony whereby the parlour became a "target of criticism virtually from the moment that making one became a real possibility for middle-class families" (1988: 211). The move from parlour to living room, especially, entailed a reduction in the number of rooms on the ground floor but an increase in the relative space used for the family, as opposed to more formal public uses of the parlour and reception hall in hosting guests and family occasions. This shift occurred within the context of a reduction in the actual size of the family houses being built between the First and Second World Wars. Charm and simplicity entered the discourse of home design and decoration at this time and operated within a wider discourse of expressivity and personality. As Grier points out:

> The argument that living rooms properly revealed the personality of a family used a twentieth-century understanding of the nature of the individual to recast the earlier argument about comfort: that a parlor should reveal a family's true character rather than its social façade (1988: 216).

The virtue and aesthetic superiority attributed to simplicity had at least two decorative origins: the distinct colonial style of the Shaker design in the USA, and the aesthetic criteria of the Arts and Crafts movement, especially in the UK. However, in its manifestation in the 1950s, it also acted as a counter to the gleeful consumption and advertising of new goods and materials. Simplicity became a way of being both modern and tasteful, not a rejection but a negotiation of the new forms of home consumption. It spoke not only to the enthusiasm but also the anxiety felt by those newly faced with such exuberant and heterogeneous forms of home decoration as a way of being able to participate in what was becoming a social as well as private from of leisured labour. Implicitly, the discourse of simplicity worked to create a sense of distinction from exuberant home improvement and the spectacle of over-consumption that many professionals criticised in the public, exterior face of the home. Such a distinction was itself distinctly classed in nature. Restraint, modesty and style were entwined in the notion both of simplicity and of beauty as this advice from Samuel Paul's *The Complete Book of Home Modernizing* (1954) demonstrates:

> [Beauty] springs from orderly simplicity. This sounds easy to achieve but may require the advice of an experienced designer. Too often we see three or four different materials on the same exterior elevation – undoubtedly intended to create interest through a wide variety of colour and texture. But the result of this effort is busy confusion, doing more harm than good to the lines of the structure. Overabundant ornamentation gives a cluttered look to the exterior. You will find that few materials and simple lines yield the best results every time [...] Lastly, don't clutter the clean surfaces of your home with a lot of meaningless frills [...] Many personal emotions will be expressed in the new design of your modernized home. Let them be translated in as simple and relaxed forms as possible (1954: 38-9).

In the move from parlour to living room, and in the idea of simplicity prevalent in DIY manuals, we can see an emphasis on the successful stylisation of home as a reflection of a distinctly modern self, one who is reflexive about their own artistry and representation. Whilst the idea of home as a reflection of the inhabitants was not a new idea, DIY (encompassing the range as well as rapidity of new product and fashion developments) meant that there was a greater array of opportunities but also expectations of self-fashioning than ever before. Like the modern self, home improvement was portrayed as an ongoing project, one that involved both activity and, just as importantly, contemplation. It was also a project that whilst deeply personalised, was also collective with many magazines of the period such as *Practical Householder* routinely showing idealised representations of nuclear families engaged together in home improvement. The increasing leisure time enjoyed by middle-class families placed demands upon domestic space as leisure activities needed to be accommodated by changes in domestic order. Leisure became more prominent within the home, and the home – especially as represented in magazines and manuals – needed to be remodelled to it. Leisure led to labour because leisure required the creation of new spaces and because it acquired increased domestic prominence. But labour also became a part of leisure with the rise of DIY as a hobby.

DIY as a hobby might be born either of necessity (for example, the increasing costs of labour), or of opportunity for self-fulfilment and self-expression. Historians such as Steven Gelber read the rise of DIY as a hobby both in the 1920/1930s and then in the 1950s as evidence of how middle-class American men could negotiate and construct their masculinity within the new suburban domestic spheres: "By taking over chores previously done by professionals, the do-it-your-selfer created a new place for himself inside the house" (Gelber 1997: 67). These new spaces were often located at the periphery of the home, sometimes on the boundary between inside and out, including for example, the workshop or den, the basement, outbuildings such as sheds, and transformed garages. However, the idea of DIY as an opportunity to work and re-assert masculine skill seems especially geared towards homeowners and to those men who did not employ manual skills in their paid work. Labouring at leisure might well have been a more appealing prospect for those who did not physically labour at work. Nonetheless, for some men DIY enabled them to beat out a gendered rhythm of suburban life. Because it was often tied to national improvement, sound economy and investment in the family's future, DIY could be regarded as a worthy and workmanlike form of consumption. Just as importantly, however, this consumption as production was often represented as itself a way of being together for the 'modern' married couple, one in which men were indeed the main actors but who were normally assisted – and very importantly, admired by – women.

DIY magazines such as *Man About the House*, *Practical Householder* and *Home Kinks* repeatedly ran front covers in which wives were pictured assisting their husbands, for example, by polishing newly laid floor tiles, or painting newly constructed banisters. DIY literature demarcated appropriate roles for men and women. Where men were portrayed as the skilled labours and instigators of projects, women were represented as cheerful assistants, whose role entailed more aesthetic tasks such as selecting paint colours, preparing fabrics and or merely making the tea. Carolyn M. Goldstein points to how this gendered division of DIY labour operated through a set of other oppositions of surface and depth, decoration and construction:

Again and again, women appeared refinishing floors, painting window trim, polishing furniture, or doing other small projects – but never actually constructing
things. In assuming responsibility for maintaining the condition of the home's surfaces, the ideal homemaker literally seemed to take charge of her family's refinement [...] When electric power tools for amateurs were introduced in the 1940s,
magazines and advertisements drew on this convention and showed women using
them only in certain circumscribed situations – to polish or buff various surfaces,
for instance (1998: 10).

Despite existing as assistants and aesthetic guides to the handyman,
the most overt contribution of women to the domestic scenes of DIY
was through their adoring looks of wonder at the handiwork of their
husbands. DIY was a gendered spectacle then inasmuch as men's
work became something to 'look at'; it became an object of a wife's
(and the magazine reader's) gaze.

For both men and women, but perhaps most for heterosexual couples, DIY has provided a space in which to produce, challenge and
reformulate sexual identity and sexual relations. The making of home
in DIY literature was repeatedly fashioned as a form of coupledom,
not just of masculine activity. Interestingly, this trend continues today.
It is striking how few single participants are screened on television
house shows; even when couples are not introduced as heterosexual
partners, we find for example, friends buying houses together, or a gay
couple as in the case of the presenters of the BBC's *Million Pound
Property Experiment* and of Channel Five's *How Not To Decorate*.
This representational emphasis on couples is not fully reflective of
social shifts as the UK bank Abbey may have realised when, in 2001,
it dropped its long established logo of a heterosexual couple walking
together under an umbrella and replaced it instead with an abstract
series of pastel colours. In Britain today we are witnessing a steady
rise in the number of single-person households, with an increasing
number of single women becoming homeowners.

The realities of women's experience of DIY were complex, not
least because the war had meant that many women had learned how to
do-it-yourself from necessity, if not also from choice. Thus we can
find examples of DIY literature that was either authored by women –
for instance Dorothy Sara's *The New American Home Fix-It Book*
(1955) – or those that addressed women specifically. It was during the
1970s, however, when DIY manuals aimed at women really took off,
including Florence Adams' *I Took A Hammer: the Woman's Build-It
and Fix-It Handbook* (1973). Nonetheless, as David Giles (2002) sug-

gests in his analysis of Channel Five's programme, *Hot Property*, the gendering of aesthetic taste continues into contemporary television representations of home improvement, with male participants often being rebuked for their poor taste and limited appreciation of colour. Where Giles sees this as a feminised televisual discourse that undermines men's aesthetic choices, an alternative view is that such programmes, like the earlier DIY literature, work performatively to reveal the uneasiness real social subjects experience with gendered domestic roles.

At the same time as DIY was operating as a site for the working through of gender divisions, hierarchies of professionalism were also being contested by the rise of home improvement. The relationship between the professional and the handyman amateur started to alter in the 1950s and 1960s and a key element in this shift is that the professional and the amateur find themselves consuming in the same space. Post-war hardware manufacturers developed new ranges of products to facilitate small-scale home improvement in a bid to create a mass-market, rather than one comprised solely of professionals. It was between the late 1960s and late 1970s, however, when the DIY industry really took off. March 1969 saw Richard Block and David Quayle open their first hardware store in Southampton, launching what was to become the B&Q chain that dominates the British DIY market. Home centres provided a new spatial experience to shoppers both in their acreage of goods stacked to the ceiling and in their vast range, cutting across the previously distinct trades of plumbing, tiling, carpentry, and so on.

Furthermore, they balance two aspects of home improvement that are paradoxical but which persist today. On the one hand, within the practice of home improvement, there has always been a strong trajectory towards frugality. Money-saving has always been a significant motive for DIY and the no-frills approach to the shop floor catered to this impulse. On the other hand, an equally important trajectory within home improvement has been towards pleasure and plenty. Whether driven by the pleasure of home improvement as a leisure pursuit in its own right or by the creative self-styling which it affords home-owners, home centres appealed to pleasure and plenty through their constant supply of a vast selection of goods which seemed to make available to DIYers a range of future possibilities and options for change. Home centres and DIY stores were important actors in the formation of the retail park landscape, often exploiting changing patterns of shopping. Via such new consumption spaces and practices of the 1970s and 1980s, the material culture of home improvement became embedded in many of the rhythms of everyday life.

Styling the Nation: Televisual Representations of Home

As Charlotte Brunsdon (2003) has demonstrated, the prime-time weekday evening slot on British television has been transformed since the late 1990s into a lifestyle zone, one characterised by a concern with aestheticised and self-conscious forms of consumption, whether of food, clothing, gardens or homes. Lifestyles, as stylised projects of consumption and self-fashioning, offer a potentially securing narrative force at a time when both our social identities and our purchase on place (including for example, the workplace) have undergone substantial change in the post-fordist era of Western industrial capitalism. Lifestyles provide patterns for the management of our quotidian relations with material objects and the myriad social meanings that our interaction with them generates. Lifestyle television dramatises this complex ordinariness, as Lisa Taylor argues:

> The 'ordinarization' of lifestyle media describes how lifestyle programmes fasten onto the sense that we are all insofar as we connect to the backdrop of everyday life, ordinary; we are all somehow anchored to routine, to a place called home and to the mundanity of daily habit (2002: 482).

First broadcast in 1996, and successfully exported to the USA as *Trading Spaces*, the BBC's house makeover show, *Changing Rooms* may be seen as the starting point for a new era of televisual representations of domesticity, and whilst the BBC announced its plans to conclude the series in 2004, there is as yet little sign of a more general decline in what we might term 'Property TV'. This refers to television that places the exchange, improvement or transformation of homes at the centre of lifestyle programming. Property TV makes the idea and material realities of owner-occupation mundane, common, exhilarating and compelling. Through its ubiquity, its repeated assertions of style and investment knowledge, and through its intimate mode of address to the viewer 'at home', Property TV establishes owner-occupation as normative and in so doing contributes to the mythology of Britain as a nation of home-owners. Of equal importance, however is the fact that Property TV places in the public sphere the narrativisation and performance of both home making and home improvement as everyday activities. Television turns the house inside out so that what happens behind closed doors becomes available for public view. In the process, it reveals both the intimate commonalties and peculiar differences of others' homes. It is this which gives such programmes their uncanny or *unheimlich* flavour – the familiarity and strangeness that animates each transformation of a domestic style that is both already known (from experience, common style knowledge, and from other such shows) and yet brand new, open for the first time to the nation's gaze. In making the domestic national, it sutures the making of home to the making of the nation, and more broadly to the making and negotiation of national belonging. More even than the DIY magazines that brought new ideas for improving the home, television has been the mass medium best able to mediate nation through the symbolism of home, and it does so precisely through its homeliness. In his *Home Territories*, for example, David Morley examines how:

> [National] broadcasting can [...] create a sense of unity – and of corresponding boundaries around the nation; it can link the peripheral to the centre; turn previously exclusive social events into mass experiences; and above all, it penetrates the domestic sphere, linking the national public into the private lives of its citizens, through the creation of both sacred and quotidian moments of national communion (2000:107).

Whilst nationalism is often easier to see in instances of the sacred – say through the Royal Broadcasts from the home of the monarch – it is just as important to recognise that nationalism operates at a low frequency, as a repetitive and often barely audible cue to belong. For this reason, Michael Billig's concept of "banal nationalism" seems especially useful here. Billig defines banal nationalism as "the ideological habits that enable the established nations of the West to be reproduced". "Daily", he argues, "the nation is indicated or flagged in the life of the citizenry" (1995: 6). Property TV can be read as an instance of banal nationalism precisely because it flags the nation in the life not only of the citizenry but of the television audience. This is achieved in a myriad of ways. For example, Property TV enables members of the nation to see one another in their own domestic space, thereby crossing domestic boundaries of the home which, given both geographical and class distances, might never normally be crossed. This relatively recent collapse of social and geographic distance is brought home when we look back to the experience of earlier commentators on home, who found it difficult to access the private realities of the domestic realm outwith the boundaries of fiction:

> There is hardly a garden in England which is not surrounded by wall or hedge or railing, the obscurer the better [...] There is hardly a window in any family house which is not curtained effectively to obscure the view of the inquisitive passer-by. And as a consequence there is no play or book or film as successful as that which deals with the intimacies of family life, which, except in one family – his or her own – are a complete mystery to the ordinary man or woman (Spring Rice [1939] cited in Hunt 1995: 301).

For some contemporary commentators, however, the journey into others' domestic lives is a limitation of the home makeover format. Munira Mirza (2001) argues that:

> The domestication of the nation's tastes has become so banal that we are content to watch, as voyeurs, a middle-aged woman on *Changing Rooms* cry for joy at her new dining room. Is a newly decorated room really that exciting? Especially when it is not even our rooms that have been changed, but those belonging to somebody we do not know.

In fact, one of the key pleasures derived from watching such shows is being able to see into other people's homes – a transgression of boundaries that makes the private world intimately known and familiar on the national screen. Intimacy and proximity are the *modus operandi* of much of the camera work of such shows, as they allow us to observe, as no polite guest could easily do, the finest of details, from bedding to coving. Such spectatorial omniscience provides the audience with a sense of commonality and knowableness, despite the diversity of participants and homes. In this way it is both deeply voyeuristic *and* idealistic – an aspirational narrative, not only for possession, but for a level of proximity that the nation itself rarely allows.

Mirza's bafflement at audience pleasure, characterised by the "cry for joy" at a transformed dining room, misses another key element of Property TV, namely its emotional range. Whilst emotion animates many Property TV shows – the moment of waiting for the offer on the house to be accepted, for example – it is in the makeover formats of the genre that emotion plays a central role. As John Ellis has suggested with regard to *Changing Rooms*:

The appeal of the programme lies in its address to questions of class and taste, style and appearance. This takes place across a powerful emotional dynamic, involving an insight into the nature of the relationships of the two couples, with their neighbours and even with the professional designers who behave with a degree of pantomime exaggeration (2000: 174).

The emotional tenor of home is played out in the makeover show through scenes both of horror and of melodrama. The former commonly entail some quite Gothic narrative movements, as presenters lead us into unknown domestic spaces containing "frightening" carpets, "scary" ornaments, and "horrendous" wallpaper that may have been concealed beneath layers of different ages and families' wall-hangings. In *Changing Rooms, How Not to Decorate* and other such shows, the repressed returns to haunt the participants and the audience alike; we all recall together the "nightmare" of avocado bathroom suites, as the presenters and experts reveal the bad taste that we endured but of which we may also be cured. Though the regulatory ripping out of carpets and replacement with wooden floors may well be homogenising, being educated in matters of taste is no small matter given that taste has itself become an important terrain for working out social difference. The horror of the home entails today a fear less of failing to be unique, and more of being like no one, of being cut adrift from the markers of community, family, and class that secure us in time and place. Makeover formats self-consciously play with the horrors and fears that our homes may house, whilst offering both narrative and stylistic resolution to keep such fears at bay. The relationship with the past, for example, is often negotiated so that whilst certain decorative decisions such as floral wallpaper are upbraided, especially when linked to a failure to 'keep up with the times', other material objects and styles are valorised for their embodiment of past aesthetics. Such objects include so-called period features – objects imbued with value because of their nostalgic purchase on the styles of the valued past – but also more personal objects such as toys, furniture, and decorative objects that act as cues for personal memories and life stories of the participants. In this regard, makeover shows construct an endlessly re-fabricated museum of the home, one that links the current home to the past, but is able to secure itself in relation to it with both postmodern irony (British readers may recall Lawrence Llewelyn-Bowen's gothic dining room), and sincere affection and attachment.

In her analysis of makeover shows on British television, Rachel Moseley (2000) has sought to distinguish these formats from the wider lifestyle genre by seeing the moment of revelation as definitive:

> [The] closeup [sic] display of the knee-jerk reaction of the ordinary person becomes a primary public spectacle, and it is in this moment of excess that the essential difference between makeover shows and cookery / lifestyle / consumer competence programmes to which they are generically related resides (2000: 312).

More broadly, however, we can note the inherent melodrama of many of the scenes of *Changing Rooms*. Melodrama as a distinct cultural form explains the emphasis in these shows upon extravagant action, sensation and emotion, as well as the excess not only of the designs themselves, but of the reactions of the participants, presenter and experts. Whilst many critics have noted the increases in the number of 'ordinary' people on television, this has tended to obscure the way in which popular factual entertainment retains and adapts aspects of fiction. The replacement of actors with 'ordinary' people does not equate with a reduction in the dramatic or narrative force of television; the conflict, desires and pleasures of the house makeover work well as fictions of reality, fictions that as they operate so much at the level of the imagination and stylistic invention. Some of the clearest examples of this may be found in the makeover of children's rooms. For example, in the 2004 Christmas Special of *Changing Rooms*, broadcast from the flood-damaged Cornish village of Boscastle, the designers produced a quite melodramatic pink bedroom, a "princesses' palace", which was described as "a very girly room for two little twin princesses who need their own space". This Cinderella narrative makes tangible a romantic fantasy of both domestic pleasure (in pretty objects and new materials) and of childhood transformation as the 'girls' become, through the imaginative labours of the designers, "princesses". Though functioning through interior design and DIY, the room makeover is cast and experienced as being as magical as a fairytale, or at least a filmic version of one, as 'magic' dust is replaced by the real thing. The excess and melodrama is counterbalanced by a more sober reflection on the durability of material objects and their stylistic arrangement in fantastical form. So, for example, the factsheet accompanying the design advises parents to "accessorise a girl's room with toys fit for a princess. Wooden dolls' houses are fantastic as they are durable and elegant, and won't date as the children grow older" (BBC 2005). The notion that a doll's house will not outlive a young girl's interest is striking not only in its gendered assumptions, but in its eerie and uncanny doubling of the domestic sphere, as the house makeover entails not only its own representation but an artefact of the idea of home, the doll's house. The material object's future life is imbued with a security and endurance that is of necessity absent from the life of the girl who is yet to become a woman. Such a negotiation of fragility and invention may have been especially appropriate for a location devastated by floods, where homes have been washed away and random objects alone survive as elegiac embodiments of home's susceptibility and endurance.

Conclusion
Historically, one of the most visible ways of marking national difference has been through dress. Sumptuary laws may now be a thing of the past in Britain, yet the eminence of media representations of domestic stylisation in the post-war period suggests that the fabrication of national identity continues through the marriage of home and high street, as a British department store's strapline, "Debenhams: Styling the Nation" suggests. Home improvement as a material cultural practice sutures the everyday shapings of house into distinctive homes with the extraordinary imaginative transformations that may be wrought by human creativity in the domestic sphere. Such transformations provide glimpses into wider social negotiations of what it is to be 'at home' in a nation, especially one where owner-occupation has become an index of status and civic inclusion. Property TV is conservative, then, inasmuch as it draws attention to the financial benefits of home improvement and to home ownership; yet its emotional range and intimacy also reveal a more democratic opening up of that most important of pieces of domestic furniture, the television, to the lives of ordinary people, whose capacity to turn a house into a home remains both a fascinating sight for viewers and a site of considerable debate for scholars.

Safe House:
Authenticity, Nostalgia and the Irish House

Shane Alcobia-Murphy

ABSTRACT

During an economic boom characterized by both an increasingly high level of owner-occupation and rising house prices due to rapid increased disposable income, immigration, low direct taxation, low mortgage interest rates and increased investor activity, the 'house' figured prominently as a thematic concern in the Arts in both the Republic of Ireland and Northern Ireland. Negative equity and unaffordable house prices in the Republic brought a new dimension to spatial politics and the question of plotting one's 'social subjectivity'. Artists and writers, such as Beat Klein, Henrijke Kühne, Vona Groarke and Seán Hillen explore the acute tension between nostalgia and authenticity in the face of globalisation and the awareness that forms of habitation arising from the emergence of Celtic Tiger economics are no less "authentic" than earlier forms. While such artists' self-reflexivity demonstrates a positive, forward-looking engagement with outworn symbols, writers and visual artists from Northern Ireland, although equally self-aware and critical, convey a sense of being trapped in a hiatus, unable to progress. The key difference between them is the presence (or legacy) of the Troubles. The image of the house may indicate sheltered domesticity, but in Northern Irish artworks by Willie Doherty, Victor Sloan, Rita Duffy and Ciaran Carson, the private realm is always under scrutiny. Inscribing into their work the physical, socio-political and psychological effects of the ongoing strife, the artists register a sense of vulnerability due to the all-pervasive gaze of neighbours, the police, and the opposing community.

Introduction

The house is the primary unit of measurement and point of reference for a spatial politics, a human scale which determines the nature of our relationship to the immediate environment and beyond that to the culture as a whole. 'Where do you live?' figures amongst the key questions which momentarily arrest the narratives of identity, how we answer determining our place within a grid of co-ordinates which plot social subjectivity (Bird 1995: 119).

Rachel Whiteread's controversial Turner Prize-winning cement cast of the inside of a three-floor terraced Victorian house on Grove Road in the London borough of Hackney (1993) presented to the viewing public mummified space and, in the words of the artist, "fucked up everybody's perception of their home, their houses, their domestic life, and their 'safe' places" (Whiteread 2001: 19). While 'home' may imply familiarity, involving as it does a set of affective relationships which ground our sense of identity, Whiteread's memorialising artefact enacted a defamiliarisation, focusing on the physicality of the walls, door frames and roof, revealing "a life-size, negative mirror image of the intangible, air-filled spaces that were once inhabited" (Schlieker 2001: 59).

The private domestic sphere we normally associate with 'home' became an exhibition space for the public gaze. Crucially, the exhibit disrupted social time-space by solidifying the living space of the house, thus creating a conceptual paradox: while *House* suggested the silencing of the house's past and the preservation of traces of its former life-patterns, nevertheless, the sculpture was also a living space, arousing debates centring on nostalgia, the degeneration of the East End of London, and the impact of local planning decisions. As James Lingwood argues, *House* was "both a closed architectural form and an open memorial; at one and the same time hermetic and implacable, but also able to absorb all those individual thoughts, feelings and memories projected onto it" (1995: 8). In contrast to the inhibiting discourses (nationalism, tourism) which seek to fix the meaning of 'place' in order to create singular, fixed identities with recourse to an essential, internalised moment, the time-space of *House* necessitated a radical re-conceptualisation, one akin to Doreen Massey's redefinition of 'place'. The singularity of place, she argues, is "formed out of the particular set of social relations which interact at a particular location"; the identity of place is, therefore, "always formed by the juxtaposition and co-presence there of particular sets of social relations, and by the effects which that juxtaposition and co-presence produce" (1994: 168-9). Open to the public's gaze and devoid of all Coventry Patmore's 'angels', Whiteread's *House* belied the initial impulse to view it as dead space. As Massey herself argues, "*House* emphasizes – indeed it throws in our faces – the fact that its meaning always has to be interpreted; that there was never any simple 'authenticity'; that the meaning(s) of home are always open to contestation" (1995: 42). In

1993, nostalgia for departed Victorian values co-mingled with the rise of the British National Party and an increased disparity between rich and poor (Canary Wharf loomed to the south of the exhibit).

The self-same re-evaluation of 'home' took place in the Republic of Ireland during the 1990s, a period in which the country "reinvented itself" (NESC 1999: 21). This second coming[1] was inaugurated by the birth of that infamous rough beast, the Celtic Tiger: its avid embrace of globalisation and informational capitalism initiated a decided paradigm shift, with a cultural discourse that prioritised "individualism, entrepreneurship, mobility, flexibility, innovation" displacing "earlier discourses prioritising national development, national identity, family, self-sacrifice, self-sufficiency and nationalism" (Kirby, Gibbons and Cronin 2002b: 13). The relationship between self and state, and the related notion of 'Irish identity', all underwent a marked change, each stage of which can be traced in the publications of Ireland's foremost cultural commentator, Fintan O'Toole. In *The Ex-Isle of Erin*, as a "placeless consumer", he experiences a defensive nostalgia for a distinctive Irishness;[2] in *The Lie of the Land*, he wholeheartedly adopts the transformative potential inherent in globalisation, noting how "cultural distinctiveness lies not in any fixed inherited tradition but in the particular way that it reacts to an overload of global stimuli" (1997a: 20-1); finally, in *After the Ball*, he demythologises the Celtic Tiger myth of prosperity and concludes that Ireland "is not exceptional" in its experience of globalisation (2003: 3). The emphasis in this last publication shares with other recent analyses a concentration on how economic disparity, fostered by a market economy, impacts upon cultural identity.[3] During an economic boom characterised by both an increasingly high level of owner-occupation and rising house prices due to rapid increased disposable income, immigration, low direct taxation, low mortgage interest rates and increased investor activity, the 'house' figured prominently as a thematic concern in the Arts. Negative equity and unaffordable house prices brought a new dimension to spatial politics and the question of plotting one's 'social subjectivity'.

In September 1998 Beat Klein and Henrijke Kühne took part in the Artists' Work Programme at the Irish Museum of Modern Art and began assembling an installation entitled *Property*, an expanding metropolis made up of photographs of buildings offered for sale taken each week from the Property Supplement of the *Irish Times*. Each

'house' was glued on cardboard, "put together in a stand-up rectangular system".[4] When this floor-mounted complex of photographic imagery was shown at the gallery's *Unblinking Eye* exhibition (18 September 2002 – 16 February 2003), a spectator could be forgiven for
thinking they had stumbled across some Lilliputian dystopia; even
with the accorded panoptic viewpoint, she he would discern little pattern in either scale or arrangement of the miniature urban sprawl. The
work's title, focusing on ownership and contractual agreement, intimates a concern with housing at the most basic level: "economically,
buildings provide for investment, store capital, create work, house activities, occupy land, provide opportunities for rent" (King 1990: 11).
Indeed, the *Property Review*, a quarterly analysing mortgage lending
trends, property completion targets and interest rate outlook, used the
work to illustrate the cover of their June issue in 2003. The sheer multitude of properties available for procurement shown by the exhibit
seemingly belies the shortage of social housing in Ireland and the devastating impact upon the populace of soaring house prices, namely the
displacement to the ever-widening commuter belts, unmanageable
debt, and homelessness.

   Yet a work focusing on the house as a material object cannot avoid
the complex meanings bound up in the relation between the built form
and its social environment. As the urban theorist Anthony King argues:

> [Socially, buildings] support relationships, provide shelter, express social divi-
> sions, permit hierarchies, house institutions, enable the expression of status and
> authority, embody property relations; spatially, they establish place, define dis-
> tance, enclose space, differentiate area; culturally, they store sentiment, symbolize
> meaning, express identity; politically, they symbolize power, represent authority,
> become an arena for conflict, or a political resource (1990: 11).

Although every house in *Property* is connected, the space is eerily
depopulated and the layout suggests the very opposite of social cohe-
sion: the high density of housing and the manner in which the work
"defines distance, encloses space, and differentiates area" suggests a
lack of what Oscar Newman terms "defensible space" (1972: 3-21)
and, consequently, indicates the potential for urban crime and social
alienation. However, the most insistent critical appraisal is reserved
for the cultural level. Referring to the material used in its construction,
Catherine Marshall, the exhibition's curator, commented that the work

"gives a playful yet critical insight into a formative moment in the property boom in Dublin in 1998" (2003: 2). The humour is compounded by the tone of the accompanying collected letters. With its mix of precise technical jargon and disingenuous euphemism, one such example offers a parody of estate agent discourse:

> Oozing potential and retaining its original pebble-dash, red-brick, Howth stone and Victorian Tudor-style architect-designed bay-window frontage, this sensitively restored high density development in its quiet terraced enclave, well located on a busy thoroughfare, has truly stunning cosy corners, an abundance of character and burglar alarms (Órla Dukes, 29 October 1998).

The eclecticism of architectural styles bespeaks a postmodern aesthetic where the lines between irony, innovation and bad taste become unclear. The sheer vibrancy and eccentricity of this new European city functions in a manner similar to all such urban conglomerations: "The cities represent themselves, accumulating a mass of vital imageries from the fluid matter of memory, nostalgia, evocation, and suturing that index of scars into the projection of the contemporary moment, the present and the presence of the city in its immediacy and urgency" (Barber 1995: 8). Yet there is little sense of suture here; rather, it points towards nostalgia for more coherent, indigenous, local forms. The myriad colours, designs and sizes of *Property*'s structures foregrounds the rationale for the current backlash against globalisation. Indeed, the emphasis on, and implied distaste for, non-indigenous design is shared by Anne Marie Hourihane's contemporaneous caustic appraisal of Celtic Tiger Ireland's housing developments. Describing the Carrickmines Wood development with its "Japanese-style pond" and nomenclature taken from the Irish literary canon (implying an unintentional artistic hierarchy: "The Shaw" is cheaper than either "The Joyce" or "The Kavanagh"), she says, "it could be a holiday village in southern Spain or perhaps Florida" (2000: 148-52). The kaleidoscopic, if not chaotic, vista presented by *Property*, allied to the unplanned, claustrophobic proximity of each building to the next in its quasi-medieval layout (the city plan is decidedly pre-Haussmann), reinforces critiques such as Hourihane's.

While the demise of de Valera's dream of an inward-looking, economically self-sufficient, and culturally distinct nation is epitomised by *Property*'s plurality of styles, other works, such as Vona Groarke's poetry collection *Other People's Houses*, betray a nostalgic longing for communal identification. In 'Open House' (1999: 16-18), the speaker may have "all the aplomb of the propertied classes", yet becoming a householder is here akin to being condemned to solitary confinement: "This neighbourly interface is forestalled / by the containing gesture of four straight walls". The material reality of the building – "breeze blocks, plaster, paint, insulation" – evokes shelter and security, but it is that of the penitentiary and, ultimately, of the crypt: "seventy-six ideal homes / laid out with the stature so many tombs" (the full rhyme with 'homes' undercuts any notion of the domestic idyll). The work encapsulates what Wendy Wheeler terms "postmodern nostalgia", namely, "the desire for communal identification"; nostalgia, she argues, "turns us toward the idea of the individual as non-alienated, as knowing and being known by others in the commonality of the community which is identified as 'home'" (1994: 40).

It is remarkable, however, that such a yearning for communal identification due to the standardising effects of globalisation is not so pronounced in Irish culture. Theorising the impact of change on European cities, Stephen Barber argues that "each living city carries the implication of its own flattening into shards of memory" and, consequently, "the speed of its transformation must make it yearn for its cities to fall away and pass into the limbo of ecstatic nostalgia" (1995: 23-4). In contrast, such transformations in Ireland have caused artists to question the validity of cultural norms, sceptically to re-examine that which is deemed 'authentic'. In his project *Irelantis* (1993), for example, Seán Hillen presents the viewer with hyper-real images of Ireland, collages of spliced together spaces reminiscent of different eras. This Ireland is "everywhere and nowhere"; Irelantis is "a world where all borders – political, cultural and psychological – are permeable" (O'Toole 1999: 5). 'The Oracle at O'Connell St. Bridge' places contemporary skyscrapers (L.A. Towers) in the same cityscape as 1960s Dublin, with Delphic columns in the foreground. At work here is what Fred Davis terms

> reflexive nostalgia […] the person does more than sentimentalise some past and censure, if only implicitly, some present. In perhaps an inchoate though nevertheless psychologically active fashion he or she summons to feeling and thought certain empirically oriented questions concerning the truth, accuracy, completeness, or representativeness of the nostalgic claim. Was it really that way? (1979: 21)

A clue to the artist's intention comes from the material used: the apocalyptic image of the sky is taken from a John Hinde postcard, an image that belongs to the discourse of tourism, promoting a 'real' Ireland, but whose colouring is patently unreal. The Ireland that is being 'lost' through globalisation may be presented as 'authentic', but Hillen's images embrace the paradox outlined by recent postcolonial theorists: to forge a nation, one must create a national consciousness and to do so requires a national, authentic art; yet this can only be constructed (Graham 2001a; Graham and Kirkland 1999). Authenticity is not a pre-existent quality; it is contextual and strategic. The Ireland projected by Hinde is as mythical as *Irelantis*. Hillen continued this critique in one of his images for the *Focail* project (2003). 'Géaga Ginealaigh – The Branches of Ancestry' is a poster that depicts a 'fairy landscape' at Lough Gur, Co. Limerick. Through the branches in the foreground, the viewer sees a five-storey whitewashed thatched cottage: while the title may emphasise the importance of the Irish language and cultural heritage, the image suggests a moving with the times. Although indigenous architecture is here incorporated into a modern design, the scene is unreal, that of a fairy-tale.

A more complex meditation on "the instability of our relationships to home, place and memory" is Brigid McLeer's visual arts project, *Collapsing Here*.[5] McLeer is an Irish artist living in London, and her work explores the concept 'being at home' and the extent to which she may be displaced, part of a diasporic community that is not quite Irish. The version in *Circa* (1998) combines text and images (of the interior and exterior of a glass house, of the sea, of landscape), each of which move in relation to each other. The 'glasshouse' is a perfect emblem with which to explore and represent that which is interior and exterior, evoking the interactions and interstices between that which we deem public and that which we guardedly affirm as private. The transparent glass is a metaphor for unmediated representation, an assertion of our ability to represent; yet this is offset by the changes of perspective, focus and scale employed by McLeer. Moving to England instigated a reassessment of her identity and the project highlights the difficulties of both fixing and representing the notion of 'here': "Here on an island of doors without houses, without insides or outsides, without openings or closings – my home (*m'anim*) is a bridge ever crossing". Playing on the signifier that identifies her ('Brigid'), she attempts to bridge the gap between the Irish and English versions of herself; yet by emphasising the paradoxical nature of *deixis* ('pointing'), namely that which fixes and contextualises, yet also only gestures towards, the project cannot define 'here' in singular terms. The motifs of journeying, of crossing or inhabiting a liminal space, of moving outwards to confront 'the other', allows the artist to actively reconfigure her place in the world rather than be passively defined by place: "I used to be a place. A territory encompassing fields, crossing walls to gardens – stepping tentatively out through the door. I used place, while leaving, as naming bridge – *droichead anseo, mise m'anim, anseo agus átha(s)* – I played with lexicons of here". The key symbol is the letter 'H', graphically signalling a bridge between two 'I's:

> My foreignness in conjunctions used to be a place. And here and where and how bridging here, meshing where once, and there together tying loose and once again – a raft to journey staying here. Where h her here, her frame for stepping her language ladder, lines stretching steps, tries tying to there – precarious tightrope flung across from side of I to other (1998: 21).

The bridge is 'precarious' and the use of a continuous present tense implies a temporal hiatus, an ongoing process that eschews the securities inherent in a Heideggerian sense of 'dwelling'. As a clue to her overall intention, McLeer incorporates into the *Perhelion* version a quotation from the architectural theorist John Rajchman: "the fold distances one from one's habitual perception and reading of space, as if to transport one to the 'elsewhere' where things go off in unimagined directions or are folded again".[6] The 'fold' (or 'perplication') negates the idea of the house as a bounded or framed space. In contrast, the 'glass house' is designed according to the principle of 'multiplicity' where unity is the "holding together of a prior or virtual dispersion" (Rajchman 1998: 15-16). The idea of 'here', then, is not a pre-defined place but a gesture towards an idea of home that is dependent on a multiplicity of factors (social interrelations, cultural determinants, recollection, imagination, etc.). While the architectural theory informing this project seems at odds with the supposed memorialising aesthetic of Whiteread's *House* and the post-modern kitsch of Klein and Kühne's *Property*, it shares with both a belief that the specificity of place is "continually reproduced" and that "it is not a specificity which results from some long, internalised history" (Massey 1994: 155).

In a Northern Irish context, to adopt Eisenman's motto regarding architectural practice – "In order to get [...] to a place, you have to [...] blow it apart [...] you have to look inside it and find the seeds of the new" (quoted in Rajachman 1998: 19) – would seem ironic, if not darkly humorous, given the violent manifestations of socio-political contestation which it has endured since the late 1960s. It has been noted that factors such as the inner city developments, incorporating high-rise buildings out of scale and sympathy with already existing edifices, and traffic pressure have each contributed to the decline in Belfast's visual character (Brett 2001: 90), but that the main contributor has been the legacy of the so-called 'Troubles' (peace-lines, sectarian graffiti, destroyed buildings). However, official responses to city planning have tended to strategically implement a policy of cultural amnesia. The graphics employed by the Belfast Urban Area Plan (1989), for example, projected "a suite of positive images of newly built or planned developments" which were "counterpointed by anaemic toned panoramas of the city of the past". As William J.V. Neill points out, all reference to "the sectarian divisions with which the city is riven was studiously avoided in both text and photographs" (2001: 47).

Counterbalancing this occlusion is a project such as John Davies' *Metropoli* (2000), which sets out "to document the multi-layered character of metropolitan areas and to produce a coherent series of images which reflect the positive achievements and realities within our continually changing urban space".[7] The black and white photographs of Belfast depict a city in transition with modern and Victorian designs co-existing; the elevated vantage point from which the photographs are taken enable Davies to capture the icons of global capitalism in the same frame as the crowded terraced houses of the Donegall Pass. Davies here combines a synchronic gaze, that which "registers the varieties and patterns of present usage", with a diachronic gaze that "opens up the urban palimpsest" and "goes back through layers and accretions, perceiving history, influence, development, change".[8] In one key image, that of an almost completed apartment block covered by scaffolding and tarpaulin, Davies, as Colin Graham astutely argues, "catches the moments in which a city's nostalgia is made, when the tarpaulin is pulled back like the curtain on an unveiled plaque, and in the midst of the achievement we feel that twinge of regret for its completion, because the future of a city space revealed is the beginning of

a life-in-death for many pasts" (2001a: 10). The tarpaulin is the photographic text's *punctum*, the expansive and metonymic detail that
overwhelms our reading of the image and raises it above that which is
merely *unary* (Barthes 2000: 32-59). Like Whiteread's *House*, the image is both a living and a dead space; the black-and-white photograph
may indicate a documenting of the past, yet it is simultaneously a
blueprint for the future.

The most celebrated chronicler of Belfast's ever-changing city is
Ciaran Carson, a poet and prose writer who "collects the bricolage of
corrugated iron peace lines, the cul-de-sacs of charred vacant lots, and
the pubs and jails strung on decades of barbed-wire rosaries"
(McDonaugh 1991: 120). For him, the city is "an exploded diagram of
itself, along the lines of a vastly complicated interactive model aircraft
kit whose components are connected by sprued plastic latitudes and
longitudes" (Carson 1997: 15). The city as a "diagram" suggests a
space that is readable, a delimitative narrative subject to fixed interpretation. Yet "exploded" denotes a chaotic element implying a self-
cancelling, ever-shifting metropolis, an impression reinforced by Carson when he immediately introduces a qualifying, supplementary
metaphor: the city, he says, "mutates like a virus, its programme un-
dergoing daily shifts of emphasis and detail" (1997: 15). Like Davies,
Carson's use of both a synchronic and diachronic gaze allows him to
depict the city in transition. In a poem entitled "Clearance", he captures the moment at which the Royal Avenue Hotel is demolished,
opening up an unexpected vista:

> The Royal Avenue Hotel collapses under the breaker's pendulum:
> Zig-zag stairwells, chimney-flues, and a 'thirties mural
> Of an elegantly-dressed couple doing what seems to be a Tango, in
>   Wedgewood
> Blue and white – happy days! Suddenly more sky
> Than there used to be. A breeze springs up from nowhere (1987: 32)

The "breaker's pendulum", indicative of the ineluctable passage of
time and its destructive effect, exposes the 1930s interior design to the
flâneur's gaze and juxtaposes it with the more contemporary features
of a "greengrocer's shop". Carson's "celebration" of the city's collapse (Johnstone 1990: 151) is not a form of macabre documentary;
rather, he revels in the materiality of the buildings and the new narra-

tives that they embody. Playfully conflating "story" with "storey", Carson states:

> The houses started to go up, attaining hitherto unknown levels. I used to watch the bricklayers ply their trade, as they deployed masonic tools of plumb-line, try-square and spirit-level, setting up taut parallels of pegs and string, before throwing down neatly gauged dollops of mortar, laying bricks, in practised, quick monotony, chinking each into its matrix with skilled dints of the trowel. Had their basic modules been alphabet bricks, I could have seen them building lapidary sentences and paragraphs, as the storeyed houses became emboldened by their hyphenated, skyward narrative, and entered the ongoing, fractious epic that is Belfast (1997: 126).

The "fractious epic" recorded by Carson pays close attention to the "expressive" nature of architecture, "the 'social meanings' that people give to the built environment" (McEldowney, Sterrett and Gaffikin 2001: 101). In certain areas and enclaves of Belfast, buildings, and their material inscriptions (murals, flags, graffiti), are not merely functional or aesthetic objects, but serve as reminders of one's political identity. Having experienced decades of conflict, the most troubled parts of the city have been "carved into mutually antagonistic 'turfs', where those who do not share an affinity with the cultural / political orthodoxy in particular neighbourhoods can feel under severe pressure, if not intimidation" (Gaffikin, Morrissey and Sterrett 2001: 159). Buildings, therefore, become sites of contestation regarding identity. In 'Intelligence', for example, Carson registers the "dense graffiti of public houses, churches [...] bonding stores, graving docks, monuments, Sunday schools and Orange halls" (1989: 81). Described as "graffiti", these buildings do not constitute "a signature without a document, an anonymous autograph" (Sinclair 1998: 1); rather, "graffiti" here is a marker "not only in the material, territorial sense but also of political possession and assertion" (McGonagle 1987: s.p.). In a poem such as 'Night Out' Carson focuses on one building, a private drinking club, and records with minute detail the security apparatus put in place to vet each customer:

> Every Thursday night when we press the brass button on the galvanized wire mesh gate
> A figure appears momentarily at the end of the strip-lit concrete passageway,
> Then disappears. The gate squeaks open, slams shut almost instantly behind us.
> Then through the semi-opaque heavy-duty polythene swing doors they might

have taken
From a hospital. At the bar, we get the once-over once again (1989: 77).

While this gritty, poetic urban realism seemingly luxuriates in the material description, the main thematic preoccupation centres on the implied psychological effects. The banality of the scene and the unthinking manner by which the protagonist reacts both to the security procedures and to the "broken rhythm / Of machine-gun fire" suggests that sectarian conflict and the consequent protective rituals have all become normalised, habitual.

Paul Seawright's *Belfast* series (2000), comprised of large cibachrome photographs of blocked-up entrances, scarred fences and security gates outside social clubs, shares with Carson's *oeuvre* a concern for the way an urban environment can both reflect and reinforce a tribal mentality. The urban landscape embodies "discourses of inclusion and exclusion" and the buildings function as "symbols of identity, validation and legitimation" (Graham 1998: 130). Four images of blocked-up windows are suggestive of forced relocation at a sectarian interface; the red white and blue UVF marking on one of them is indicative of a reflexive nostalgia for past glory, a statement of defiance and a warning. All of the images, taken in Loyalist areas, connote defensiveness and decay. As Colin Graham argues, "the blankness with which the cages, gates, bricks and corrugated iron all respond to the camera is defiance devoid of substance, and it leads the viewer to increasingly see these images as reflective of a bewilderment, a lost stand still being made, its symbols decaying" (2003: 159). At each juncture the viewer's gaze is blocked and the material constructions themselves represent a mentality that underpins conflict. The 'house' here is not 'safe', yet it is utterly resistant to change.

The key difference between the Irish and Northern Irish house, and their representation in art, is the presence (or legacy) of the Troubles. The physical, socio-political and psychological effects of the ongoing strife are most noticeable at the interfaces between loyalist and nationalist communities. In a number of localities in Belfast physical barriers ('peacelines') separate the two communities and, as Brendan Murtagh's research has shown, they affect "nearly every aspect of daily life":

Peacelines demarcate production and consumption patterns in the city, they intensify poverty ad isolate people. They concentrate violence, cut through housing markets, blight land and project negative images to visitors and investors. But they also protect, build solidarity and enhance cultural identity (2002: 63-4).

The barriers at these junctures reinforce a sense of an embattled ethnic identity whilst simultaneously constructing the neighbouring community as 'other'. At the same time, the Housing Executive has transformed "the sociologist's concept of 'defensible space' into the policing convenience of 'containable space'" (Brett 1991: 32). The sense of alienation and defiance is captured in Rita Duffy's 'Territory' (1997), a work comprising fifteen drawings on gesso panels, each one featuring a cartographic representation of houses and streets situated near peacelines. Inscribed across the boards are selected lines from Seamus Heaney's 'Act of Union': "His heart beneath your heart is a wardrum"; "And ignorant little fists already / Beat at your borders"; "your tracked / And stretchmarked body, the big pain" (1975: 50). Heaney's text presents the 1801 Act of Union in terms of a rape, a clumsy psycho sexual allegory that attempts to explain the origin of the Troubles. Duffy's artwork retains the corporeal metaphor (land-as-body), portraying the peace lines as stretch marks indicative of Heaney's "opened ground"; the blood-red pigment and the violently rubbed surface of each board indicates the ongoing nature of "the big pain".

The image of the house may indicate sheltered domesticity, but in Northern Irish artworks the private realm is always under scrutiny. Poets register an acute sense of vulnerability due to the all-pervasive gaze of neighbours, the police, and the opposing community. Grainne Toibin's 'Family History' depicts the moment when the domestic realm becomes unsafe:

Leaving that evening,
Ashamed to be seen,
(the word was out
our houses was next to burn) (2002: 22).

While the family avoid "our attackers", they come under renewed surveillance from the authorities: "Police weighed up our load, address and destination". The individual's behaviour within the house becomes regulated as if within a panopticon. To express this debilitating unease (and to escape from it), another poet, Medbh McGuckian, inhabits the rooms once occupied by her literary exemplars; embedding unacknowledged quotations from their works allows her to empathise with their feelings of being placed under watch. In 'Balakhana' (1988: 39-40), for example, she cites from a passage referring to state surveillance in the first volume of Osip Mandelstam's biography, *Hope Against Hope*: "In the years of terror, there was not a home in the country where people did not sit trembling at night, their ears straining to catch *the murmur of passing cars or the sound of an elevator*. Even nowadays, whenever I spend the night at the Shklovski's apartment, I tremble as I hear the elevator go past'.[9] Similarly, in 'Yeastlight' she quotes from passages referring to the intrusive searches of Mandelstam's apartment and his subsequent arrests:

> During the search of our apartment in 1934 the police
> agents failed to find *the poems I had sewn into*
> *cushions or stuck inside saucepans and shoes* (271).

> When M. was arrested again in 1938, they simply
> *turned over all the mattresses . . .* (9).

> . . they *shook out every book . . .* (7).

Compare with:

> ... When I found
> In the very cup of the town those poems sewn
> Into cushions, or pushed into saucepans or shoes,
> I took the arm of someone I didn't know
> Who turned over all my mattresses
> And shook out every book.

The house in each of these poems become an unsafe site.

In his visual artworks Willie Doherty deploys the image of the house under a watchful gaze to explore the deleterious, self-regarding identity formations determined by "a society in which surveillance is the prerequisite for control" (Green 1996: 56). In works such as 'Blackspot' from 1997 (2002: 158), Doherty portrays the intrusive gaze of the security installations on top of the Derry Walls: the viewer experiences an unsettling voyeuristic pleasure as he watches the unedited, real-time thirty-minute video projection: the houses seem peaceful, yet the inhabitants are aware at all times that they are being watched. However, for Doherty, the conflict does not simply reside in political differences. Rather than presenting the viewer with an outworn media cliché of Northern Ireland as war-torn place in which the conflict is solely between two rival factions (Catholic and Protestant),

Doherty makes the viewer question our received perceptions. 'God Has Not Failed Us' from 1990 (1999: 54) is a black-and-white photograph of a house with barred and broken windows overlooked by a fortification flying the Union Jack and adjacent to a wall and high railings. The text ('God Has Not Failed Us') is written across the image acting as "a sort of screen though which visual perception must pass before it can come to terms with the image itself" (Cameron 1993: s.p.). As always, "the picture demands a context" (Erävaara 2002: 73): here we have a house situated in The Fountain, a Protestant working-class area on the river Foyle's west bank in Derry. The text, taken from a sermon protesting against the signing of the Anglo-Irish Agreement, suggests that God will protect the Protestant privileged position in Northern Ireland; the image, however, indicates economic decline and the state's refusal (or unwillingness) to ameliorate the condition. As Maite Lorés has argued, Doherty's "images of a scarred urban environment hint not only at the endemic nature of violence, but the equally corrosive effects of economic depression" (1999: 116).

All of the examples provided in this chapter suggest perhaps the crucial distinction between recent engagements with the house North and South of the border: whereas the latter's self-reflexivity demonstrates a positive, forward-looking engagement with outworn symbols, the former, although equally self-aware and critical, convey a sense of being trapped in a hiatus, unable to progress. Many others could have been cited. Victor Sloan's c-type print 'House, Edenderry, Portadown' (2001: 141), for example, presents a close-up of a scarred wall of a house. Unlike his previous work in which he did violence to the negatives, scratching them with a pin and applying toner indicating both his anger at and critique of the scenes depicted, in the series from which this photograph is taken "[the] violence has already been done to what is depicted, and what is depicted is invariably flat, is itself all surface, a plane, a fragment of wall or ground. All photographic content has been, so to speak, compressed into this place, a surface which is essentially a mute repository of history" (Dunne 2001: 122). The wall acts as a record of and memorial to the violence in Northern Ireland, and the current political impasse in which the anomalous State finds itself is symbolised by the inability of the viewer's gaze to move beyond the wall's surface. The image is reminiscent of Willie Doherty's early photo-text 'Closed Circuit' from 1989 (1990: s.p.) which shows, in the midst of metal barriers and security cameras, the Sinn

Féin Advice Centre in Short Strand. The image highlights the way the inhabitants of this nationalist 'house' must protect themselves; but the text implicitly criticises the cyclopic, self-regarding ideology of nationalism, with its siege mentality, unable to engage with either the British Government or the Protestant community. However, the most recent text to incorporate the house as a central trope demonstrates a distinct shift in emphasis. Glenn Patterson's extraordinary novel *Number 5* (2003) traces the history of the different occupants of a terraced house in Belfast from the 1950s to the present day. While the house becomes a relatively unsafe space during the years of the Troubles, Patterson's broader perspective allows him to portray differing social dynamics and, ultimately, what one of the characters terms "the Peace Dividend". The location may be singular, yet each occupant's sense of place and their corresponding idea of identity is shown to be different. As with Whiteread's juxtaposition of different time-frames within the same work, Patterson's novel demonstrates that place depends on the co-presence there of specific "sets of social relations" (Massey 1994: 167-72).

Notes

1. The first coming was announced in T.K. Whitaker's famous 1958 White Paper on *Economic Development*.

2. O'Toole 1997: 28. For a general commentary see Harvey 1989.

3. See the essays by Peader Kirby (21-37) and Michel Pellion (54-68) in Kirby, Gibbons and Cronin 2002.

4. This description is by Klein and Kühne from a letter dated 24 December 1998 that was included in a book of letters entitled *Property* which formed part of the exhibit.

5. The quote arose in conversation with the artist. This project exists in print form in four versions: *Circa, Coil, Performance Research* and *Perhelion*. The print version in *Circa* indicates the directions in which text and images move. A web version previously existed on the *Stunned Artzine* (stunned.org).

6. See heelstone.com/wherewewere/brigid/brigidpoetry.htm. The quotation comes from Rajchman 1998: 23.

7. John Davies, daviesphoto.demon.co.uk/metropoli.htm.

8. For the distinction between the two kinds of gaze see Barry 2000: 224-6.

9. Mandelstam 1971: 349. The italicised words are the ones reproduced in McGuckian's poem.

'The house […] has cancer':
Representations of Domestic Space in the Poetry of
Carol Ann Duffy

Mari Hughes-Edwards

ABSTRACT

This article evaluates the diverse representations of urban domestic space in the work of the poet Carol Ann Duffy. It examines the ways in which Duffy connects imagery of the heart, hearth and home, sometimes offering the reader the comfort of the house as refuge, at other times affording glimpses into far less comfortable fictional worlds; the worlds of the inhabitants of the houses of the strange, the lost and the beautiful. It evaluates above all the ways in which Duffy uses houses as metaphors for the relationships played out in them. It demonstrates that the health of the home and the health of the heart are cast in her work in a mutually referential relationship. It proposes therefore that Duffy's constructions of the presence or absence of a happy home life are fundamental to her depictions of the human condition. Finally, it argues that representations of house and home are crucial to the meaning of, and motivation behind, the poet's work as a whole.

Introduction

The purpose of this essay is to examine the ways in which Carol Ann Duffy represents domestic space in some of her key poetic works. It will explore the extent to which her portrayal of house and home intersects with, and impacts on, her central, crucial interests in complex human relationships in their cultural, social, sexual and political contexts. I wish to analyse the ways in which these relationships are formed, played out and reflected in the domestic arena, and to explore the extent to which the home functions as a microcosm of the society upon which Duffy seeks to comment.

Born in 1955 in Glasgow, Carol Ann Duffy was raised in England, and published her first pamphlet of poetry, *Fleshweathercock* in 1973.

In 1985 she published her first mature collection, *Standing Female Nude*, which won the Scottish Arts Council Award. Later collections, almost all of which have won major poetry awards, include *Selling Manhattan* (1987), *The Other Country* (1990), *Mean Time* (1993), *The World's Wife* (1999) and most recently *Feminine Gospels* (2002). A significant number of Duffy's poems refer explicitly to the house or contain household imagery. Since love is of central concern to the poet, the home frequently acts as a locus of love, or the lack of it in the lives of her characters. As each one of Duffy's six major verse collections uses the home in this way, it would be impossible to evaluate the numerous references made in every collection. Only her first four collections will be examined here.

Duffy's use of house and home in these works can only be appreciated if attention is first drawn to some key general significances of contemporary domestic space. All interpretations of the house and home are necessarily subjective. This is entirely as it should be for the home is of huge personal significance – decorated, shaped and interpreted by those to whom it belongs. It is an intensely private space to those who inhabit it or co-habit within it, reflective not simply of the personality of those individuals, but their emotional, psychological, intellectual, material and even physical health. They are also signifiers of social status and permanence. In the context of western society the house has long been a symbol of hierarchy, of gender and power (im)balance; ideals which are entirely interwoven with ideas about nationhood and community. Thatcher's Britain, which provides the socio-political backdrop to Duffy's earlier collections, highlighted the central importance of home-owning as part of the rise of its aggressive, self-orientated, reactionary brand of capitalism. The concept of renting became conversely an indication of impermanence and instability, while the notion of homelessness developed into a symbol of failure and degradation. Linda A Kinnahan, in an article on the discourse of nationalism in Duffy's writing, is right to site the interests of the poet in this as part of "a larger crisis of national identity brought on by the decolonization process following the second world war" (2000: 208).

The central paradox of the interpretation of domestic space is that the home is intensely private and yet concurrently a public arena. Richard Gill, remarking on the tradition of the British country house, declares: "Like a great stage, it quite literally gathers people together and shows them meeting, separating, colliding, uniting" (1972: 15). To allow access to the home is an intimate and potentially precarious act, rendering the individual vulnerable and visible. A guest must acknowledge certain protocols and respect the hospitality of the host(s). Housebreaking and burglary therefore are not simply a violation of material goods and property, but an assault on the personality, integrity and even the humanity of the homeowner. A fundamental difference exists between the home as it is experienced by its creator and shaper, and the home as it is experienced by outsiders who gain entry to it, whether they are intimates or strangers. The most vulnerable places and spaces within the home are without a doubt the boundary lines that divide the inner from the outer world. The doors and windows through which guests and strangers, uninvited or not, may gaze and / or enter physically, are therefore fundamentally important; at the same time, they are also the most vulnerable points in the house. Victor Turner's famous anthropological theory attributes a liminal status to boundary lines and to those who regulate them:

> The attributes of liminality or of liminal *personae* ('threshold' people) are necessarily ambiguous, since this condition and these persons elude or slip through the network of classifications that normally locate states and positions in cultural space. Liminal entities are neither here nor there; they are betwixt and between the positions assigned and arrayed by law, custom, convention and ceremonial (1969: 95).

The delicate balance of protocol and the importance of these ambiguous, potentially liminal, boundary lines make abuse within the home all the more unacceptable. This points us to the fundamental difference between a house and a home: a house is merely a repository for personal and cultural artefacts and items – a space wherein to perform primary functions, such as eating and sleeping; a home is a place bound together by love and mutual respect; a place of safety, of refuge, of emotional grounding and warmth. Paul J. Pennartz's study of the experience of atmosphere within domestic urban culture argues (after the urban sociologist Herbert Gans) that "the manmade 'potential' qualities of architectural characteristics are transformed into an 'effective environment' […] empowered on the individual's conceptual level" (1999: 102). Put simply, it is the interaction between individuals within the building that determines the extent to which it is a home. There will always be a disparity between the ideal and the reality; no one knows what goes on behind closed doors. "There's no place like home", as the proverbial saying has it: perhaps, unless it is shared with an incompatible partner, family member or friend, unless that home has become a place of abuse, prejudice, anger, hatred, self-hatred or violence. John Rennie Stuart, in the foreword to an important volume on the anthropology of domestic space, writes:

> Home is often idealized. What isn't? But it is idealized more often than other places [...] In the early seventeenth-century John Fletcher wrote: "Charity and beating begins at home" [...] Domestic abuse and child abuse are nasty in themselves, but public outrage is often heightened by the fact that they take place in the home. It is like a murder in the cathedral; a sacred place defiled [...] The image of a serene home life haunts our collective and individual imaginations (quoted in Cieraad 1999: x).

If the home has become the sacrosanct space that has, potentially, eclipsed the church in our national consciousness, then its violation says much about the health of the society in which we live and for which we are all responsible. It is in response to this question that Duffy's poetry about the home begins to come into focus.

This essay is divided into two sections, both of which consider Duffy's representations of domestic space. The first considers Duffy's use of the dramatic monologue; the second explores her seemingly autobiographical poems, those in which the use of personal pronouns tempt the reader to apply them to the poet herself. In reality it is as much a mistake to read the latter as autobiographical simply because they appear confessional and personal, as it is to assume that the dramatic monologues are entirely fictional and can tell us nothing of the poet's perspective. Both poetical approaches reflect implicitly and explicitly the views of Duffy's own persona, and both dramatise the perspectives of other deliberately constructed and fictional personae. Both approaches, despite their difference in form, reflect Duffy's commitment to use the simplistic everyday speech with which she has become identified and through which she strives to show the extraordinariness of the ordinary and *vice versa*.

Domestic Space and the Dramatic Monologue.
The monologue, for which Duffy has become justifiably famous, provides the ideal vehicle for the most immediate, dramatic and arresting perspectives of a host of characters whose opinions are often intended

to provoke opposition in the reader. Duffy's command of this form of writing has earned her valid comparisons with Browning. Danette DiMarco suggests that she, like Browning before her, engages in the language and form of self-empowerment, and quotes Lynda Nead's conclusion that "'to represent is to take power – it is to tell your own stories and draw your own lines, rather than succumb to the tales and images of others [...] there is a risk involved; you might not end up telling a fairy tale with a happy ending, but at least you are [...] in control of the means of narration'" (1998: 35-6). These poems offer a glimpse into fictional worlds – or more accurately, into fictional houses. The first-person narrative offers the poet a form through which she can articulate the perspectives of the disaffected, the marginal, the prejudiced, the criminal and the dispossessed. Deryn Rees Jones describes the monologues as acts of ventriloquism, noting that Duffy has acknowledged (in an interview with Jane Stabler in 1991) "an initial, and often quite powerful, empathy or identification" with the characters to whom she gives voice: "the dramatic monologues [...] are, yes, objective; but closer to me as the writer than would appear" (Rees Jones 1999: 23). The reader has to work with the poet to complete their meaning. The poems offer implicit judgements intended to act as triggers to the reader's own judgement system. It is in this context that Ian Gregson argues that "there is a powerful dialogic element" in Duffy's monologues – that they are in part designed as responses to "a monologically masculine aesthetic" (2000: 101). The meaning of these poems arises chiefly from the intersection between the views of writer and reader. Where each reader's perspective differs from that of another, or where the views of a given reader change over time, the poem is remade, reinterpreted. As such, this poetical form assumes a textual life in which meaning is not fixed but organic.

The voices heard in Duffy's monologues can usefully be divided into those that are forceful and sometimes aggressive, and those that are more passive, even fragile. Perhaps the most dramatic exploration of the frequently extreme relationship between domestic space and aggression is found in 'Education for Leisure',[1] a poem affording a glimpse of the madness that is played out unhindered behind closed doors. It features an unnamed, unemployed, unstable figure whose gender is unspecified. This speaker unleashes vengeance upon the domestic pets that as faithful family companions would, in an ideal world, symbolise domestic harmony. In this distorted environment however they represent the only things over which power can be exerted: "Today I am going to kill something [...] today I am going to play God" he / she declares. A strong connection is evident between the loss of perspective inside the home and the speaker's sense of isolation from, and rejection by, the world outside it, implicit in such statements as "I have had enough of being ignored" and "[the dole office] don't appreciate my signature". The speaker, "a genius" and "a superstar", glories in the feelings of strength and control which are reborn within through murder, using clipped, active and powerfully business-like language and tone: "I pour the goldfish down the bog. I pull the chain. / I see that it is good". The absolute power exerted inside the home is in perfect counterbalance to the inadequacy experienced outside it for much of the poem. However, in the final stanza these two worlds collide sharply, as the speaker makes contact with the outside world and the blood-lust enacted within the house, symbolised by "our bread-knife", is carried forth into the street: "The pavements glitter suddenly. I touch your arm". The poem calls into question here the link between the mentally vulnerable and the society that fosters their isolation and which therefore potentially fails them. The effect of this seems to be to intensify the need to understand society's role in creating and perpetuating or simply ignoring the misery that contributes to their downward spiral. At the same time the randomness of the connections made in the mind of the speaker, and the swift escalation of the violence from the killing of a fly to the (implied) attack on a passer-by seem to suggest that there is no possibility of understanding such actions. The creative force of the poem resides in its ambivalence, an ambivalence that lends itself to constant reinterpretation.

Absolute power exerted within the home is a recurrent theme elsewhere in *Standing Female Nude*. 'You Jane' (*SFN*: 34) deliberately genders that power, however, in a way in which 'Education for Leisure' does not. It is the aggressive narrative of, as its title suggests, an animalistic, Tarzan-like male who is "Man of the house. Master in my own home." His masculine authority is rooted in the body, in its physical strength and also in its ability to withstand alcohol. Such masculinity is therefore precariously sited and requires frequent reaffirmation. Repeated references to the speaker's physical strength in this narrative of an implicitly abusive marriage therefore interrupt his train of thought, resulting in almost random juxtapositions: "Australia next year and bugger / the mother-in-law. Just feel those thighs". This is a home where everything is reduced to the level of physicality and where the speaker, as the stronger, reigns supreme. Implicit threat is detected in colloquialisms like "[she] knows when to button it". Clearly this is not a loving home; indeed, it is not a home at all, merely a house. Sex, which carries the implicit but nonetheless strong threat of violence, is reduced to a function, one where consent is barely heeded: "I wake half-conscious with a hard-on. Shove it in. / She don't complain". His wife, who remains unnamed throughout, is demeaned as sexual object in a description which unintentionally acknowledges the precariousness of siting authority in the unstable flesh: "Although she's run a bit to fat / she still bends over of a weekend in suspenders". The husband, of course, misses the point: if his wife's body has run to fat, his own, wherein is sited his concept of masculinity and attendant self-esteem, may well do so too. There is vulnerability in the final line: "When I feel, I feel here / where the purple vein in my neck throbs"; but it is more faithful to the context of the poem to read it as further evidence of the speaker's absence of emotion. 'Feeling' for him is reduced to physical function, as are sex and (dreamless) sleep. His is a house of actions, not emotions, and this reflects the power imbalance of its central relationship. At its epicentre is a man who is mentally distorted, although, dangerously enough, in a far more culturally acceptable and insidious way than the protagonist of 'Education for Leisure'. In an exploration of subversive strategies in contemporary women's poetry, Liz Yorke speaks of the communal responsibility of a poet who explores "unspeakable" realities. Such writers (in which we can surely include Duffy) "speak out of the 'silences' of culture. The subversive power of the revisionary poet in finding words [...] to bear witness to social oppression [...] provides the impetus [...] whereby the 'not-said' may become audible and public" (1991:16). The speakers of both the monologues considered thus far share the conviction that they are at the centre of their universe just as they are at the centre of their house. Both use their dominance and oppression of those who share that house to enhance their own sense of power. They consequently take the sense of selfhood acquired through the power imbalance of their domestic environment out with them into the outside world.

Other monologues using household imagery, and also giving voice to varieties of aggression, are in evidence in Duffy's next collection,

Selling Manhattan. 'Yes, Officer' (*SM*: 31) recounts the story of a man framed by the police. He protests his innocence and distances himself from a statement concocted by others in a dramatic metaphor which trades on the reader's understanding of the intimate bond between home and the individual. He exclaims: "Without my own language, I am a blind man / in the wrong house". The link between language and location is here made explicit and through it the disorientation and terror of the verbal and physical onslaughts of others is made powerfully clear. We meet a genuine criminal in 'Stealing' (*SM*: 38). The poem, voiced apparently by an adolescent male, opens with the theft of a snowman, which is later violently destroyed in the backyard of the speaker's home. Examples of housebreaking and burglary are recounted colloquially:

> Sometimes I steal things I don't need […]
> break into houses just to have a look.
> I'm a mucky ghost, leave a mess […]
> I watch my gloved hand twisting the doorknob.
> A stranger's bedroom. Mirrors. I sigh like this – *Aah*.

Such actions (as remarked above) represent a violation of all the protocols that should govern the safety of the home's boundaries. The thief's sigh can be read both as a sigh of relief at entering undisturbed and as a dark parody of a legitimate guest's sigh of pleasure at their entrance to the room. Boredom, rather than malice, is the motivation given for this kind of life. Again, the reader is encouraged not to judge but to understand, while at the same time accepting that she may never truly understand. The final line: "You don't understand a word I'm saying, do you?", obliges the reader to accept her own culpability in society's desire to punish aberrations from the 'norm' and to ignore difficult language. It bespeaks the failures and breakdown in communication, particularly between different social spheres and generations, which have alienated one individual from another. A sense of community is entirely absent from this poem; there is nowhere better to show it than in the violation of the home.

Not all of Duffy's monologues feature such aggressive speakers, however. Of her more passive voices the one which is the most closely related to the home is that of the seemingly elderly woman who narrates 'Whoever She Was' (*SFN*: 35). The sense of this speaker, and therefore of the poem as a whole, is difficult to pin down.

Nonetheless, it can be usefully read as a metaphor for the retrospective idealisation of the childhood home by adults: "When they / think of me I'm bending over them at night, / to kiss. Perfume. Rustle of silk. Sleep tight". The speaker stands for all the stereotypical mother figures, pegging out clothes, cleaning wounds, cooking: "They see me always as a flickering figure / on a shilling screen. Not real". It is not clear if the speaker is living or dead. Her narrative is frequently confused and confusing and switches from the first to the third person and from the past to the present tense. If she is still living then she has been left behind by children grown into adulthood, who nonetheless will always remember her as children, frozen in time: "forever their wide eyes watch her / as she shapes a church and a steeple in the air". If dead then she both haunts and is haunted by a past that she is impotent to re-enter. Whether living or dead, however, it is clear that hers is a house of memory, of loss and of sadness and one in which she may as well be dead, as impotent as she is. Indeed, her own impotence is mirrored by that of the house to which she seems held hostage. Empty, dusty and neglected, this is a family home without a family; a grotesque parody of itself. The disused playroom stands as testimony to the absence of the children for whom it was intended, and the house, in sympathy with its occupant, is haunted by the echoes of the lost childhood which ring through the rooms and garden, by the "little voices of the ghosts / of children on the telephone".

One issue which preoccupies Duffy greatly in these collections is that of cultural displacement. The monologue 'Deportation' (*SM*: 59) is written from the perspective of a foreigner who has been branded "*Alien*" and seeks to come to terms with his isolation both from his former culture and the adoptive home from which he is threatened with deportation. In the absence of a cultural location in either country and without a house / home to which he has a natural or adoptive right, love emerges as the key to the concept of the home, and as the only location which signifies any kind of permanence. Its vulnerability is all too evident, however: "we will tire each other out, making our homes / in one another's arms. We are not strong enough", he declares sadly.

'Translating the English, 1989' (*TOC*: 11) dramatises similar notions from a different perspective. Its speaker describes with bitter irony the consumer culture which has eroded England's cultural heritage. In broken English the poem builds up to its dark conclusion:

"Plenty culture you will be agreeing / Also history and buildings […] / Filth. Rule Britannia and child abuse […] plenty rape". Both these monologues widen the concept of home to its (inter)national, rather than simply its national context. The collections from which they are taken, *Selling Manhattan* and *The Other Country*, are those in which Duffy focuses most intensively upon the home. Angelica Michelis ties these two collections into a mutually referential relationship; both are about cultural "alienation and displacement", but in the latter collection especially, she argues, "Britain has become the other country, a place which is defined by exclusion and division" (2003: 91). The implications that this has for the home are bleak indeed.

Duffy's monologues, then, are as much about understanding the perspectives of their speakers as they are about judging them. She certainly communicates the perspectives of the morally dubious, the prejudiced, the violent. Yet the voices of the habitually silenced, the isolated and the breathtakingly sad are also heard. The monologue form allows Duffy to articulate the perspectives of often wildly divergent individuals in such a way as to let them condemn themselves, if condemnation is necessary. More frequently, however, this poetic form allows her (and us) to have empathy with the speakers even when they are aggressive and repellent. If we understand their condition, and their position, then we cannot simply condemn them. In an interview with Andrew McAllister in 1988, Duffy spoke explicitly about the ambivalence of a form that allows her to bear witness to human experience by getting relatively close to the individual speaker while still preserving an inevitable degree of separation:

> When I'm writing them [the monologues] I'm not thinking about a critical description or analysis of them. If you push me this far I would say that all of us are outside of everything else. Even if you are in bed with your beloved there is a sense in which you are forever excluded from any sort of contact. That is the condition and tragedy of us as humans (McAllister 1988:70).

Examining the speakers of the monologues within their own domestic settings also forces us to an understanding of the role of society in shaping such individuals however. These speakers unsettle and trouble us, because however unpleasant, sad or frustrating it may be to hear them, and however much the human condition effects a separation between one individual and another, we cannot ignore the validity of their experience. Neither can we distance ourselves from our own part in the society reflected in and distorted by their narratives.

Domestic Space and Autobiography

Duffy's apparently autobiographical poems present us not with her 'voice' (whatever that may be) but with another of her fictional voices: herself as created entity, as a textual, or rather a poetical, persona. As she remarked in an interview for *Young Writer Magazine* (2002): "I haven't felt vulnerable in anything I have written so far. There have been subjects that I haven't written about because of the feeling of privacy [...] But once I begin a poem it becomes a literary problem rather than a personal one" (Bentham 2002). It is not possible to read these poems as straightforward autobiography, then; but it is nonetheless the case that in their reliance for the most part upon the use of personal pronouns, they have been constructed to *seem* autobiographical. It would be wrong to suggest that all such poems should be read as unquestionably about Duffy's own life and experiences; rather, it is the case that they *could* be and that they have been constructed in such a way as to seem so. Michelis argues that "Home [is not] a fixed state but a process [...] the different poems [...] oscillate thematically between past, present and future interconnecting the personal history of the poet [...] with that of national history and identity. To define oneself in relation to home [...] is here developed as a journey in time" (Michelis and Rowland 2003: 92). The latter half of this essay explores that journey. Duffy's autobiographically constructed poetry is a journey through a woman's life, seen in all its beauty and ugliness, engaging with her emotional, intellectual and sexual aspirations, with her sorrow, hope, fear, disappointment and fulfilment. The bond between the central speaker (referred to as Duffy's persona) and her domestic space will be explored in detail. Since these poems chart, in a non-sequential way, the trajectory of a woman's life, they will be separated here into those dealing with childhood and those which focus on adulthood.

Domestic Space and Childhood

The poetry articulating Duffy's childhood persona communicate an inner longing for a lost past which is deeply bound up with the retrospective idealisation of house and home. Most of these 'autobiographical' poems of childhood are in fact seen through the eyes of an adult recalling a lost past. The poet Susan Wicks, describing her own writing processes, makes a point which is surely also applicable to Duffy. For Wicks, somewhere in the relationship between poetry and poet is "the child, perpetually reaching out, trying to make contact, frustrated by a world which doesn't match any of the templates she holds up to it" (2000: 21). If anger frequently characterises Duffy's monologues – anger at power imbalances between the genders, poverty, prejudice and abuse – then it is grief that is the overwhelming force here. 'Originally' (*TOC*: 7) mourns not simply the loss of a childhood home, but the loss of a former identity bound up with space and place. The speaker asks: "Do I only think / I lost a river, culture, speech, sense of first space / and the right place?" It is the move not just from one home to another but from childhood to adulthood that is to be regretted most. If, as the poem states, "All childhood is an emigration" then the loss of identity in which it results forces her to falter: "Now, *Where do you come from?* strangers ask. *Originally?* And I hesitate". In sequencing this poem to begin *The Other Country* – a collection which, more than any other is about alienation – Duffy signals from the very beginning then that this is a collection about the search for identity, about the fragility of the self, and about the desire to heal that which has been ruptured from childhood onwards.

The relationship between mother and child is central to the house of childhood in the 'autobiographical' poems. In them, women both symbolise and maintain the moral health of the family home, and therefore of the family. The father figure is noticeably absent from Duffy's work and it is the mother who is authority figure and disciplinarian. The mother / daughter relationship is frequently shown to be fraught as a consequence. 'Mouth with Soap' (*SM*: 44) is, on the surface, a darkly humorous exploration of the sanitisation of language within the home. Although its female subject is never explicitly identified as the speaker's mother, she certainly seems to assume the authority of that role. Duffy's persona declares: "She was a deadly assassin as far as / words went […] Watch out / for the tight vocabulary of living death". If we recall the strong links made elsewhere in *Selling Manhattan* between language, location and identity (in poems like 'Yes, Officer' [31]), it may be seen that this is a poem about far more than social niceties. The irreconcilability of vocabulary points to the irreconcilability of personality – to a clash of identity. Duffy's persona insists, in colloquial terms, on telling it like it is and in taking this honesty to extremes. "Saturday night, / when the neighbours were fucking, she *submitted to intercourse*" she declares of the mother figure, insisting on candour that the mother will not own. Their linguistic struggle in this first stanza, in which colloquially crude descriptions and their sanitised counterparts (the latter italicised) are batted back and forth, is part of a larger struggle for honesty and for identity in a poem about anger and denial. This is a poem about one woman's resolute refusal to acknowledge the messy, difficult, and downright dirty aspects of life. We are told in a dark parody of housewifely duties that instead "she / bleached and boiled the world". Nonetheless this is also a poem about another woman's refusal to collude with that sanitisation in retrospect. A life without honesty of communication, where even cancer is sanitised as "*The Big C*", is a "living death" for Duffy's persona, as she seems to construct herself here.

The conflict of identities sited within a house of crippling courtesy is one to which Duffy returns in her later collection *Mean Time*. The poem 'Litany' (*MT*: 9) again seems on the surface to be darkly humorous but in fact goes straight to the heart of a bitter linguistic power struggle between mother and daughter. It builds up, in its final stanza, to the scatological verbal outburst of a "thrilled, malicious" moment when Duffy's childhood persona speaks out sensationally to a roomful of tightly constrained adults: "*A boy in the playground*, I said, *told me / to fuck off*". Yet exactly the same power struggle is seen here as in 'Mouth With Soap', centring upon the need for linguistic honesty on behalf of Duffy's childhood persona and an equally intense need, on behalf of her (here explicitly identified) mother, for polite superficiality. Where 'Mouth with Soap' focuses only on their personal relationship, however, into the domestic sphere of 'Litany' come others – the Mrs Barrs, Mrs Hunts, Mrs Emerys and Mrs Raines of the world – who corroborate the mother's perspective. The kinds of women who congregate in 'The Lounge' (capitalised and forbidding) are, we are told, stiff-haired with "terrible marriages" and "eyes, hard / as the bright stones in engagement rings". The "sharp hands" described in 'Mouth with Soap' are used here too, as the ladies take tea together without being drawn by a need for mutual support, friendship or honesty. These women speak without communicating, locked as they are into the artificial world of the consumer catalogue from which springs the litany of domestic objects of the poem's title – "*candlewick / bedspread three piece suite display cabinet*". The poem 'Litany' reflects and reinforces, savagely in places, the materialism and artificiality of a life lived without the exchange of truth. The heart of the poem is not its final sensational section, but unquestionably its third stanza in which we see the bitter effects of the same desperate conflict that went on between mother and daughter in 'Mouth with Soap'. The poet writes starkly:

> This was the code I learnt at my mother's knee, pretending
> To read, where no one had cancer, or sex, or debts,
> And certainly not leukaemia, which no one could spell.
>   (from *Mean Time*, 1993: .9).

The "mass grave" of wasps trapped within their glass prison recalls the glass of the window against which the child of 'Sit at Peace' presses herself, staring, unable or unwilling to leave the house by which she is ensnared. The butterfly which stammers in her hands in 'Litany' reflects the fragility and vulnerability of her own language in the face of the dominant force of the mother and her so-called friends. There is a sense in which it is clear that it is these women, and not Duffy's persona, who are trapped within the confines of a world of nothingness which they themselves create and perpetuate. The child is, as yet, no match for these women however, but there is a strong sense that the storm which attends her outburst (during which she is made literally to experience the taste of soap), is the precursor of an adult life lived honestly and articulated openly, and publicly, at the personal cost that that always brings. Against this, the sanitised power of the mother within the childhood home washing her daughter's mouth out literally and / or metaphorically and insisting on the trite euphemisms of denial falls short. Horrific as the idea of conversation without communication is undoubtedly shown to be in these poems and the collections in which they are included, such a waste of life – and of the ability to speak of it with passion and integrity – seems more worthy of compassion than condemnation.

Domestic Space and Adulthood
The intersections between adulthood and domestic space in Duffy's 'autobiographical' poems are many and varied. Some reveal the connections made between the poet's persona and friends, their bonds forged, fostered and challenged through their relationship with the home. Others explore interactions between Duffy's persona and chil-

dren, animals, neighbours, relatives and other members of the community. It is however with the exploration of the significant and intimate sexual and emotional connections made in the home between lovers that these intersections emerge most distinctly.

Duffy's reputation as one of the most accomplished love poets of modern times comes at least in part from her characteristic insistence on honesty, and on her realistic interpretation, in matter-of-fact language, of the powerful and often contradictory experience of love. Rees-Jones writes of the dominant force of Duffy's "preoccupation with finding a safe place in which to love [which] cannot be removed from the realities of the world in which she lives and in which she may be oppressed for expressing the full range of her sexuality" (1999: 44). These poems reveal passionate attractions between lovers, their domestic harmonies and tensions, the gradual degeneration of some relationships and the strengthening of others, and the sometimes rapid death or surprising rebirth of such bonds. It has been well documented that Duffy's partner is the female writer and poet Jackie Kay. In 1999 Duffy was passed over for the post of poet laureate in favour of Andrew Motion and at that time she was aggressively pursued by the tabloid press, who focused on her sexuality rather than her work. As a Downing Street official told a reporter: "Blair is worried about having a homosexual as poet laureate because of how it might play in middle England". The decision was infamously labelled, as Katherine Viner (1999) reported in *The Guardian*, "a bag o' shite". Duffy has also had intimate heterosexual relationships in the past, notably with the poet Adrian Henri. Her experience of both gay and straight sexual relationships renders her highly qualified to reveal and explore love in all its forms, and she speaks of both heterosexual and homosexual love with honesty and an authority born of personal experience. In fact, she does not appear to impose any great distinction between homosexual and heterosexual desire; in her work all love is simply, wonderfully and terrifyingly celebrated *as* love, as indeed is the physical expression of love in sex.

The couples and couplings articulated in these poems can be usefully separated into three categories: those dealing with lust, longing and loss. This essay will focus on representations of loss in detail, but of those poems dealing with lust and longing (which may or may not be reciprocated) the most extraordinary is perhaps 'Words, Wide Night' (*TOC*: 47). In this short but sharply vivid and effective poem

Duffy's persona attempts to give voice to that which cannot be voiced in a room which turns "slowly away from the moon". The final lines "For I am in love with you and this / is what it is like or what it is like in words" make a vital distinction between the richness of love as an experience and the comparatively impoverished attempts to articulate such an experience, which will always fall short of the sensation itself. Language cannot convey that which is beyond language, and love is, Duffy's work suggests, beyond language although it is her task as poet to shorten the gap between the two, the reward for which is the process itself. It is imperative for her as poet *and* as poetical persona to keep on trying to get closer to the accurate articulation of the experience even if it is impossible. In 'The Windows' (*MT*: 47) she articulates a deep, almost physically painful, longing for the family life born of the intimacy of lovers, glimpsed through windows by a stranger: "How do you earn a life going on / behind yellow windows [...] How do you learn it?" The vulnerability of windows as a place of silent appeal and of (literal and metaphorical) self-reflection has already been noted in the monologues and the poems about childhood. This is not their only manifestation, however. It is possible to see in through them as well as out. They also offer glimpses into a world that, for Duffy's persona at this time, seems out of reach. She constructs home in terms of the five senses. We share her pleasure / pain at the noise of the doorbell, the feel of warm linen, the scent of hyacinths and taste of food and of the lover's kiss and the sight of it all. This poem dramatises the inner / outer dichotomy upon which much of lovers' lives are chiefly predicated. Such love often seeks the inclusion, and absorption with, each other and the relative exclusion of the world, which makes the unit of the lovers concurrently strong and yet potentially vulnerable.

There is no doubt that it is in the articulation of the torment of lost love that Duffy's strength as a poet lies. Pain circulates throughout her work just as it circulates throughout the body of the abused and abusive lover. 'Naming Parts' (*SFN*: 21) depicts a man and a woman at breaking point, their domestic space apparently distorted by violence. The bruised woman lives in a broken home – that is, a home literally and metaphorically broken open by rage. She cannot bear to be alone in that home, her hands reaching "sadly for the telephone"; yet, potentially at least, she can find comfort in domestic tasks. The voice, which may be that of Duffy's persona, declares:

This is another fine mess
Perhaps soup will comfort them.
To have only soup against such sorrow.

Mean Time is the collection in which the death of once vital love is explored most tellingly; moreover, images of house and home are frequently deployed by Duffy to render the pain of lost love in all its visceral intensity. Poems such as 'First love' (*MT*: 27) and 'Close' (*MT*: 37) locate the suffering inherent in the severed connection to a lost past firmly in the context of the home. The poem 'Never Go Back' (*MT*: 30-1) is a darker exploration of the return to a house of trauma. Duffy's poetical persona admonishes sharply: "Never return / to the space where you left time pining till it died". The third and fourth stanzas of this poem are central to her exploration of the intersections between pain and the home. The house is personified and "prefers to be left alone / nursing its growth and cracks, each groan and creak / accusing you as you climb the stairs". In one of her most brutal lines she declares "The house where you were one of the brides / has cancer". The house is sick with "all the lies / told here, and all the cries of love". The compelling power of loss felt by the central figure combines with a sense of threat and danger that escalates as she walks through room after room. Such is the sense of sorrow and of distress in the place that everything from the broken plasterwork to the ornaments or "objects held / in the hands [...] fill a room with pain". The window is blinded and "myopic with rain". This diseased house should be left to die in peace. Duffy's persona declares emphatically:

Baby,
what you owe to this place is unpayable
in the only currency you have [...]
So drink up. Shut up
[...] And never go back.

This chapter concludes with an examination of the poem 'Disgrace' (*MT*: 48-9), a text deploying an extended house metaphor which tropes the disintegration of a relationship in terms of the disintegration of the house wherein it is conducted. The two are cast in a mutually referential relationship as the reader moves from room to room though the home of a couple at breaking point. The house, like the relationship, has begun to atrophy and decay: "the fridge / hardened its cool heart, selfish as art, hummed / To a bowl of apples rotten to the core". Put simply, this poem proves the point made in 'By heart' (*SM*: 57): love truly does make buildings home. Conversely, therefore, if love has died or is dying, the home disintegrates and dies too; the building reverts to a house once more. This, for Duffy, is a "disgrace". Linguistic breakdown is prefigured in the poem by physical breakdown and we see again the link between language and location made clear: "And how our words changes […] nothing we would not do to make it worse […] / Into the night with the wrong language". Breakdowns in relationships are linked to breakdowns in the home and breakdowns in language, and *vice versa*. We leave Duffy's poetic persona at the vulnerable window, "counting the years to arrive there faithless, / unpenitent".

Conclusion

Using the home as a microcosm of wider society allows Duffy to signal her unease with the social and cultural health of society and at the same time it facilitates her celebration of human imperfections and of the richness of human relationships, in particular those founded on love in all its forms. Duffy's constructions of the presence or absence of a happy home and of the health of the life within it are, in this context, fundamental to her depictions of the human condition. To understand how Duffy uses domestic space in her poetry, then, is to understand what motivates and characterises her writing as a whole.

The two kinds of poem focused upon in this essay (the dramatic monologue and the seemingly autobiographical poem) use techniques that are very different to explore domestic space in ways that in fact offer similar social and cultural comment. Both give voice to the often contradictory perspectives of individuals contextualised within their domestic environment, and both engage with the confusion and contradiction inherent in modern life. Ultimately the *same* kinds of domestic space are revealed in both kinds of poem, even though the form and the technique of their revelation is different. There is a shared similarity of purpose; yet the same distinction between house and home is maintained. The same celebration of domestic harmony is evoked in and through Duffy's relation of love, the lover and the home. The same distortion and power imbalance is evoked through Duffy's depiction of the cessation of love, or through systematic abuse. The same emotions are experienced in all their delicacy and brutality, and the same complications and contradictions in the relationships played out within four walls are shown to have the same impact – devastating or enriching by turns – on the individual and on society as a whole.

In revealing the same kinds of domestic spaces through two different forms, Duffy points to the importance of perspective and of the contextualisation of the individual in society. Her focus is on the normal everyday life of people who spend a great deal of time in their houses, and whose domestic arrangements reflect their emotional, intellectual and physical health. In her insistence on such commonplace language and imagery, the poet shows us that honesty – even (or especially) when it becomes contradictory, confusing or downright uncomfortable – is essential to an understanding of the human condition. One central message of the poetry of Duffy's first four collections is that if we could understand and accept the plurality of different social, cultural and political identities, and understand our own role in creating, shaping and perpetuating human relationships and the environments in which they are sited, we might go some way to changing it where it needs to be changed and celebrating it, as she does, where it deserves to be celebrated.

Notes

1. In Duffy, *Standing Female Nude* (1985), p.15. Further citations of individual poems will be included in the main body of the essay as an abbreviated collection title followed by page reference, thus: *SFN*: 15.

Building, Dwelling, Moving:
Seamus Heaney, Tom Paulin and the
Reverse Aesthetic

Scott Brewster

ABSTRACT

This essay explores figurations of the house, the shelter and the resting-place in the work of the Northern Irish poets Seamus Heaney and Tom Paulin. It puts Heaney and Paulin in dialogue with Bachelard and Heidegger in order to examine the relationships between refuge and incursion, homeliness and estrangement that have been negotiated to an acute degree in the North over the last thirty-five years. The chapter first traces how Seamus Heaney develops a sense of dwelling that is future-oriented rather than regressive, and in which the poetic self experiences the intimacy of homelessness. No matter how far Heaney's poetry has travelled, it has constantly circled back to the omphalos of the farmhouse, the heimlich *habitation commemorated in the early essay 'Mossbawn'. Tom Paulin's work has shown an increasing preoccupation with the potential of makeshift and prosaic locations, spaces where belonging and identification are apparently refused, yet spaces which represent the very condition of living 'in' history, with its terrors and possibilities. The neglected interiors and peripheral structures that litter these poetic landscapes challenge the desire for rootedness and authenticity, but such buildings can nonetheless "quicken into newness" (Paulin 1994: 13).*

Introduction

Both the subject matter and the scholarly fashion dictate a turn to the personal, so I feel obliged to begin with an anecdote. In *The Poetics of Space*, Bachelard proffers an aesthetics of intimacy, an archaeology of the unlearned, centred on that most secure and estranging place: one's place of dwelling. The house image, he writes, "would appear to have become the topography of our intimate being", and thus there is ground for taking the house "as a *tool for analysis* of the human soul" (1994: xxxvi, xxxvii, original emphasis). I began writing this essay whilst my study lay in ruins, its renovation long overdue, eagerly anticipated but nonetheless untimely in its disruption to scholarly routine. I moved to another room, and was temporarily lodged amidst boxes, clutter, disassembled (or unassembled) furniture: this stopping point, merely a storage depot for anomalous lumber, a disordered and slightly unsettling space, was obliged to function as a space of contemplation and the discomforting intimacies of thinking. It became tempting to translate this fairly humdrum household condition into a metaphor for what we carry with us, for the unfamiliar that remains, even if our dwelling-places speak of other resonances and continuities. The house represents retreat, security and secrecy, yet it is a structure whose physical and symbolic fabric must weather the storms of history. We can renovate an interior but can never remove ghosts, creaks, layers of alteration, accretions of the past or of previous occupancy. Houses are repositories of the historical archive, what Bachelard calls "abodes for an unforgettable past"; the dwelling-places of the past "remain in us for all time" (1994: xxxvi, 5). These memory-hoards drawn from the remotest past, however, retain the power to startle us with their closeness and latency: the return can defamiliarise our sense of the present, can demand that we reconceive our cherished notions of domestic space. The sense of the unhomely is tied up with the experience of immediacy, the sense of inhabiting a house *at this time*, *now*, even as the weight of other moments crowd for attention.

Viewed in this way, we might read the house in terms both of aftermath and of the sudden, surprising arrival: with its haunting or spectral logic the house can transmit its 'before' into a future. This double temporality is acutely felt in a moment of historical transition, where optimism mingles with painful memories of the recent past, in which the home has at times offered only partial shelter from turbulence 'outside'. In the literature of Northern Ireland, the domestic attachments and investments of the private sphere have often been interpreted as purely reflective of conflict in the public domain. The house in Northern Irish poetry is not the symbol of embattled authority, like the Yeatsian tower: it provides no immunity from violent incursions, as elegies such as Michael Longley's 'Wounds' and 'Wreaths' strikingly depict (1998: 36, 60). Thus the phrase 'safe house', like the *unheimlich*, can invite a number of ambiguous and contradictory definitions. Unavoidably, many Northern Irish poets have questioned the categories of 'home' and 'house', and the extent to which the physical and emotional fabric of domestic space forms the basis of cultural retrieval or transformation. This essay will concentrate on the topoanalysis of the house in the work of Seamus Heaney and Tom Paulin, particularly their different articulations of 'home ground' at various junctures in the North's recent history. At a moment in which the faltering peace process, and the fragile 'normality' it fosters, both impels and imperils the questioning of things closest to home, it is timely to turn to the house and the interior.

The house is both an overdetermined site, and a curiously overlooked space, in Irish culture. The predominant affiliation in cultural representation has been to landscape rather than to buildings. Eamonn Hughes remarks that place is habitually conceptualised in Ireland "within the terms of custom, convention and community rather than in terms of law, polity and society" (1999: 162). Place is not "merely where one lives, nor even just a metonym for a set of communal relations; it is understood to stand for an authentic identity, beside which such issues as legal title, citizenship and social relations are mere contingencies" (163-4). For the Free State, nation and family were inextricably interwoven, and hearth and home became the symbolic bedrock of the state. Any 'fresh' return is always already foreclosed or inhabited. In Ireland and elsewhere, the topophilia of home can easily become territorialisation, a matter of exclusion, silence and vulnerability as much as of security, routine and connection. As Gerry Smyth comments, poetry labours more than any other cultural practice "under the weight of a supposed 'special relationship' between place and Irish identity" (2001: 56). Yet, as Kathy Mezei and Chiara Briganti emphasise, it is the novel rather than poetry that invites a household perspective on literature, furnishing an extensive critical architecture within which fictional texts and houses are perceived as similar intimate interiors (2002: 838-9). Poetry, in contrast, is a space that does not permit ready entry.[1]

For both Bachelard and Heidegger, however, the house or dwelling is intrinsically poetic: inhabiting the space of the home is not only a matter of empirical living, but also a matter of feeling, remembering and imagining. The intensity of poetry, its power to transform our vision and 'reveal' the world, means that the house is not to be understood in terms of daily experience or personal narrative: poetry opens up an "immemorial domain [...] beyond man's earliest memory" (Bachelard 1994: 5). Bachelard argues that it is in poetry that we appreciate most fully the emotional investments bound up with the house: the poet speaks "on the threshold of being" (xvi), and through the poetic imagination, more than recollections, "we touch the ultimate poetic depth of the space of the house" (6). This poetics of the house opposes itself to "the lazy certainties of the geometrical intuitions by means of which psychologists sought to govern the space of intimacy" (220).

For Heidegger, language is the house of Being, and there is a fundamental interconnectedness between language, being and dwelling. He traces this through the etymology of the modern word *bauen*, to build: it is derived from the Old High German, *buan*, which means to dwell. The extent of the essence of dwelling is expressed in the word *bin*: hence *ich bin* means both "I am" and "I dwell". Building is not viewed as "an art or as a technique of construction; rather, it traces building back into that domain to which everything that *is* belongs" (Heidegger 1993: 347, original emphasis). As Joanna Hodge outlines, this interconnectedness is also illustrated in Heidegger's thinking on ethics (*ethos* means abode, dwelling-place) by the play on *Halt* (retention), *verhalten* (conduct), *Hut* (shelter), *behüten* (to shelter), *Haus* (house) and *Behausen* (housing) in his 'Letter on Humanism' (Hodge 1995: 101). It is the poet, even more than the philosopher, who finds homecoming through poetic power, thus achieving the transition from merely living to full dwelling.

Omphalos, Utopos: Seamus Heaney
In 'Building Dwelling Thinking' Heidegger distinguishes between two senses of building. In the first definition, one builds in the sense of "preserving and nurturing", tilling the soil, cultivating the vines: this is a matter of tending, cherishing and protecting; the second sense of building relates to construction, such as shipbuilding or temple-building. Both of these meanings are comprised within genuine building, but they are building only in a narrow sense. By claiming the name *bauen*, these activities obscure the proper sense of *bauen*, dwelling. "We do not dwell because we have built, but we build and have built because we dwell, that is, because we are *dwellers*" (1993: 350, original emphasis). We might compare Heidegger's sense of dwelling to Seamus Heaney's remarks at the end of his essay, 'The Sense of Place': "We are dwellers, we are namers, we are lovers, we make homes and search for our histories" (1980: 148-9). In Heaney's

formulation, although it is the land that is treated as the "stable element", that which provides continuity, the house and its natural surroundings meld into each other through the invocation of dwelling. Dwelling is our primary state: history is 'made' subsequently. Yet the act of homecoming is not simply temporal regression: the return is also a beginning. As Heidegger puts it, "[only] if we are capable of dwelling, only then can we build" (Heidegger 1993: 362). Via Heidegger and Freud, Richard Kearney has read homecoming in Heaney as uncanny and ambivalent, involving "an unresolved dialectic between the opposing claims of home and homelessness" (Kearney 1988: 102). Homecoming is the "possibility of the advent" rather than an actual event (103), and his poetry is about transit rather than place and rootedness:

> If Heaney insists that one of the tasks of the poet is to recover a sense of belonging to a shared past – "an ancestry, a history, a culture" – he construes this task as a *project* rather than a *possession*, as an exploration of language rather than some triumphalist revival of a lost national identity [...] Poetry, in short, comes to express the sense of 'home' less as a literal (i.e. geographical, political or personal) property than as a metaphorical preoccupation. Home is something that cannot be taken for granted as present. It must be sought after precisely because it is absent (103, original emphases).

Kearney identifies two competing myths of grounding in Heaney's writing: one is a revivalist return to the source, the other is future-orientated, open, *u-topic*. Kearney has subsequently amplified this latter sense of myth: "In contrast to the ideological use of myth to reinstate a people, nation or race in its predestined 'place', utopian myth opens up a no-place (*u-topos*). It emancipates the imagination into a historical future rather than harnessing it to the hallowed past" (1997: 122-3). Utopian myth represents stories in unfamiliar form, with "a shock of alterity at the heart of the habitual" (123).

We can see how Heaney grounds his poetic in the house and its surroundings in the opening passage of the essay 'Mossbawn'. As American bombers fly over the family farm, and American troops manoeuvre in neighbouring fields, this "great historical action does not disturb the rhythms of the yard". The pump outside the back door of the house marks "the centre of another world":

> Five households drew water from it. Women came and went, came rattling between empty enamel buckets, went evenly away, weighed down by silent water.

The horses came home to it in those first lengthening evenings of spring, and in a single draught emptied one bucket and then another as the man pumped and pumped, the plunger slugging up and down, *omphalos, omphalos, omphalos* (1980: 17).

Heaney emphasises that the pump "centred and staked the imagination, made its foundation the foundation of the *omphalos* itself" (20). The pumping of water is a synecdoche of the farmhouse's self-sufficient power "to let earth and sky, divinities and mortals enter in simple oneness into things". In the terms established by Heidegger in 'The Question Concerning Technology', the pump does not 'challenge' the water supply, does not store and plunder its plenitude: it reveals the essence of the water. The working of the pump is at once *poēsis*, and *technē* in its original sense: a "bringing-forth of the true into the beautiful" (Heidegger 1993: 339). The pump epitomises a craft "sprung from dwelling", characterising for the generations their "journey through time", since it connects earth and sky, mortal and divine, past, present and future. The pump / *omphalos* discloses the fourfold. Its plunging action performs a homecoming that may be, in Kearney's terms, a project rather than possession, but it is nonetheless presented as a bringing-forth or unconcealment (*aletheia*). His later collections have widened the cartographic and thematic range, but the locale remains as "the great domain of the undated past" (Bachelard 1994: 141). The poetic trajectory might be figured as concentric circles, rippling out like reverberations from the pump in Mossbawn. Heaney's poetry (and his critical reception) is about coming back for more: from the early celebration of lore and craft, through the mythopoeic bog poems, the turn towards elegy and ethics, then the ascent to the airy and luminous, everything homes in towards the defamiliarised spaces of childhood. For Bachelard, "[all] really inhabited space bears the essence of the notion of home"; this space carries with it "the various dwelling-places in our lives", a "community of memory and image". Wherever Heaney the poetic persona has ventured, he has consistently travelled back to "the land of Motionless childhood", an immemorial space that retains "the treasures of former days" (Bachelard 1994: 5).

Heaney has been regarded as both the exemplary poet of place and the "transatlantic poet laureate" (Fennell 1991: 25): his poetry and criticism is saturated by non-indigenous literary histories and influences – Wordsworth, Robert Frost and Robert Lowell, Derek Walcott, poets from Eastern Europe – and his translations include the Gaelic *Buile Suibhne* (*Sweeney Astray*), *Beowulf*, and sections of Dante's *Divine Comedy*; yet he is enduringly celebrated for a fidelity to place. He may be one of the most marketable products in international literary culture, but his prominence is nourished by, perhaps dependent upon, the constant invocation of what Lyotard terms the *domus*. Lyotard describes this notion of the domestic community as "a mode of space, time and body under the regime (of) nature. A state of mind, of perception, of memory confined to its limits, but where the universe is represented" (Lyotard 1991: 191-2). The "temporal regime of the *domus* is rhythm and rhyme" (192), a poetry determined by the seasons, cultivation, custom and memory. Over centuries, the city has gnawed away at this domestic community, encroaching on its fields and woods: the city "stifles and reduces *res domesticae*, turns them over to tourism and vacation" (193).[2] Now, the *domus* can only be understood from the vantage point of the "human world become megalopolis [from] after the end of the houses" (194). The *domus* may never have existed, but the nostalgia that it awakens for those lodged in the megalopolis shows that the house 'haunts' thought: "it is impossible to think or write without some façade of a house at least rising up, a phantom, to receive and to make a work of our peregrinations. Lost behind our thoughts, the *domus* is also a mirage in front, the impossible dwelling" (198). Our domain is the awakening of this nostalgia: "So only transit, transfer, translation and difference. It is only the house passing away, like a mobile home or the shepherd's hut, it is in passing that we dwell" (198). Heaney has tended to this *domus* throughout his career, and we return now to this inaugural moment of cultivation.

'Digging' (1966: 1-2) has become one of Heaney's defining poems, laying bare the contours of his poetic. The commemoration of place, community and rural tradition, the interlinking of poetic and agricultural craft, co-exists with a defamiliarising break with origins, a recognition that this putatively shared history is neither readily available nor necessarily productive. Thus the poem evokes a past and anticipates a future. Like so many Heaney's poems, 'Digging' excavates the linguistic and affective etymology of home, reminiscent of Heidegger's sifting of *bauen*. The energetic diction and rich assonantal and consonantal patterns evoke the sensory impressions and effort of agricultural labour, but for all the immediacy of the text's present participles, the father's effort is recollected in the tranquility of the writer's study. Just as the father is depicted digging under the son's window, so the poet gazes down on the remembered scene. In spite of the stress on fidelity and continuity, writing inescapably makes a decisive break with custom and inheritance. The house becomes a retreat from 'building', and the poet's return is less an effort to 'make' history – the "curt cuts" that bring disturbance and discontinuity – than an attempt to give thought to his homelessness (Heidegger 1993: 363). Exploratory and confirmatory, breaking from the past within the structure of tradition, the poem acknowledges ancestral tradition whilst severing that connection. The home-place is at once foundational ground, and merely a transit-point, for poetic self-definition. It is in passing that the poet dwells. Far from exemplifying the homely nature of Heaney's poetry to come, 'Digging' constitutes an ambivalent severance from the domestic, leaving a house divided against itself.

'A Sofa in the Forties' (Heaney 1996: 7-9), published thirty years after 'Digging', calls at a distance to the earlier poem. In its spontaneous (re-) encounter with the momentary, with quotidian objects and the numinous, 'A Sofa in the Forties' is typical of Heaney's work since *Seeing Things* (1991). The poem can be read as an expression of the inextricable link between being, dwelling and language postulated by Heidegger. It simultaneously inhabits two different temporalities: it meditates on historical transition, and on history as 'becoming'. As such, the poem is an exercise in anamnesis (Docherty 1991), disclosing the "presence of the past". Object of childhood play and imagination, of calendar events and of hospitality, the sofa undergoes constant metaphorical transformation, whether as train, ghost train, "Death-gondola" or model of poetic experience. It rests under the "wireless shelf", and it is here that the speaker is transported into the estrangements and wonders of language. As part of one *omphalic* cord, the radio conjoins the sofa and the inhabitants of the house with the surrounding sky: a meeting-point between nature and culture, mortal and divine, the aerial wire "Swept from a treetop down in through a hole / Bored in the windowframe". The movement of the wind and the sway and swell of language become indistinguishable: both wind and words speak at once of great distance and intimate proximity. Capable of travelling "inestimable" distance yet holding "out as itself", intimately appreciated yet "stood off in its own remoteness", we might compare Heaney's sofa to Heidegger's peasant jug; the sofa is hardly unmobilised by modern technology, but it is "redolent of the human activities in which it plays a part" (Taylor 1992: 264). The sofa is not merely a context-free object, nor part of the standing-reserve; it retains both its everydayness as furniture and its poetic power of disclosure. While it lacks the overt religious and moral significance of Heidegger's jug, the sofa is "Potentially heavenbound, earthbound for sure", and like the pump in 'Mossbawn' gathers to itself the fourfold.

In the various stations of Heaney's career – the cherished topography and place-lore, the mythopoeia of the bog poems, the turns to elegy and ethical reflection, the aerial and numinous 'marvels' of the most recent books – the poetic self has constantly sought grounding and been rendered homeless. It is no surprise that the poetry still circles back to the *omphalos* of the farm-house, the most homely and estranging habitation, across a lifetime: nostalgic and estranging, the *domus* has always represented the impossible dwelling, but perhaps Heaney's poetic power derives from the fact that we have never moved away.

Tom Paulin: The Reverse Aesthetic
Writing "from within the belly of the system" (Paulin 1984: 22), Tom Paulin has long positioned himself as both outsider and critical insider, developing a poetics of awkward *location*. His work has shown an increasing preoccupation with the potential of makeshift and peripheral structures that are to some degree placeless. The mobile 'homes' surveyed in his poetry seem to thwart any sense of affiliation, yet these often anomalous and 'inauthentic' spaces symbolise the condition of living 'in' history. Paulin's poetry scans a range of topographies shaped by historical and political contingencies: civic architecture, urban streets, a Martello Tower, country houses, Anglican manses, holiday cottages, Army checkpoints, Nissen huts, new bungalows or wind farms. Whilst these practical buildings, isolated or derelict sites and tense frontier zones initially appear to be devoid of meaning, in his poetry such places can "quicken into newness" (Paulin 1994: 13).

It can be said that Paulin is "hypnotized by the gaze of the solitary house" (Bachelard 1994: 36). Of particular interest here is Paulin's analysis of Louis MacNeice's 'House on a Cliff' (MacNeice 1988:

129), published in his essay collection *Ireland and the English Crisis* (1984). The poem, which he terms "one of MacNeice's finest achievements" (1984: 78), dramatises the obvious cultural affinities between Paulin and MacNeice: both are Protestant writers of the left, making a career in England, constantly crossing the water physically and imaginatively and thus never fully within or beyond Ireland. Yet it is the specific setting of 'House on a Cliff' that engages Paulin's attention, since it portrays the house as a site that simultaneously refuses to provide secure ground for, and to relinquish its claims upon, its inhabitant. The dialectic of placelessness and liberation in the poem is played out in a space that is both precarious refuge and prison, "ancestral curse-cum-blessing". The speaker is trapped inside by existential crisis, and faced outdoors with a heaven that is an "empty bowl". The light that "keeps vigil on the far horizon" (Bachelard 1994: 37) is reduced to a "tiny oil lamp" answered only by the "winking signal on the waste of sea" (MacNeice 1988: 129). While there may be a "concentration of intimacy in the refuge" (Bachelard 1994: 37), there is at the same time a chilling loneliness. Paulin notes the poem's "terrible stoic isolation"; there is a "freedom in its intensity that transcends its unflinching sense of cosmic indifference", an ambivalent freedom born of its "derelict" quality (Paulin 1984: 78-9).

In its apparent hostility to ideas of grounding and embrace of dereliction, MacNeice's poem in Paulin's reading would seem to abjure the comforting sense of refuge and shelter conveyed by Bachelard and Heidegger. Heidegger in particular has been a figure of caricature and opprobrium in Paulin's poetry and criticism. The most prominent example is the essay 'Dwelling Without Roots: Elizabeth Bishop', in *Minotaur: Poetry and Nation State* (1992), where Paulin 'visits' the Black Forest farm invoked by Heidegger at the end of 'Building Dwelling Thinking'. For Heidegger, the farm is the essence of building in the ancient meaning of *bauen*: "Here the self-sufficiency of the power to let earth and sky, divinities and mortals enter in simple oneness into things ordered the house." The farm is situated on a south-facing, wind-sheltered slope, its roof able to withstand the burden of snow. It makes room for "the altar corner behind the community table [...] the hallowed places of childbed and the 'tree of the dead' [a coffin]". The farm epitomises a craft "sprung from dwelling", a bringing-forth that combines community and destiny: "it designed for the different generations under one roof the character of their journey through time" (Heidegger 1993: 362). The simplicity of the structure, a close relative of the primitive shelter, makes it akin to Bachelard's characterisation of the hut, which "appears to be the tap-root of the function of inhabiting [...] a centre of legend" (1994: 31). Heidegger's farmhouse creates its legend by effacing the labour of construction: the dwelling seems to emanate from the earth itself, a natural feature of the landscape.

When Paulin crosses the threshold of that Black Forest farm, he opens a veritable door into the dark. His Heidegger wanders in the woods, exalting the "earthly ancientness and provenance" of *Grund*. He views technology as inimical to authenticity, craft, folklore: notions that easily "take on the stink of power politics and genocide" (Paulin 1992: 190). Language may be the "house of Being", but this dwelling "isn't an abstract concept – it is a Black Forest cottage whose walls are impregnated with race memories" (191). Paulin poses a rhetorical question:

> Is it possible to contemplate such an image without smelling the burnt flesh that clings to certain German place-names? And – to push the question further – doesn't this exaltation of the poet reflect two centuries of *European* aesthetics? If it does, how can writers come to terms with this tainted cultural inheritance? To rip up all those deep-laid roots like so much worn electrical cable is to place oneself in a minority and erect a makeshift building nowhere (191, original emphasis).

Elizabeth Bishop constructs such a building in her poetry, rejecting the "dangerous cultural lumber" of *Volk* and rootedness. Her typical house (strongly influenced by her experience of shanty-towns in Brazil) is "a warm and fragile shelter that gives what protection it can against the hurricane of history" (194). The fragile, deracinated shelter is an apposite description of Paulin's ideal structures. Yet Paulin's rejection of Heidegger's cottage in favour of Bishop's transient refuge is not unproblematic. The rootlessness and retreat of Bishop's dwelling suggests the solitary, untutored and primitive forms of making celebrated by Romanticism, from which emerges the same 'tainted' roots that clutch at European aesthetics and bedevil ideas of foundation. Equally, the desire to break from these roots is hampered by the critique of 'progress' implicit in Bishop's shelter, which exemplifies sustainable and low-impact living, rather than the exploitative development and 'inauthentic' space of late modernity. For Paulin, the makeshift building represents a way of making a home by using the materials to hand: in connecting nature, culture and artistic craft, it recalls Heidegger's arguments in 'The Question Concerning Technology', where *technē*, like *poēsis*, belongs to bringing-forth, a poetic mode of revealing or unveiling (Heidegger 1993: 317). This contrasts with modern technology, which is a "setting-upon" of nature, a "revealing that orders" (324) – precisely the instrumental design that Bishop's house refuses. It is not therefore surprising that the simile linking "deep-laid roots" with "worn electrical cable" can only tangle together the organic and the prosthetic, the renewable and the transitory.

The unresolved tension between Enlightenment rationalism (with its exploitative and instrumentalist potential) and Romanticism (with its emancipatory and irrational aspects) is an acknowledged feature of Paulin's thought. As Patricia Horton remarks, this tension is symbolised by the staging of Paulin's 1985 play *The Riot Act*: its neoclassical architecture and masonic trappings (Paulin 1985: 9) represent the clash between the Law of the State (Creon) and the 'law' of the unconscious passion and atavism (Antigone). Elmer Andrews notes too the ambivalent fascination with geometry, masons and designers in Paulin's poetry (1997: 133-4): pattern can be imposed on 'unordered' space in the service both of improvement and tyranny. Horton explores Paulin's affinity with Shelley's republicanism and, increasingly, with Hazlitt's suspicion of the 'Gothic' excesses of unfettered imagination. Hazlitt sees the Gothic as a form that privileges "the rough, the uneven, the unfinished" over smoothness, order and completion (Paulin 1998: 203), and this reorientation of the Gothic towards a tradition that is "democratic and regional" (Horton 2001: 417) has particular implications for Paulin's topoanalysis of the house. The unfinished making of Gothic architecture recalls Bishop's dwelling, and describes the recurrent design pattern of buildings in Paulin's poetry. It is also connected to his interest in the artist Paul Klee, whose avant-garde experimentation with the line works against instrumental rationalism.[3] Yet again, too, there is an unexpected echo of Heidegger, who argues that building in its authentic sense is closer to "the essential origins of 'space' than any geometry or mathematics" (Heidegger 1993: 360).

The reconceptualisation of living space is a central feature of historical transformation in Paulin's poetry and criticism. In the introduction to *Ireland and the English Crisis* (1984), Paulin outlines his version of an imaginary "fifth province" in Ireland founded on values of reason, pluralism and social justice, a visionary and incipient concept initially advanced in 1982 in the journal *The Crane Bag* (Kearney and Hederman 1982). Stressing the imaginative possibilities of the fifth province, Mark Patrick Hederman argued that whilst the concept is attached to "real provinces", it is also metaphysical, transcendent (1985: 115). For Paulin, the fifth province rejects "the nationalistic image of the four green fields" (1984: 17) that has traditionally symbolised an organic, homogenised culture: this 'province' imagines a pluralist sanctuary where cultural identity constitutes a process rather than a fixed essence, a space of possibility rather than stasis. This idea of the fifth province emerges out of a dialogue between imagination and reason, "Enlightenment-derived civic republicanism" (Hughes 1998: 168) and Romanticism; as Bernard O'Donoghue observes, in its mutual reinforcement of artistic imagination and political commitment, Paulin's work has remained "true to the central European traditions of Romantic realism" (1992: 187).

By the time this credo appeared, Paulin had already begun to interrogate the concept of the house, and to trace new spaces of possibility in his poetry. In *The Strange Museum* (1980), 'Going in the Rain' (21) alludes to Yeats's 'Ancestral Houses' in surveying a fading Protestant architecture in Northern Ireland. The implanted style of Georgian designers, who crossed from the mainland to build a culture "brick by brick", is slowly being erased: the state to which they 'grafted' reason is in terminal decline. *Liberty Tree* (1983) explores its "aspirational" history (E. Longley 1994: 159) through architecture and interior space, although it is still to an extent dependent on organic metaphors. It contrasts the rusting mission hut built from "flattened tin cans" in 'Manichean Geography I' (32), a forgotten outpost of Empire characterised by mercantilism, *ersatz* culture and febrile evangelical dependency, with the austere yet inspiring interior in 'Presbyterian Study', which chooses "the free way, / Not the formal" (49). Yet this room lacks song, favouring a "dream of grace and reason", and the last stanza waits on nature in the hope that the seed of radical dissenting culture will germinate again. In 'To the Linen Hall', the poem that ends the collection, the design of the late eighteenth-century building exemplifies the republicanism of the United Irishmen, their radicalism shaped by reason rather than the "philosophies of blood" that are banned in the library. Yet the style

phies of blood" that are banned in the library. Yet the style and discipline of the library finds its "tongue" in the scholars who fret to "taste
the true vine / and hum gently / in holy sweetness" (77).

Paulin's later collections have progressively left behind the territorial traces that surface in *Liberty Tree*. They explore alternative forms
of aesthetic, political and philosophical grounding by journeying
through extemporised, prosaic or abandoned places. The fragile, temporary or informal spaces scrutinized in *Fivemiletown* (1987), which
situates the sense of embattled desperation felt by the Protestant
community in the wake of the Anglo-Irish Agreement in 1985 within
the wider historical context of central European Protestantism, offer a
mixture of confinement and liberation, idealism and inauthenticity.
The décor in 'Bungalow on the Unapproved Road' (1) – wallpaper
adorned with "tequila sunsets / on the Costa Brava" – bespeaks incongruity and adulteration, but only perhaps in the sense that it do-
mesticates an 'exotic' location which has become already all-too-
homely and 'inauthentic' due to mass tourism. The defenestration of
Prague in 1618 is a recurrent spectre in the collection, not least because some Unionist figures responded to the Agreement by invoking
this memory to describe their vulnerability. In 'The Defenestration of
Hillsborough' (54), the open window is figured both as a tenuous,
temporary location and a desperate avenue of escape. For Paulin, the
imaginative leap out of historical stasis is the precondition of the fifth
province: "it is impossible to achieve a cultivated cosmopolitan outlook without beginning – like a diver kicking off a springboard –
from the idea of a secular republic" (1984: 18). Given the precariousness of the window ledge, however, the flight to salvation for Northern Protestants might seem a critical utopia inaugurated by urgency
and necessity rather than reflection and debate.

The long poem that closes *Fivemiletown* (1987), 'The Caravans on
Lüneberg Heath' (55-66), focuses on two moments of crisis in German history. It features the poet Simon Dach, who wrote during the
Thirty Years War when Protestantism fought for survival during the
Counter Reformation, and Heidegger, whose philosophy Paulin links
directly with National Socialism. (At the end of World War II, German forces surrendered to the Allies at Lüneburg Heath.) The poem
indicts Heidegger's complicity with the Nazi regime, despite his plea
of philosophical detachment from historical events and attributions of
guilt. Dach and Heidegger represent antithethical versions of cultural

renovation and civil society. Dach is part of the Cucumber Lodge, a Konigsberg literary society that met in a garden overgrown with cucumbers and pumpkins. This retreat into a privileged aesthetic space and an organic imagined community appears to embody Heidegger's mystic primitivism, yet the pumpkin hut and garden do not survive Konigsberg's post-war reconstruction. In its transience, the Cucumber Lodge constitutes an unrealised idea rather than a solidly rooted site, an interim refuge where it is possible to "speak plainly for a new civility" (Paulin 1984: 22). This community of artists (significantly all Protestants) attempts to construct a shelter of imagination and reason that contrasts with a destructive and attritional war.

While Dach's beleaguered status in the besieged city may allude to the anxieties of the Protestant community in Northern Ireland in a moment of political change, it also suggests the radical transformation implied by the fifth province. Rather than ceding to traumatised historical consciousness or the consolations of an epic narrative, the poem ends by proposing that "there's still time to stop over / on the road to Damascus" (Paulin 1987: 66). Deferring destiny or divine teleology, the text suggests more provisional, exploratory forms of salvation. The final voice rewrites history in an aluminium classroom, an extemporized structure of hardboard and scrap fuselage that seems to refute organic foundations and formal harmony. This unprepossessing construction is reminiscent of the caravans in the poem's title: these temporary shelters and prosaic mobile homes are also evocative of exotic journeys, marking the transition point from a disastrous historical moment to a possible new beginning.

Paulin's subsequent work – particularly *Walking a Line* (1994) and *The Wind Dog* (1999) – surveys functional, ugly, or temporary structures with increasing fascination. Importantly, each place is a space in which one can forge a poetic – in the double sense of fabrication – even if it is "not the kind of building you'd assent to" (Paulin 1994: 13). There is "something strained something perky but daft" in 'The Firhouse' (16-18), a "curious" house situated in a flat East Midlands landscape, dominated by squares, triangles and permanently unfinished outbuildings. The owner's forced politeness emphasises a sense of partition and exclusion ("who wants a stranger / in their own house?") but the speaker remains fascinated with writing this anonymous terrain, where the door may open onto a vacuum or a secret, "a sort of riddle". Rather than hovering on the threshold, 'Priming the

Pump' (56-64) vigorously renovates an interior that refuses the conventional markers of domestic attachment, and in some respects offers a clear contrast to Heaney's pump-*omphalos*. The room begins as a "grincing dusthole", before the removal of curtains makes the space "brimful of new light / like a studio" (61). As "slodgy dollops" of wet plaster are hurled onto the wall, a "graceful shape / faint and half-classical" begins to stick. In its arbitrariness, this "art-work" recalls the unbounded expressiveness of Jackson Pollock, a figure on the 'dark', irrational side of Romantic creativity but one nonetheless celebrated in a previous poem, 'I Am Nature' (Paulin 1987: 32-4). This preoccupation with a raw house style is also evident in later poems such as 'Sentence Sound', which depicts another "uncurtained" space of making in which the "raspy texture" of the diction matches the rough surfaces of the interior (Paulin 1999: 11). 'Door Poem' (43-50) recalls first reading Heaney's *Door into the Dark* in a "creaky Georgian farmhouse / maybe near Limerick", where the uncertain location betrays a wider reluctance to name "what patch of ground / now thirty years later" (46). Nonetheless, as the closing lines suggest, the opening of doors can unleash a "particular pong" that is like "coming home / and knowing it is home".

'History of the Tin Tent' (Paulin 1994: 3-4) provides the most appropriate place to stop over in this discussion of Paulin's alternative domestic economy. The Nissen hut is a serviceable product of war that acquired a "throwaway permanence": with its military and civilian utility, "complete societies / could be knocked and bent / into sudden being". It looks back to 'The Caravans on Lüneberg Heath', in which Paulin cites Heidegger's denial of the groundedness of modern, technological constructions: "Bridges and hangars, stadiums and power stations are buildings but not dwellings; railway stations and highways, dams and market halls are built, but they are not dwelling places" (Heidegger 1993: 347). Like 'The Caravans on Lüneberg Heath', however, 'History of the Tin Tent' does not lament 'dehumanising' technology. In a sense, its prosthetic, self-assembly culture constitutes the Enlightenment ideal of a rational state, in contrast to Romantic notions of authenticity and rootedness. Half submerged, the huts have merged into the landscape, challenging distinctions between nature and technology. The poem's flatly descriptive language is pitched somewhere between social history and a design manual; just as Nissen huts break with traditional notions of organic community, so the poem articulates a new aesthetic: "they're almost like texts / no-one wants to read / – texts prefabs caves / a whole aesthetic in reverse" (Paulin 1994: 4). Nissen huts may constitute the archaeological remains of military emergency and the imperatives of the national state, yet the poem extends a degree of sympathy to this abandoned experiment, born of historical necessity. The throwaway landscape answers the question asked a decade previously in 'Yes, the Maternity Unit': "can this nissen plain [...] *really* be a poetic?" (Paulin 1983: 36, original emphasis). Such forgotten structures challenge the 'tainted' concept of rootedness in European nationalism and in poetic tradition, since they 'concretise' the dialectic of the formal and informal that shapes the idea of the fifth province. The DIY community, transiently inhabiting the mass-produced, 'inauthentic' spaces of modernity bespeaks a poetic of "rational mutability" rather than "absolutist stasis" (Hughes 1998: 185).

Paulin returns to assembly-line buildings in 'Schwarzwald oder Bauhaus' in *The Invasion Handbook* (Paulin 2002: 88-93), where he has Heidegger musing on Le Corbusier's "serial house" or residence machine. Le Corbusier "prefers to live / in a nomad's tent / of concrete and glass"; this space of pure function has not grown from the earth, and is thus robbed of "heimlich charm". In its suspicion of Heidegger's 'primitive' groundedness, Paulin's poetic inclines to this triumph of 'civilized' design. Yet it must be remembered that in 'Building Dwelling Thinking', Heidegger is not expressing outright opposition to functional building; the lecture was presented to the Darmstadt Symposium on 'Man and Space' in 1951, part of a series of lectures dominated by figures of myth and poetry rather than by technical-philosophical language (Krell in Heidegger 1993: 344). The lecture addresses the post-war housing shortages in Germany and the problems of reconstruction for a society emerging from the ruins, and seeking to find home ground again. As such, it reflects on building from crisis, a sustained theme in Paulin's own poetry.

As Julian Holder observes, post-war prefabs were regarded with precisely the ambivalence reserved for the Nissen Hut in Paulin's poem. Prefabs offered the "Modernist dream of the factory-made house that Le Corbusier's sought in his dictum that a "house is a machine for living in" (Holder 1998: 86). Modernism marked an acute break between art and the conventional design of the house. The anti-domestic and anti-humanist tendencies of the modernist house, with its steel and glass, made it hard to leave any human imprint, and worked to expunge the uncanny (Reed 1996: 7-11). Prefabs could be regarded as the mass-production expression of this aesthetic. Yet Holder argues that the prefabs, so apparently inhospitable to the attachments and intimacies of the house or dwelling-place commemorated by Bachelard and Heidegger, ironically became too domesticated in popular consciousness, suffering a nightmare inversion of their rationale into a suburban ideal: "[the] functional was subverted by the small-scale symbolic in the name of instant domesticity" (Holder 1998: 86). The ambivalence felt towards these structures has largely disappeared, a significant rise in fortunes after W.G. Hoskins had declared the prefab, the Nissen Hut and the electric fence the predominant violations of the English landscape in the twentieth century (Hoskins 1955). While the afterlife of these makeshift structures continues to fascinate, prefabs still rank low on an architectural scale measured through organicist and sacralising notions of making and dwelling: "Conception and creation is privileged over use and abuse, the permanent over the temporary" (Holder 1998: 86). Nonetheless, prefabs question value distinctions between the monumental and the mundane, between craft and mass-production. They became an icon for peace and reconstruction, for building *in extremis*, with the materials to hand, a reminder of living with and living through emergency.

The reverse aesthetic of the Nissen Hut expresses linear rationality rather than mysticism, construction rather than origin: apparently antithetical to Heidegger's notion of locale and dwelling, the prefabricated building is nonetheless a space that 'makes' its surroundings, inaugurates transcendent possibility, and discloses a poetic 'truth'. A recent Paulin poem, 'Shades Off, No Sheds' (Paulin 2004: 5), stages a stand-off between corrugated iron sheds and an adjoining farm-house. The sheds are "bodged" and lack "the barm / that belongs to a dwellingplace", but what in contrast constitutes the "real presence" of the house remains uncertain. The speaker imagines turning the earth to find the shards of belonging, fragments cast "straight in the midden / like casualties after some battle". The poem wonders whether this act of recovery begins "whatever it is those sheds [...] are trying so hard to block out?" The markers of 'authentic' habitation represent the debris of history, and the poem's texture and colour is to be found in the empty sheds and barns. In Paulin's representations of the house, geometric design and sensuous attachment, dynamic makeovers and comforting refuge, vie for supremacy as models of living space. Whilst his deep suspicion of the poetics of grounding sets him apart from Heaney, both poets regard the house as *u-topos*, a space that cleaves, an impossible dwelling that perpetually excites our critical nostalgia. As Northern Ireland emerges tentatively from a moment in which the ground of home has been overshadowed by claims to 'home ground', the returns to the idea of the house offers fresh ways of thinking about identity, community and affiliation. As Bachelard says: it is by remembering houses and rooms that we learn "to abide within ourselves" (1994: xxxvii).

Notes

1. The intricate interplay between invitation and exclusion, exposure and conceal-ment in the poetry of Medbh McGuckian would repay detailed consideration in this regard.

2. One might think here of the 'Heaney' tourist trail around the Bellaghy area in County Derry; see Sharrock 1995.

3. See 'Klee / Clover' in *Walking a Line*, 1-2.

Troubled Places:
Domestic Space in Graphic Novels

Jeff Adams

ABSTRACT

This paper discusses the depiction of domestic space in contemporary graphic novels (comic books). Joe Sacco's Palestine *and Chris Ware's* Jimmy Corrigan, the Smartest Kid on Earth *are used as examples of graphic novels that use space as an innovative means of constructing a narrative and as a way of representing the psychological condition of their characters. These are analysed using the following concepts: Scott McCloud and the temporal use of frames and sequence; Gaston Bachelard's interior / exterior oppositions; George Perec's ideas of the space of the bed and its relation to memory; Barbara Ehrenreich's theories of the vulnerability of the working poor; Edward Said and the concept of min al-dakhil ("from the interior") in relation to Palestinians' lives, and Michel Foucault's heterotopia of deviation applied to Sacco's depiction of refugee camps. Frames and sequence, the relationship of text and image and cinematic graphic techniques are discussed and their role in depicting the anxieties that occur in relation to domestic spaces in these narratives. The conclusion suggests that these graphic novelists use the ambiguities of spatial depiction to explore psychic fragility and tension.*

Introduction: The Graphic Novel Medium

In recent years scholars in the field (Sabin 1993; Barker 1989) have commented on the preference of a number of graphic novelists to construct autobiographical and documentary narratives centred on traumatic events and social crises. Examples of this are Keiji Nakazawa's *Barefoot Gen* (1972-73) on the atomic bombing of Hiroshima; Art Spiegelman's *Maus* (1986, 1992), which explores the Holocaust and its effects on subsequent generations, and Joe Kubert's work on the Bosnia war, *Fax from Sarajevo* (1998). These are but a few examples of this development, and for the purposes of this essay on the representation of domestic space, I have singled out the work of Joe Sacco and Chris Ware. These two writers / artists have created graphic novels that have attracted wide critical attention for their willingness to tackle unpalatable social issues: Sacco for his work *Palestine* (2003, fig.2), which inspired the late Edward Said to write a foreword (2003), and Ware for *Jimmy Corrigan, the Smartest Kid on Earth* (2001, fig.1), which won the *Guardian* first book award in 2001. Although very different in conception and structure, they share an interest in exploring space in relation to their documentary or fictionalised narratives.

Sacco's novel is an account of domestic experience in the confined and threatened spaces of the occupied territories. His choice of a documentary structure, interviewing people in their homes, helps to emphasise this sense of confinement. Ware, on the other hand, creates a fictional epic that jumps abruptly back and forth between generations. His protagonist Jimmy is a member of a dysfunctional family, whose attempts to establish emotional bonds with his relations are largely unsuccessful, and he exists in a continuous state of dissatisfaction and anxiety. This experience is played out in the spaces of capitalist display such as the vast *fin de siécle* exhibition halls of Chicago, or within bland suburban interiors.

Like many of their contemporaries Ware and Sacco exploit the distinctive features of the graphic novel medium to construct their narratives. Both authors utilise these with an adroitness born of many years' labour and experience. In particular they develop the idea of sequence, a fundamental characteristic of the medium. This allows for image and text frames to be arranged in temporal intervals that may be tightly governed by the novelist. As Scott McCloud (1994: 100-03) and Fusanosuke Natsume (2002) have demonstrated, the control that the writers appear to exercise over time is great: moments that may be inferred as lasting seconds may be explored by spreading them over many frames for several pages; conversely days may be condensed into a single space between frames. Ware and Sacco are adept at pacing their narratives by utilising this device, sometimes extending moments of reflection or even boredom with a sense of psychological time passing or arrested, all integrated into the virtual space of the page.

Both writers are concerned with the relationship between text and image, a necessary requirement of the graphic novelist. The integration of the two is extremely varied, but their approach has, in common with many of their contemporaries, a dynamic interplay between the virtual space of the image and the flatness of the text. Whereas this may have been formerly thought of as a disadvantage of the medium, with clumsy speech and thought balloons 'floating' over a character, for both Sacco and Ware this is turned to advantage by an emphasis on the distinctive illusionist anomalies to which it gives rise. The simultaneous creation of text and image enables these writers to posit ideas of space that, in the case of Sacco and Ware, refer to its political connotations and the way that domestic space may be represented as the site of solidarity, resistance or alienation. For each the effects and characteristics of the medium, such as sequence, the integration of image and text and the anomalies of illusionist space are fundamental to their work.

Anxious Space

Jimmy Corrigan is remarkable both for the sheer range of represented spaces and for the contrasts between them, and this variety is often used to imply the psychological state of the novel's characters. Ware atomises time in some sections, devoting dozens of frames to his protagonists' emotional states as they are inflected through small moments of physical change. Jimmy inhabits a variety of domestic and public spaces, many of which he is shown as knowing intimately, yet from which he is alienated by his psychological discomfort. Ware uses vivid colours, printed flat and entirely bereft of any modelling through shading or cross-hatching. This is not to say that Ware avoids depicting three-dimensional space. On the contrary, he deploys an extensive range of virtual spaces throughout the novel, including illusionist conventions such as linear and aerial perspective. The effect of using flat colour with regular, mechanical outlines is reminiscent of the techniques used for drawing utilitarian art forms, such as diagrams, posters or maps. Genealogical structures are displayed diagrammatically, for example, and inserted at intervals through the text along with bogus cut-out models of buildings and objects. Ware creates striking visual contrasts between the vast new architectural constructions of the late nineteenth-century exhibition spaces, and those of the cramped interiors of the suburban houses where the Corrigan family members interact and play out their fantasies. Such contrasts are emphasised by Ware in his creation of dreamlike spaces, where fantasy events are on equal terms with reality events, with no obvious distinction made between them. The anonymous and vacant spaces of contemporary offices and public housing are the spaces where present and past Corrigans struggle to come to terms with their perceptions of the errors and disappointments of their lives. The flat colour, the emphasis on outline and the overtly *printed* character of the pages all serve to reinforce the anonymity of the spaces.

At one key moment in Ware's narrative the middle-aged Jimmy, recently reunited with his stepsister and grandfather, is shown breaking down (fig.1). His part in the reunification of the family has inad-

Figure 1. A page from the kitchen scene where Jimmy breaks down. Illustration from *Jimmy Corrigan: the Smartest Kid on Earth* by Chris Ware published by Jonathan Cape. Used by permission of The Random House Group Limited.

vertently had disastrous consequences, which prove to be fatal for his father. The scene is played out in a kitchen interior, and the space is visualised through a large number of panels. Here Ware uses *aspect-to-aspect* and *moment-to-moment* transitions, favoured devices that he deploys throughout the novel. In these models the temporal interval implied by the spaces between the frames is greatly reduced (McCloud 1994: 70-93). Ware employs these techniques here to slow the pace of the narrative, allowing him to analyse spaces that his characters occupy. Some of the breakdown scene, where Jimmy expresses his self-pity and his responsibility for events, has frames within frames as Ware utilises the architecture of the room itself to reframe the characters. Jimmy is viewed though the opening in a partition wall several times; he also draws us back and forth with distant views followed by close-ups of objects, which themselves have additional framing devices: the repetition of the cupboards, fridge and chair backs, for example, have this effect. Each of these forces us to re-visualise the characters as they uneasily wait for the moment of Jimmy's discomfort to pass. Ware repeats the same or similar pose and position of the characters many times over across a sequence of four pages, which has the effect of making time seem to pass slowly and making us acutely aware of their mutual embarrassment.

The ability to seem to control time through the spacing of the frames and the turning of the pages is one of the fundamental characteristics of the graphic novel medium that artists like Ware are able to exploit in their narratives. Once again Ware employs moment-to-moment transitions in the scene where Jimmy is waking in his father's house as breakfast is being prepared for him in a ritualised manner, deliberately reminiscent of his childhood. He is depicted rising from his sofa bed to the realisation that his father's cooking is an attempt to re-establish a child-parent relationship. The meticulous visualisation through many frames allows for a sense of psychological space, as Jimmy is able to reflect on their relationship during these routine movements. The conversation, depicted through text bubbles at the top of each frame, establishes Jimmy's emotional ambivalence towards his newly rediscovered father.

It is often in the space of a bed that important moments occur in Ware's narrative, bearing similarities with Georges Perec's interest in the topic (1997). Perec accords to beds and bedrooms significance for the invocation of domestic memory, discussing many rooms that he recalls from his past, and playfully muses on the possibility of making an inventory of all the beds that he has ever slept in (1997: 22-3). He makes the important point that the act of recalling past beds and bedrooms spatially facilitates the recall of a myriad of related people and events, as if the space of the bed in our memory forms a significant link in a chain of spatial memory moments. Ware's bed events take place in a variety of bed types, including makeshift beds under tables, hospital beds, narrow single beds and vast double beds viewed from the ceiling. These beds become theatre platforms, where events like sickness, anxiety attacks and sexual liaisons are acted out, the rectangle of the bed giving yet another framing device for the staging of the performance. Perec's recollections of the formative imaginings that occurred in his former beds have a more sinister parallel in Ware's bed scenes, where the beds signify the site of unresolved psychic events. The temporal transitions between sections of the novel, from present day to past, at first appear to acquire continuity by the reoccurrence of bed scenes. This sense of continuity is destabilised, however, by the underlying narrative of psychic fracture, as each generation struggles to maintain its family or community identity.

Another feature of the depiction of the psychic disruption that accompanies Ware's narrative is his use of snow in several sections of the novel. Graphically, Ware's snow is distinguished by the absence of outline as well as that of modelling. Although bestowing snow with allegoric qualities in the manner of Gaston Bachelard, Ware nonetheless resists the interior / exterior oppositions that Bachelard sets up in his discussion of snow in relation to the 'dreamer of houses' (1994: 40-1). This somewhat nostalgic concept of the house besieged by snow enhances the contrast between inside and outside:

> In any case, outside the occupied house, the winter cosmos is a simplified cosmos. It is a non-house in the same way that metaphysicians speak of a non-I, and between the house and the non-house it is easy to establish all sorts of contradictions [...] As a result of this universal whiteness, we feel a form of cosmic negation in action. The dreamer of houses knows and senses this, and because of the diminished entity of the outside world, experiences all the qualities of intimacy with increased intensity (Bachelard 1994: 40-1).

Whilst his graphic snow conforms to Bachelard's idea of the non-house by concealing detail and texture, Ware's does not otherwise function in the same way. This is because the interiors of Ware are the largely unadorned apartments of public housing schemes for the low-waged, and by rendering them in a flat, hard-edged outlined geometry they function as a metaphor for the minimised luxury of their underprivileged inhabitants. The epilogue to *Jimmy Corrigan* depicts such a bleak interior, completely bereft of surface texture. Here Ware's room reverses Bachelard's model entirely: the snow scene outside is enriched by contrast. This acts as a metaphor for Jimmy's unfulfilled desire, his life empty not only of family, but also of community. This individual is delineated in his solitary existence, in the presence of a community to which he is unable to belong. Occasional distant views of the large tower block where Jimmy has fantasised over his suicide are partially concealed by snow in large, half-page frames towards the end of the novel. This contradicts the "diminished entity of the outside world", for here Ware creates buildings of overwhelming proportions that are the projection of Jimmy's compelling fantasy of escape by suicide, as he dreams of falling from the pediment.

Ware's characters inhabit spaces that are more akin to those described by Barbara Ehrenreich (2000) in her account of low-wage women workers in the U.S.. Ehrenreich gives detailed accounts of her experience working 'undercover' (in the sense that she conceals her wealth and class privileges from those with whom she worked), documenting the dismal conditions that she and her colleagues have to endure. Often the only spaces available for people on these rates of pay are motel rooms, more permanent spaces being beyond the means of the working poor. In one particular case, which Ehrenreich describes with great distain (2002: 150-3), the motel room space is dilapidated and exposed, and she complains of her feeling of vulnerability. Apart from the dirt and the absence of comfort, she has no lock on her door and her windows cannot be screened. She is exposed literally as well as figuratively. The room, once lit, displays her like a beacon. From this situation Ehrenreich correctly asserts that her feeling of exposure is a fact of poverty: the lack of privilege is also the lack of domestic security:

> Here, only the stuffiness of the air with the window shut reminds me that I'm really indoors; otherwise I'm pretty much open to anyone's view or to anything that might drift in from the highway [...] Sometime around four in the morning it dawns on me that it's not just that I'm a wimp. Poor women [...] really do have more to fear than women who have houses with double locks and alarm systems and husbands and dogs (2002: 152-3).

In the earlier scenes of the novel the suffering that Ware's characters undergo reflect their poverty and that of the dwellings they inhabit. The small child Jimmy has to sleep under the table and endure the sounds of his father's sexual activities with temporary partners in the adjacent bed. Abuses increase and anxieties are generated as the domestic space becomes less stable. The sanitised and bland housing that they inhabit in later generations may have improvements in security, but fails to ameliorate their deeply embedded anxieties.

Threatened Spaces

Sacco gives us a glimpse of how much worse these anxieties must be
in the occupied territories of Palestine, in the extreme poverty that is
exacerbated by the ever-present threat of violence. The concepts of
domestic space and refugee camp space have a tension between them
to which he returns at stages throughout the narrative. The contingencies of living in a condition that is, by definition, temporary and subject to the vagaries of a tempestuous political situation, bring a
singularity to his portrayal of the Palestinians' plight. Sacco explores
their domestic existence by means of stark juxtapositions, comparing,
for instance, the appalling sewage flood stains on the walls of the
houses contrasting with the delicately adorned interiors (2003: 218-19,
187).

In *Palestine* the graphic novel medium is frequently exploited in a
cinematic way, offering a plethora of perspective viewpoints that explore equivalents to the dynamism of film. Sacco achieves this by devices that make direct reference to film techniques – especially the
characteristics of the camera lens and its movements. These are but
some of the many features of film production that contemporary
graphic novelists have attempted to simulate, as far as this is possible
within the confines of a static medium. The desire to emulate film has
an effect upon the realisation of space, especially that of room interiors. Sacco's repertoire of viewpoints in such interior scenes is great,
as he depicts the restricted spaces of the Palestinians into whose
homes he is invited for his interviews. He "pulls up" the viewpoint to
give aerial views of his hosts and himself (Adams 2000), or drops the
angle to give floor views, or zooms in for extreme close-ups of his
interviewees' faces. All of this may occur within the space of a double
page spread as he extrapolates an extensive virtual space from the con-
finements of a cramped room in a refugee camp (Sacco 2003: 66-7).
Like Ware, the utilisation of these visual dynamics is directed towards
the exploration of the psychic experience as much as that of the physical space. This becomes evident through comparison with Bachelard's
experiments with space as representative of psychic conception.

Bachelard's concept of the oneiric house is founded upon the idea
of the house as protective, offering the physical and psychic manifestation of shelter: "[If] I were asked to name the chief benefit of the
house I should say: the house shelters daydreaming, the house protects
the dreamer, the house allows one to dream in peace" (1994: 6). The

homes that Sacco depicts in *Palestine* are almost the antithesis of shelter, particularly in the sense of psychic security that Bachelard refers to above. Instead they are susceptible to attack, the target for demolition, as well as the object of deterioration through poverty. Bachelard's shelter for the daydreamer becomes, in Sacco's hands, the site of anxiety and psychosis. These homes are often in camps like Jabalia (2003: 184), crammed together with makeshift doors, widows and roofs. These camps have, in some cases, existed for over fifty years. The original tents have been replaced by brick structures with weighted metal roofs, yet the houses retain the appearance of the temporary, the contingent. This is a result of the poverty, over-crowding and lack of maintenance that prevails there. Sacco's friend Sameh has a home in Jabalia camp in which the roof leaks around its ill-fitting edges and the room is depicted giving direct access to the cold night through a gap at the top of the wall (2003: 181). The temporary nature of the room is evident in other signs of contingency in Sacco's drawing: the oil lamp on the arm of the sofa, the corrugated metal roof, the exposed wiring; all of this is amplified by white diagonal streaks representing hail stones entering the room and falling upon the occupants. The sense of incongruity between the temporary and the permanent is heightened by Sacco's depiction of the pictures on the walls, the potted plants on tiered stands, the rugs, bedspreads, blanket cupboard and patterned soft furnishings: "He'd created as much of a refuge for himself as circumstances allowed" (2003: 187, fig.2).

Domesticity is, as Edward Said pointed out (1993), not merely evident in Palestinian homes but proclaimed therein by a variety of decorative means. For Said these have come to represent solidarity, belonging to a Palestinian interior life, as well as a resistance to living in threatened accommodation under military occupation (1993: 51-62). Said speaks of the term *min al-dakhil,* which he translates as "from the interior" (1993: 51), as having a special resonance for Palestinians. Originally designating Palestinians who lived within the 1948 boundary of the Israeli State, he discusses the way that the term acquired new meanings as Palestinian territory diminished, with the

Figure 2. The interior of Sameh's home. Illustration from *Palestine* by Joe Sacco (2003) published by Jonathan Cape, p.187. Used by permission of The Random House Group Limited.

corresponding number of those living in appropriated territories or in exile increasing (1993: 51-2). He goes on to argue that this term has further connotations that refer to specific social codes, such as those of recognition and the solidarity of shared experience, particularly that of loss. Said later ventures the idea that the interior decoration of Palestinian homes may be in some way representative of these ideas, a material expression of this sense of social interiority:

> The oddness of these excesses, and asymmetries, their constitutively anti-aesthetic effect, their communicated insecurity seem to symbolize exile – exile from a place, from a past, from the actuality of a home (1993: 61).

These contradictory domestic Palestinian spaces, interiors that may be at once expressing exile as well as interiority, are an important feature of Sacco's work. Key meetings in these interior spaces attenuate his narrative. Each occasion is marked by the characteristics upon which Said commented: too much tea, offerings of comfort in excess of that available to the inhabitants, hospitality that is almost imposed as a mark of defiance. In the tea-sharing sequence at Nuseirat, for instance, Sacco demonstrates his bewilderment at the repetition of ritual and anecdote that he encounters as they discuss their plight (2003: 152). Sacco also explores the idea, which Said articulated (1998), that amongst many Palestinians who have been evicted there exists a condition of waiting: waiting to return. This persists from generation to generation, and Said gives the example of the retention of deeds of houses reoccupied or destroyed by the original occupants long after all possibility of actual reclamation has gone.

One of Sacco's methods for depicting their temporary homes includes layering text boxes to work to facilitate his depiction of space. Thus the interior of the Palestinian home in Nuseirat refugee camp (2003: 152), for instance, is plastered with text cartouches that dominate the image beneath. Reminiscent of the confident displays of text in the European political cartoons of the eighteenth and nineteenth centuries (those of James Gillray, for example), this device has the effect of creating the equivalent of a window through which we peer. The picture plane is revealed and simultaneously the illusion of the space beyond is heightened; added to which is the occlusion of people and objects within the frame, brought about by the vertical line of the text cartouches themselves. These are parcels of information that occupy the flat space of the picture plane and represent Sacco's private thoughts, which are also those of the guiding narrator. Simultaneously he develops the virtual space of the room, with the tea ritual and the anecdotes in full flow. Using shading by means of cross-hatching, he adds pictorial depth in the scene and allows us, the viewer / reader, to inhabit the space vicariously from this high vantage point. The exploration of the interior of the home is induced by these means, as the reader is stimulated to imaginatively complete the missing parts of the space, thus corroborating the illusion created by the artist.

The idea of the refugee camp accords with the concept of the heterotopia, first mooted by Michel Foucault in 1967 (1998: 176-85). Foucault speculated on the existence of specific places common to all historical formations wherein particular kinds of social relation are expressed. The examples he gives are "crisis heterotopias" and "heterotopias of deviation" (1998: 179-80). The latter are those spaces created to accommodate groups considered deviant, as an expression of their relation to dominant accounts of normality: such spaces are prisons and psychiatric hospitals in Foucault's examples (1994: 179-80). The social relations expressed in Sacco's representation of the refugee camp of Jabalia seem to comply with this heterotopic model, whereby the inhabitants' perceived status and culture runs contrary to the dominant social group, making them, de facto, deviant. The refugee camp contains and renders anodyne the threat of this deviance, and may be maintained indefinitely or relocated at the behest of the more powerful social group. One of Sacco's declared aims (Adams 2000) in writing *Palestine* was to resist the containment that such an ideological imposition implies, the privileging of one group and the impoverishment of another, resulting in the forced persistence of a huge and unwilling social configuration, the refugee camp.

Sacco's resistance to the refugee camp heterotopia in the *Palestine* narrative is achieved partly through depictions of the domestic and interior life of Palestinians. At home in the camps the Palestinians are frequently depicted partaking in the ubiquitous tea ritual of hospitality. Their detailed anecdotes are interpolated as short sequences within the larger sequence of the autobiographical narrative. This often has the effect of creating imagined space inserted into the domestic space: the virtual boundary of the interiors are disrupted by the intensity of the inserted tales of desperation and crises, as they relive their experiences, depicted as if taking place at the moment of interview. Thus the domestic space is invaded by vicarious experience, just as the transient space of the refugee camp is susceptible to violation by the occupying soldiers or the local militias that rule in the absence of effective civil institutions protecting human rights.

Irreconcilable Spatial Ambiguities
In their own distinctive ways both of these authors have manipulated the medium of the graphic novel to particular political and fictional ends, yet each is concerned with the space in which their characters dream, conspire or fail. Like many of their contemporaries, Sacco and Ware have found that the effectiveness of their narratives are enhanced, rather than diminished, by exposing many of the ambiguities of visualising and rendering space graphically on the page. By pushing the boundaries of the medium and resisting orthodox approaches,

even where it would be more economical to do so, they have both created singular works. In each, the concept of *domestic* space is tested by setting it against antithetical social positions: the space of the refugee or of the disempowered. The dramatic tensions set up by these and other oppositions enables an exploration of the profound consequences of social interaction and disjuncture.

The graphic novel medium is distinctive in that the authors are compelled visually to organise a visual, virtual space in conjunction with their narrative. Within these limitations Ware's and Sacco's visual styles appear strikingly different: Sacco uses only black and white with his detailed 'etched' finish using illusionist cross-hatched shading; conversely Ware employs vivid colours with heavy outlines and an emphasis on poster-like flatness. Textually they also differ, with Sacco's extensive narration texts opposed to Ware's clipped narrative and spare speech bubbles that convey only minimal dialogue, supplemented by numerous 'asides' in the form of labels, notes and instructions scattered throughout the novel. Yet they are similar in their willingness to expose and declare the restrictive material properties of the medium. Rather than by attempting, through illusionism, to give the appearance of a reconciliation of image, text and sequence, they instead exploit its potential for ambiguities, creating metaphors from these visual double meanings.

This enables the authors to deal with paradoxical conditions like those of the heterotopia or *min al-dakhil*. The conceptual inconsistencies are rendered material through translation into visual / sequential dissonances: hence the discordance between picture plane illusion and 'floating' text boxes in Palestine acts as a metaphor for the imaginatively emancipating anecdotes of the refugees in their confined and curfew-restricted spaces. Similarly, Ware renders concrete the material limitations of Jimmy's life through the literally and explicitly two-dimensional world that he inhabits on the page. Even the physical act of the turning of the page, analysed as being of critical importance to the medium by Natsume (2002), affects the viewing of the page as the authors shift from 'splash' pages (large frames that either fully or mostly fill the page) to long sequences of small repetitive frames. Narrative time is thus slowed or accelerated accordingly. This material experience is then amenable to translation as metaphors like anxiety or lethargy, crucial to both narratives where the protagonists are forced to live in a normality of exclusion.

All of this is heavily dependent on the visual and textual experience of the reader in a specific cultural context. Those familiar with
Japanese comics (*manga*) and its western derivatives will be more
likely to assimilate the fluid and rapidly transforming characters, the
rapid change in the temporal pace and the cinematic dynamism that
characterise both novels. Once learned, these conventions may be
added to the repertoire of experience exploited by the authors and assimilated by their audience. The rate at which one convention is ex-
changed for another is high, and graphic novel readers are frequently
called upon to translate these variations or adaptations. This fluidity
necessitates a vigilant and attentive audience, perhaps making the psychic space that Ware and Sacco wrestle with still more appropriate for
this tricky medium.

The domestic spaces represented by each writer are often rendered
in a state of unsettled transience, ranging from the sterile to the dilapidated, and often these sites of disquiet and unease are in keeping with
the theories of ideological space put forward by Said and Foucault.
Bachelard's daydreams are replaced by anxieties and psychoses in
these spaces, and the irreconcilable ambiguities of illusionism act as a
metaphor for the uncertainties of lived experience, offering us a bleak
concept of domestic space.

Householders:
Community, Violence and Resistance in
Three Contemporary Women's Texts

Peter Childs

ABSTRACT

This essay will consider the struggles over houses and their significations in Michèle Roberts's Daughters of the House, *Pat Barker's* Blow Your House Down *and Toni Morrison's* Paradise. *All three texts concern domestic spaces inhabited by women and threatened by male violence, typically sexual. The essay will discuss the positioning and representation of the 'house' as symbolic and contested space within these texts, exploring how the home is usually thought to be gendered feminine but has been subject to patriarchal authority. All three texts also contest the public / private binary and proffer affirmative images of female communities as alternative social forms.*

Introduction

> For me, writing is a way of keeping house; building myself the house I felt, deep inside, I wasn't allowed to have because I was a kind of monster raging with forbidden desires and feelings, tearing it down and re-building it (Roberts 1994: 174).

Reminding the reader that the house is both symbol and location in women's writing, Lorna Sage comments that "'the house of fiction' isn't, for my purposes, only a metaphor for containment. It's a reminder that fiction isn't placeless" (1992: ix). The house as place within the house of fiction is the primary subject of this essay. As Sage suggests, the novel like the house has often been a male bastion, inasmuch as men have sought to define it and delimit it as property, and also a place of female confinement. Women writers have frequently shown the domestic home as a prison-house, but also as a possible women's refuge, as peaceful or besieged sanctuary. The house in fiction in this essay is therefore construed as a site of contestation, a place of gender retreat or struggle, a paradoxical symbol of safety and threat, inclusion and exclusion, peace and violence. In *Psychology of the House*, Olivier Marc writes that "[to] build a house is to create an area of peace, calm and security, a replica of our mother's womb, where we can leave the world and listen to our own rhythm; it is to create a place of our very own, safe from danger" (1977: 14), but this creation is far more the expression of a desire than its achievement – such that the houses in the texts examined in this essay are places of danger as well as safety.

The narratives of the three novels, Pat Barker's *Blow Your House Down*, Toni Morrison's *Paradise* and Michèle Roberts's *Daughters of the House*, concern struggles over houses and their significations: domestic spaces inhabited by women and threatened by male violence, typically sexual violence. The essay will discuss the positioning and representation of the 'house' as symbolic and contested space within these texts, exploring how, as Nancy Duncan writes, "[paradoxically] the home which is usually thought to be gendered feminine has also traditionally been subject to the patriarchal authority of the husband and father" (1996a: 131). All three texts also contest the public / private binary and proffer affirmative images of female communities as pointing towards alternative social mores if not models.

Blow Your House Down

[Faced] with the bestial hostility of the storm and the hurricane, the house's virtues of protection and resistance are transposed into human virtues. The house acquires the physical and moral energy of a human body (Bachelard 1994: 46).

Lawrence Stone (amongst others) has suggested that the drive for increased privacy in domestic spaces came to the fore with the formation of the European nation-state: attempts were made by both the state and the domestic household to bolster the family as an institution and to limit state control of reproduction within the family (1977: 133-42). The private space of the home can therefore also be considered in terms of the problematics of consent, as "a place where aggressive forms of misogynous masculinity are often exercised with impunity" (Duncan 1996: 131). This is central to Pat Barker's *Blow Your House Down* (1984), which is concerned with the relationship between domestic violence and the social control of individual women's economic and sexual lives within the context of different social spaces, defined as private or public and separated into the responsibility of the individual or the regulation of the state. The text offers a fictionalised parallel-account of murders attributed to the Yorkshire Ripper, Peter Sutcliffe.[1] Unusually for an account of a serial killer, Barker's narrative focuses on the victimized community and not the assailant. It is therefore presented with a very different focus from works on the same subject by men: David Peace's novel *Nineteen Eighty*, Gordon Burn's psycho-investigation *Somebody's Husband, Somebody's Son*, and Blake Morrison's long poem 'The Ballad of the Yorkshire Ripper'.

Barker's novels have a common theme of violence, usually but not always male in origin, but their author seems less interested in what provokes the violence than in how that violence comes to affect people – namely, the assaulted individuals and those around them. So, for example, while we learn about a community of women in Barker's novel, we are told almost nothing about the man who has attacked several of them; the reader is presented with a section of the narrative from his perspective but knows nothing of his life, motives or personality. Barker also puts forward a positive image of community and social networks struggling against an intrusive but ineffective public welfare system that treats her characters as second-class individuals.[2] Barker suggests the mechanisms by which violence, here construed as a kind of monstrosity, can spread across society, not only through actions but also through fears and suspicions.

Blow Your House Down foregrounds the ways in which street prostitutes contravene the socio-spatial rules of domestic sexual practices and transgress the public / private divide, also undermining the dictates and principles of male sexual control, especially the traditional insistence that to be a respectable woman is to be sexually submissive to one man, in *his* home. In 1984, this perspective carried an added resonance in the broader context of Thatcherite policies explicitly aimed at reversing the liberal social trends of the previous twenty years, including female sexual independence. Sutcliffe's attacks on prostitutes are construed in the novel as symptomatic of wider patriarchal strictures, a campaign directed at re-domesticating sexual transactions.[3] To explore the archetypes underlying the sexual politics of the relations between the women, their men, the Ripper and the police, the book invokes in myriad ways the story of the 'Three Little Pigs' (in its English variant, the written versions of the folk tale go back at least to James Orchard Halliwell's *Nursery Rhymes and* to James Orchard Halliwell's *Nursery Rhymes and Nursery Tales*, circa 1843). In early renditions, the two pigs who build their fragile houses are eaten by the wolf,[4] while the third, in a house of stone or brick, is protected. The third pig in turn eats the wolf who arrives down the chimney into a waiting cooking pot.

Barker's novel is divided into four parts and the reader has to consider the relationship the book has to the three-part structure of the tale. Seemingly, the first two parts, ending in murders amid derelict housing, correspond to the stories of the two little pigs eaten by the wolf, while the third sees one prostitute fighting back when she kills a man she takes to be the Ripper. Part four appears to reach beyond this implied male-female binary division between terrorised and rapacious animals, women as passive or vengeful victims and men as violent assailants.

The standpoint of the novel is summarised by its Nietzschean epigraph from *Beyond Good and Evil*: "Whoever fights monsters should see to it that in the process he does not become a monster. And when you look long into an abyss the abyss also looks into you." The women in the novel thus try to guard or fight against the 'monster' of the story, but Barker widens her narrative in such a way that the reader understands how the division between victim and victimiser is socially and economically determined, and fuelled by a fear that can poison all heterosexual relationships ("If you listened to them every stupid little prick with a few pints inside him was the Ripper".[5]) She connects what happens on the streets with what happens in the home, what affects society with what affects the individual, and the world of the narrative with the world of the reader. It is only in the last part of the story that one woman draws back from demonising everyone around her even though the "abyss was at her feet, and she could do nothing except stare into it" (156).

Part one of *Blow Your House Down*, which is narrated in the third person and largely focused on a single-mother, Brenda, who turns to soliciting, leads up to the ferocious and explicitly described murder of the prostitute Kath, a woman alone; part two, also told in the third person but deliberately including a wider circle of women, in Audrey, Elaine, and Jean as well as Brenda, culminates in the murder of another streetwalker, Carol, one of a pair of female partners; part three ends with Jean, its narrator, going missing after she has killed a man, who may or may not be the murderer of the first half of the novel; part four returns to third-person narration and moves away from a focus on the women of the earlier parts who have turned to prostitution for a source of income, to discuss a fellow factory worker, Maggie, a woman who, attacked by an unknown assailant, subsequently becomes estranged from everyone around her. It is part four of the novel that forces the reader explicitly to think through comparisons or connections between the murderer and other men as well as the prostitutes and other women, just as it widens the circle of violence and hate so that the reader realises that the book is not simply about murder but about the pervasiveness of social cruelty in many forms. The killer appears to be an extreme case of the violence that starts in the home, where child minders and the social services can exploit the vulnerability of single-parent families, but is also inflicted on the prostitutes on the streets by clients and the police.

Drawing much of her imagery from the animals of fairy tales, Barker's chief metaphor in the book is the licensed slaughter of the chicken factory where many of the women work but where "Killing's for the men" (34). Symbolically opposed to the chickens are the starlings (111) who are "blown across the sky like scraps of burnt paper" (163) and who appear to usher in the night-time world, unacknowledged by the "hurrying people" who seek shelter: "unnoticed, unless some stranger to the city should happen to look up, and be amazed" (170). Barker also employs the image of the fox's rabbit-kill for food in comparison with human cruelty. In part four, Maggie notes that the fox she glimpses is carrying a still-twitching rabbit in its jaws but feels "respect for this life that was lived apart from man" (164).

The attitude to prostitution put forward in the book is largely concerned with the causal factors of economic necessity and poor social welfare – suggesting that selling sex is for women a logical conclusion of working-class gender relations in a time of mass unemployment under a system where men are considered the source of money, even by the social services: "they went on about being married, but when you got right down to it, past the white weddings and the romance and all that, what they *really* thought was: if you're getting on your back for a fella, he ought to pay" (30, original emphasis).

Consequently, the novel develops in two ways from its initial portrayal of female victims on the one side and male abusers on the other. First, it presents the women's strength in community and numbers (most novels have one hero or heroine, but *Blow Your House Down*

has several protagonists), flocking together like the starlings, and second, it concludes with the reconciliation between Maggie, whose
problem is how to look into this abyss of violence and not turn mon-
strous, and her husband Bill, who is suspected of the assault by the
police. When Maggie is attacked she finds herself potentially joining
the conveyor belt of female victims of male violence, but then realises
that 'evil' can come from anyone, on any day:

> across her mind's eye moved a line of faces, all women, young, old, fat, thin,
> smiling, serious. She knew who they were: she'd seen them in the papers, as eve-
> rybody had, but then it had just been a story, something that happened to some-
> body else, always to somebody else. But now it was real because it had happened
> to her. The image faded and was replaced by a line of chickens waiting to be
> killed. In each eye the same passive uncomprehending terror. Mrs Bulmer's voice
> went on, and on. You thought evil was simple. No, more than that, you *made* it
> simple, you froze it into a single shape, the shape of a man waiting in the shad-
> ows. But it wasn't simple. This woman, this wheezy middle-aged woman, with
> her corrugated-iron hair and her glasses that flashed when she looked sideways to
> see how you were taking it, she knew what she was doing. And she was enjoying
> it. You couldn't put evil into a single, recognizable shape (155-6).

The redemptive conclusion of the novel picks up this comparison between women on the streets, at risk of attack from men, and slaugh-
tered chickens in the factory production line. Maggie is described in
ways that liken her to one of the factory chickens, with puckered skin
and thin legs, as Bill washes her down until he reaches "her feet which
he cradled, one by one, in his lap" (169). No words can be said to
break the silence, but Bill's Christ-like gesture enables Maggie to
reach out her hand for his.[6]

Ending on this scene, set in the couple's home, underscores the
novel's emphasis on the ineffability of violence but also the silent acts
of domestic love that heal. Barker tenders no solutions other than to
offer love as an equal presence in the world beside the will-to-
dominance (consequently Maggie can identify with the image of
Christ-in-suffering she sees in a church but not the figure of Christ-in-
majesty). But she also seeks to persuade the reader that a social system which makes women economically dependent on men, and which
also devalues male feelings of self-worth by defining them economically but also depriving them of socially useful work (the majority of
men in the book are infantilised), creates the conditions that foster violence.

Within this picture of contemporary society, the image of the house appears in several ways beyond that of the women's homes (which are defined by absent or present males in order to be *homes* because "of course two girls living together is a brothel" [111]). The house variously features as a vulnerable icon of the reader's domestic security, hence the title, as the house of God that Maggie enters, and as the abandoned and boarded-up houses that the prostitutes use with their clients.

To accentuate the title's symbolism, the first part ends with Kath's murder in her home, an abandoned and dilapidated windswept house down an alley; the second with Carol's murder on wasteland beside derelict houses. On the evening she is murdered everyone else in the city runs for their own safety from the elements:

> All over the city people are hurrying to get out of the wind. A few take shelter in doorways, but most make a dash for home. Soon the streets are empty [...] In the silence between one commercial and the next it howls and moans around the house and the people inside look up and say, "Listen to the wind" (90).

The third section ends with Jean directing a new client she is suspicious of to a place where she will kill him because she suspects he is the Ripper:

> This time he did brake a bit quick because he had no way of knowing which road I would choose. It wasn't much of a choice. All the houses round here are bricked up and waiting to come down, though it never seems to happen. They're all dead-ends (130).

Overall, the narrative portrays a divided society in which the dream of the house providing security is contrasted with a reality of street-murders, domestic abuse and state intrusion. But in its fourth part, developing beyond the dynamics implied by the fairy tale from which the novel derives its title, *Blow Your House Down* attempts, just as it seeks to prevent the image of monstrosity poisoning all heterosexual relationships, a recuperation of the house as a site of male-female love and support in Maggie's acceptance of Bill's tender care.

Paradise

> Not a house in the country ain't packed to its rafters with some dead Negro's grief (Morrison 1989: 5).

The girl's memory in the house is a sickness – everywhere and nowhere (Morrison 1993: 28).

Paradise (1998) is the third novel in a trilogy, after the Inferno of *Beloved*[7] and the Purgatorio of *Jazz* – two novels whose assigned role for houses in relation to a 'Divine Comedy' is implied by the quotations above. No less haunted by loss and violence, Morrison's 'Paradisio', whose title up until publication was 'War', is an exploration of religious devotion and a sustained contrast between the principles of an exclusive heaven and an inclusive haven. Carole Boyce Davies notes that "The representation of the house as source of self-definition occurs with some frequency in the literature of Afro-Caribbean / American women writers" (1994: 126). In *Paradise* Toni Morrison offers two key communities, one decisively founded as an act of self-definition based on exclusion, the other unconsciously developed through a spirit of inclusion: the isolationist town of Ruby, built as the last stronghold of black purity, and the nearby Convent, which houses five women but embraces all the grief brought to its door. The book culminates in the massacre of the latter by men from the former.

Pertinently, bell hooks writes that because public space can be hostile to African Americans, the home is a significant site of resistance with a radical political dimension, but she also acknowledges that the black home can be a place of patriarchal domination (1990: 110). It is this that links *Paradise* to *Blow Your House Down*, as both examine male violence against females whose economic independence is resented and whose sexual independence is perceived as threat. While Barker considers a socially hidden community of prostitutes and working women in a northern English town, Morrison similarly portrays a society whose isolation – ninety miles from the nearest other town – is entwined with men's violence against women. As Kate Crenshaw writes, "this sense of isolation compounds efforts to politicize gender violence within communities of color, and permits the deadly silence surrounding these issues to continue" (1994: 111). In her novel, Morrison uses racial politics and the history of black America to explore the deleterious effects of segregation, while offering the feminised domestic space of a house without a patriarchal presence as a truer image of the precepts of Christianity and the US Constitution, as well as a perceived challenge to patriarchy which male violence will seek both to find culpable and to destroy as vulnerable.

The Utopian all-black town of Haven has been relocated and re-named as New Haven, then Ruby, but its ideals apply far more to the Convent, which effectively becomes, until the second centenary of US Independence in early July 1976, a haven for persecuted women. Also the town's motto 'Beware the Furrow of His Brow' ostensibly be-comes a warning to the Convent against patriarchal violence, while the younger generation's belief that it reads 'Be the Furrow of His Brow' is adopted by Ruby.[8] The Convent, seventeen miles from Ruby, was originally an embezzler's refuge, a bullet-shaped mansion deco-rated with erotic pictures, statues and furnishings, situated in Okla-homa, "a state shaped like a gun" (16). It is replete with images of female sexual subservience and exploitation, from ashtrays shaped as vaginas to carvings of women offering up their breasts.[9] When the house was taken over by a small order of nuns who recreated it as a missionary school for American Indian girls it became known as 'the Convent'. Later, after the school closed, only the mother superior, Mary Magna, remained, cared for by Connie (Consolata), a street-orphan she rescued in Brazil. In the present of the novel, 1976, though 'Mother' is dead, the Convent has become a home to Mavis Albright, Grace (Gigi), Seneca, and Pallas Truelove: all of whom have been assaulted in the past and will now be murdered by nine men from Ruby.

All the Convent women (have to) lose homes to find a new one. Their story is a variant on that of Haven / Ruby, as they too have trav-elled across a hostile country to found an isolated community as a sanctuary, but their community is based on care and freedom, not rule and restriction. They each have suffered abuse in other houses or in other places, and now develop a new kind of convent(ion). Mavis has suffered at the hands of an abusive husband, and fears she will be fur-ther maltreated when her twins, Pearl and Merle, suffocate in her parked car while she is shopping for food – she also suspects that their children, who watch her humiliation, may soon join Frank in killing her. Gigi, with a father on death row, witnesses at close hand the 1968 race riot shootings in Oakland (170) and has been abandoned by her jailbird lover. She shifts from marching on Civil Rights protests to languishing at the Convent, unable to commit herself to anything, and hit by her lover K.D., one of the men who attack the house. Seneca is a self-harming foster child abandoned by her mother at age five. Re-peatedly sexually abused by men, she also becomes an in-house prostitute, kept by a sadistic wealthy woman while her husband is away. Pallas, who has left her home because her lover has started an affair with her mother, is brought to the Convent after she has been found sexually attacked in the road. Connie, the emotional centre of the Convent, was sexually abused when only eight years old (228), which gave rise to thirty years of celibacy.

The Convent is not free from hostility, which is especially notable in the relationship between Mavis and Gigi, but its presiding influence remains Connie, who epitomizes the virtues of care and comfort. Connie thus takes on the role in the house of the maternal figure that she inherits from 'Mother'. Connie's position is important in itself but is also symbolic as a definition of the Convent as refuge, sanctuary or female home; as Boyce Davies notes "In any writing of home by women writers in patriarchal or matriarchal cultures, the challenge to the meaning of the mother attains symbolic importance in terms of definition and redefinition" (1994: 128). Defining the spirit of the maternal home, Connie has healing powers and is able, among other things, to restore the women to full physical and spiritual health. She tells them of her vision of Piedade, a divine female force who herself seems embodied in Connie. Pallas decides of the Convent that "the whole house felt permeated with a blessed malelessness, like a protected domain, free of hunters but exciting too" (177). By contrast, when the men come they bring with them the sense of righteous crusaders who see themselves as the scourge of the greatest evil they have faced since they established Ruby: "Who could have imagined that twenty-five years later in a brand-new town a Convent would beat out the snakes, the Depression, the tax man and the railroad for sheer destructive power?" (17).

Paradise may appear to be a novel about race but emerges as a narrative about the ways in which the rallying cry of race covers over gender oppression:

> From Haven, a dreamtown in Oklahoma Territory, to Haven, a ghosttown in Oklahoma State. Freedmen who stood tall in 1889 dropped to their knees in 1934 and were stomach-crawling by 1948. That is why they are here in this Convent. To make sure it never happens again. That nothing inside or out rots the one all-black town worth the pain (5).

To accentuate the point, Morrison leaves open the question of the five Convent women's colour. The novel opens with the sentence "They shoot the white girl first" (3), but never reveals which of the women this is. Morrison is far more interested in the ways in which patriarchy projects on to all women its twin desires for purity and depravity:

> What, he wonders, could do this to women? How can their plain brains think up such things: revolting sex, deceit and the sly torture of children? Out here in wide-open space tucked away in a mansion – no one to bother or insult them – they managed to call into question the value of almost every woman he knew (8).

With considerable irony, Morrison exposes the thought processes by which the assailants from Ruby conceive of a binarised world in which others and not they themselves are predators: "From the beginning [Ruby's] people were free and protected. A sleepless woman could always rise from her bed [...] walk out the yard and on down the road [...] Nothing for ninety miles around thought she was prey" (8). In their righteous rage, the nine men are unable to see the way in which they themselves are the ones who shoot at the principles of their town. "God at their side, the men take aim. For Ruby" (18), the narrative explains, suggesting they are committing violence both 'in Ruby's name' and 'at Ruby'.

The men attack the Convent for several reasons, mostly to do with the Morgans and the Fleetwoods, Ruby's principal dynasties who have become feuding families. All four of the Fleetwood children are dying of a congenital disease and scapegoats outside of Ruby are needed. Arnette Fleetwood has been beaten, and the real culprit, her lover K.D., the only remaining male Morgan heir, blames the women at the Convent; Arnette also claims the women forced an abortion on her; the Convent women have been sexually involved with men from Ruby (e.g. K.D. and Gigi were lovers) and have assisted women from the town when they have needed help, though Sweetie Fleetwood claims she was not helped but 'snatched' by the Convent women. The attacking men conclude "the one thing that connected all those catastrophes was in the Convent. And in the Convent were those women" (11). While the women of Ruby are emotionally distant from their men, because they are treated with condescension, the Convent women emerge as scapegoats for the problems Ruby has created for itself but repressed, not least because Ruby's focus on blood-purity has led to a proprietary, often misogynistic attitude towards women, stereotypically construed as protection. For this reason, Ruby is seen as "deafened by the sound of its own history" (306), demonising the Other as the source of all that goes wrong in Ruby in order to preserve its own sanctity.[10]

The book ends with Ruby's outsider-within, Billie Delia, a virgin seen as a whore, hoping the women from the Convent will return to destroy the town's violently oppressive, patriarchal social structure. Rejected because of her innocent sexual pleasure and her lighter skin colour, Billie Delia understands Ruby as a male-run community that maintains itself by controlling and grading those within while rebuffing those without. To a degree, the book thus contrasts a patriarchal, Christian all-black patriarchal society with Connie's all-embracing matriarchal one.

The sections of the book each take their name from one of the women within the narrative, with the exception of the last, which is untitled. At the end of this coda, the reader is presented with a spiritual image of a paradise attained after death. The singing Piedade (whose name means pity or mercy) cradles a woman in her arms on a tranquil beach. Such a conclusion has been prepared for earlier by Connie when she performs a ritual over the women in the Convent's cellar: "she told them of a place where white sidewalks met the sea and fish the color of plums swam alongside children [...] Then she told them of a woman named Piedade, who sang but never said a word" (263-4).

Though it is unclear whether the final page contains an image of Connie / Consolata cradled by Piedade or whether it is someone else held in this pietà image in a paradise for the "disconsolate" (318), the other four murdered women return quasi-apocalyptically at the end of the novel: Gigi, Mavis, Seneca and Pallas. While it is generally acknowledged that the women seek out contact with their family in this coda, critics have not so readily drawn attention to the fact that all four women are now linked with violence and weapons, either for protection or vengeance. Grace / Gigi has a gun; Pallas has a sword (as goddess of war); Mavis is pleased that her ex-husband has married a woman who "kicks his butt" and "packs a gun" too; the self-harming Seneca is pictured with "blood running from her hands", supposedly because she fell on glass.[11] The women return for reconciliation but also for Morrison to stage their resurrection before Piedade offers all the disconsolate 'solace' in song: "the unambivalent bliss of going home to be home – the ease of coming back to love begun" (318).

If Morrison's novel has a precursor it is Zora Neale Hurston's 1937 *Their Eyes Were Watching God* which uses the image of the house in a similar way, Boyce Davies observes, as

> the sign of the colonized male's entitlement and concomitant female disempowerment. The 'Big House', as acquired by the Black male, then becomes in literature by black women a trope for Black / African nation(alism) and the parallel locus of final destruction of any positive relationship between Black men and women as Black manhood aligns itself with male dominance (1994: 66).

Like bell hooks' criticism, Morrison's novel argues for the need to reaffirm the house as a site for organizing political solidarity and re-grouping for gender resistance because "the devaluation of the role black women have played in constructing for us homeplaces that are the site for resistance undermines our efforts to resist racism and the colonizing mentality which promotes internalized self-hatred" (1990: 45).

Daughters of the House

> I'm buying a little house in France (my maternal country in which I speak my mother's tongue) and that, I know, because I shall own it and it will be *mine*, I will dust and paint and polish to an inch of its life. Because it represents the maternal body; the body of love; once lost and damaged; now found again, made reparation to. That's the house in which I hope to write my next novel, in which I shall dust, polish and paint words (Roberts 1994: 175).

Michèle Roberts's *Daughters of the House* (1992) is a richly symbolic psychological study of the search of two cousins, Léonie and Thérèse, for both the(ir) mother and the(ir) home. Invoking sibling rivalry, disavowed knowledge, abandonment and domestic secrets in its construction of two contrasting but connected identities, the book mixes a Freudian and Jungian reading of the deep associations between wartime events at the girls' childhood home in France and their mental landscapes as adults. Also heavily indebted to the work of Lacan and Kristeva, Roberts explores the mythical and psychological significance of domestic space and the desire for roots / origins.[12]

Concentrating on the daughters' repressed memories and the hidden history of the house, Roberts works at the intersection of different meanings of the 'home': "Philosophically speaking [...] the real return home or recurrence of the uncanny [*unheimlich*] is a move forward to

what has been repressed and never fulfilled" (Zipes 1991: 176). This
view of the house primarily suggests Thérèse's story. Thérèse is introduced to the reader returning home from the convent where she has
spent her adult life, in order to confront a past that is buried in the
house in which Léonie still lives. The return, physical and mental, will
culminate in her setting fire to the local Church, most likely killing
herself, as an act of sacrifice, remorse and protest against a priest's
betrayal of Jews hiding from the Germans in the house forty years earlier. However, her return will also precipitate a capitulation by Léonie,
who has herself "fought against a memory which was coming too
close" and now loses the battle she has fought to contain emotion
through materialism:

> Something was going to happen, to be upset. Léonie lay back, tried to reassert
> control over her world. She applied her usual formula for overcoming anxiety.
> She wandered in imagination through her house. She listed her numerous posses-
> sions one by one […] It was hers. It was her house. Her kingdom, firmly in her
> control. Peopled with daughters who looked like their mother and loved her com-
> fortably and did as they were told.[13]

Roberts has said that "The story of a woman obsessed with material
possessions *had* to be told as an inventory of the contents of her
house" (1994: 171, original emphasis). Leonie thus thinks of the inventory to comfort herself, but the solidity of things is unable to qui-
eten the house and she ascends the stairs, in a reversal of Thérèse's
earlier descent to the cellar, to acknowledge the voices (of the hiding
Jews) that she has repressed, in the final chapter entitled 'The Words'.
Because all the previous chapter titles throughout the book, contrast-
ingly, name household items, they compare and contrast language
with the world, evoking the duality of Léonie and Thérèse, with their
different emphases on the material and the immaterial. By entitling the
final chapter 'The Words', Roberts draws attention to the human and
spiritual presence that Léonie otherwise denies, and to its equal part in
the inventory of the house. Roberts has commented elsewhere upon
the relation between the mind and the house evident in Léonie's life:
"The housewife creates order out of chaos […] My room reminds me,
contentedly, of my unconscious: chaotic, in need of a sorting-out"
(1983a: 62-8). Léonie's old room at the top of the stairs is indeed her
unconscious, but the traumatic memory she wishes to repress is linked

to the question of the identity of her mother, the answer to which is contained elsewhere within the memory of the house.

The narrative starts with a series of comments about the house that suggest its personification. First, that "It was a changeable house. Sometimes it felt safe as a church, and sometimes it shivered and then cracked apart" (1). Second, "What bounded the house was skin. A wall of gristle a soldier could tear open with his bear hands. Antoinette laughed" (1). Third, "The house was strict. The rules indicated the forbidden places" (1). Each of these statements figures the house as physical or spiritual mother, as a changeable, strict but vulnerable parent – but there is also a suggestion of the house bounded by a membrane like the foetus or Anzieu's skin-ego (1989). As Clare Hanson has noted, in Roberts's novel "[the] house is a metaphor for the body of the mother, and the project of the novel, metaphorically speaking, is to define the relationship of two daughters to a lost mother" (2000: 238). The narrative on one level therefore progresses as an exploration of Léonie and Thérèse's identity in relation to those who have played this role, variously presented as physical maternal figure (whether birth-mother, surrogate mother, or primary care giver), as the image of an Earth Mother or the Virgin Mary and the Church (164-5).

The opening to Roberts's novel, described above, is narrated as Léonie's dream, and it is she who has remained in the house for twenty years, while Thérèse has been away. It also foretells what happens to the mother of the house, Antoinette, who may have been attacked by a soldier. This is important to the book's preoccupation with secrets. Thérèse is the daughter of Antoinette and Louis. Léonie is the daughter of Antoinette's sister Madeleine and her English husband Maurice. However, both girls were as babies cared for and fed by a local French peasant, Rose Taille: "Rose, foster-mother, mother-in-law, second mother, fostering mother" (169). It also later transpires that, according to letters Thérèse has found and since burned, the two girls are Antoinette's twins, whose father may be Louis but could be a German soldier (150-2). This secret is associated with the cellar, where it is supposed Antoinette and the soldier conceived Thérèse and Léonie. The thematic and emotional significance of this question rests on whether – and how – Antoinette is positioned as good mother and bad mother (70, 132).[14] This is a matter that relates to the visions that the cousins have in the neighbouring forest, where Léonie (who has an intuitive sixth sense, 171) sees a red, and Thérèse a blue, virgin.

Thérèse's revelation is later exposed as a mistake or lie (158), but at the time it is taken as a miracle, while Léonie's is considered to be fallacious because blasphemous. It later transpires that the Church has in fact demolished and buried in the house's cellar the pagan statue of the sensuous harvest virgin from the forest that inspired Léonie's vision of the "goddess […] with a dark face", who represents the repressed feminine principle within the novel (160-2), including Antoinette's secret history.

As though twins, the girls are indeed presented as two halves to one person by Thérèse:

> Thérèse thought: in the darkness we're equal. One married and one not, one plump and one thin, one truthful and one a liar, one who belongs and one who doesn't. It doesn't matter any more, our difference. It's all flattened out. Like wearing the habit. No bodies you have to notice. Freedom. Sisters under the skin, made identical (21).

But this is not something Léonie is prepared to admit, as is suggested when she sees birds in the country fields and wonders what the necessary degree of closeness is to make one magpie and then a second one be considered together: "When did one magpie become part of two? […] She preferred saying one-and-one to two. She knew what she meant. Two was blurry and made her anxious" (97). Léonie consequently rejects Antoinette as her mother: "all those lies you tried to make me swallow about Madeleine not being my real mother. About being adopted. About Antoinette being raped by a German. Your big hysterical drama. Just because you were jealous" (158). While the women call each other a "hypocrite" (159), their parentage emerges as undecidable, but the house itself hides these secrets, including that contained in the room at the top of the kitchen stairs, from where "the words" escape. Here it emerges is the secret of betrayal that may be linked to Antoinette's interest in distracting or compromising the German soldier stationed in the house, because in this room the Jews and their French helper, who was both Rose's husband and the father of Léonie's future husband, spent their last night before they were executed.

Olivier Marc's *Psychology of the House* argues:

> We construct ourselves according to a diagram of growth which the house discloses, and dreams about houses reveal, as Artemidorus Daldianus observed, different stages in the elaboration of the self. As we dig foundations, erect the

framework, build the walls, inspect the cellars, discover unknown rooms, and paper the walls, the unconscious reveals to us the different stages of our psychic development, in the course of this voyage in search of ourselves (1977: 72).

Particularly through Léonie, Roberts interrogates the importance of household objects and the meanings of the relative spaces of the home. As Andrea Nye writes: "Unlike an object, which can be imagined to have a unique presence of its own, spaces are defined reciprocally, by the boundaries between them. One space requires the other space which defines it" (1994: 169). *Daughters of the House* operates in this way by juxtaposing images: of Antoinette as good and bad mother, of Léonie and Thérèse, of the cellar and the upstairs room, of pagan and Catholic religions, of English and French languages and identities.

The domestic setting of the novel is to a degree a battleground ("that old war", 4) in which the objects named in the chapter titles can be weapons, mirroring the contests fought elsewhere in the novel by its many opposed individuals and groups. Sarah Sceats argues that "the balance of power in [Léonie and Thérèse's] relationship shifts and slides throughout the novel, as they play and strive for supremacy in the kitchen" (1996: 125). Illuminating this shape to the novel's construction, Roberts has herself said:

> The history of my own spirituality necessarily includes the history of my struggle
> first to name and then to integrate what have felt like warring, separate parts of
> myself: body, soul, intellect, emotions. These conflicts name me as a child of the
> Judeo-Christian tradition, which, to put it very crudely, operates within a dualistic
> and hierarchical system of concepts: soul is better than body; be guided by intel-
> lect, not by intuition (1983: 51).

This dualism pervades *Daughters of the House* and includes gender, which is relevant to the question of homeownership that runs through the three books I have examined. Roberts says she writes novels to answer questions, including: "Does a woman belong in this world and is she allowed to have a house of her own? (I realized only recently that all my novels feature homeless women, that novels are the paper houses I build, then inhabit)" (1994: 171). In relation to the modern heroine going abroad in romance novels, she also argues that: "Her being *abroad* means that she lacks a home, a family, the Ideal Home that the perfect hero will provide for her. And of course this home is based on the model that the white middle class family is supposed to aspire to" (1986: 225-6, original emphasis). In each of the novels examined in this essay, women – a majority of who are homeless – instead set themselves up in their own homes, in female environments to which males lay siege or have inflicted violence. The house thus becomes a very different kind of environment: one that is celebrated for its independence and self-dependence, but which is assaulted for the sexual temptation and moral contamination it is supposed to 'house'. In *Daughters of the House*, though the violence committed against the Jews who sheltered in Léonie's room is not in doubt, the narrative leaves unresolved the question of Thérèse's story about Antoinette and the German soldier, which may be a projection, as Roberts has said of her own history:

> My heterosexual desires had to be crushed, for I was still unconsciously in the grip of the Catholic divisions of the psyche: allowing men to see me as sexual meant that they would also name me as Other, inhuman, bestial, part of nature to be raped and exploited, lacking a soul. By fleeing from this definition, I accepted it. My feminism at this time contained enormous rage at the wrongs perpetrated on women by men (1983: 60).

Finally, Roberts considers the borderline between separation and duality that defines the daughters and their own negotiation of disabling boundaries between the spiritual and the material, the psychological and the physical. What emerges out of her book is a story of complicity. The separateness of nations, religions, and cousins, of body and spirit, is gradually eroded. Léonie's final decision to record, or confess to herself, the knowledge she has buried of the Jews' exposure and murder, a fact that has led to Thérèse's death, is the culmination of a slow exhumation of her own identity, moving her from the periphery of the story to its physical and emotional centre. She has previously refused to remember the terrible past of the town, whose mayor is now her husband: "You don't care about the dead Jews either [...] All you care about is your position in the village", says Thérèse (159). Both cousins / sisters have to acknowledge and confront their part – through silence and lies – in sublimating the murders, even though the Jews were betrayed by the Church Thérèse loved and they were killed with the father of the man Léonie loved. While representing aspects of duality and loss, the house is ultimately a metaphor for division and denial as well as an image of the mother: "Roberts invokes the figure of the home as emblematic of a Europe that has repeatedly disavowed the 'strangers' in its house" (Luckhurst 1996: 257).

In *The Poetics of Space*, Gaston Bachelard writes that

> the house is one of the greatest powers of integration for the thoughts, memories and dreams of mankind [...] Past, present and future give the house different dynamisms, which often interfere, at times opposing, at others stimulating one another. [The house] is a body and soul (1994: 6-7).

The three novels discussed in this essay are geographically differentiated by their national settings, in England, the US and France, but topographically linked by their use of the house as body and soul as well as locus of protection and persecution. Through their widely different invocations of the home as female space violated and appropriated by male incursions, the three writers also picture visionary ways in which the house can be re-appropriated for female agency. Roberts does this through psychological recuperation and the recovery of repressed personal and public histories; Morrison through an affirmative vision of an earthly paradise based on love and protection; and Barker through an alliance of female solidarity but also heterosexual recovery through realigned sexual and gender relations.

Notes

1. Sutcliffe brutally murdered (at least) thirteen women, most of whom were prostitutes, in northern England between 1975 and 1981.

2. The domestic home of presumed co-habitation – where the necessary male is simply defined as present or absent by social services – is contrasted with the matriarchal environment of the Palmerston pub, owned by Beattie Miller, where the women meet without men.

3. On the streets, violence is almost expected: "You expect a certain amount of violence in this job, you expect to get slapped around" (109). "I've been slashed, punched, kicked, slapped, raped, oh, yes, *raped*, it does happen to us too" (131). However, the home is associated with violence as much as the streets: "You know, sometimes I think people run away with the idea that Dave's forcing us to go out, but he's not. It isn't to say 'cos he hits me it's always about that. He's very jealous. You know, he's only got to see me with another man and that's it. So he must think a bit about me, mustn't he?" (83). Similarly, Brian 'belted' Brenda (21).

4. In *The Uses of Enchantment* Bruno Bettelheim positions the wolf in the story as representing both the "stranger" and "the enemy within" (82-5).

5. Pat Barker, *Blow Your House Down* (1984), 13. All subsequent references will be given in the text.

6. Although Maggie is not one of the prostitutes, she is linked to them by the attack on her and by the repeated phrase "Maggie May, why have you gone away", which is derived from an old Liverpool seaman's song about a prostitute with the refrain "Oh Maggie May, they have taken her away".

7. According to Kadiatu Kanneh, *Beloved* "theorises a Black conception of the body and of home as realities formed in the shape of past experiences, which insist upon their place in the present through exigencies of grief and anger" (1998: 119).

8. Toni Morrison, *Paradise* (1998), 86-7. All subsequent references will be given in the text.

9. It is the overt sexuality associated with the house, designed by the embezzler, defaced by the nuns, that is denounced by the attackers from Ruby who take its opulent sensuousness to be a manifestation and confirmation of the convent women's depravity.

10. Whereas, in fact, the convent has been a refuge and haven for many of the town's inhabitants, Deacon, K.D., Arnette, Billie Delia and Menus, all of who visit the Convent for reasons to do with sex; and the women have helped numerous others, from Soane to Sweetie Fleetwood.

11. Seneca's name brings to mind the Roman philosopher but more pertinently the Iroquois confederacy of peoples known as the Five Nations, or the League of Five Nations: the Mohawk, Onondaga, Cayuga, Oneida, and Seneca.

12. For a discussion of the novel in these terms see Hanson 2000: 229-47.

13. Michèle Roberts, *Daughters of the House* (1993), 168. All subsequent references will be given in the text.

14. For discussion of the 'good' and 'bad' mother see Klein 1986: 176-200. Roberts has said about her own experience: "During all those years when my emotional and sexual feelings for my father were interwoven with an acceptance of him as Patriarch, as Law-Giver and Judge, I was vulnerable to the critical words he punished me with: mad; foolish; whore; ignorant; bad; immature. I couldn't be indifferent to these words: I allowed my father to represent my conscience, and then fought back, angry and despairing and hurt. Even when I began to reject this way of relating to him, I continued, for some time, to accept the patriarchal and Catholic morality which divides women into madonnas and whores, good married women and bad sexually free women" (1983b: 108).

Sonic Architecture: Home Hi-Fi and Stereo(types)

Ron Moy

ABSTRACT
This essay is concerned with the relationship between sound and domestic space. It argues that ways of consuming audio have changed over the past two decades, with a mode of distracted or ambient 'hearing' partly replacing the focused close 'listening' associated with what can be termed the 'Hi-Fi generation' who came of age in the 1960s and 1970s. Audio must now compete with other media in an increasingly saturated domestic situation, and thus listening to music becomes part of a multi-media environment that encompasses computer games, online radio and mobile phone use. This has an effect upon the type of listening, and the resulting status of music. The essay argues for the continuing importance of close analysis of musical texts and sound production. For many young people this denaturalised experience has important pedagogic and socio-historical implications and casts important light upon areas such as gender, domesticity and 'audience affects' theory. The essay foregrounds the lack of research in this particular area but argues the need for the rebirth of the active listener at the expense of the passive hearer.

Introduction

Recent studies of popular music suggest the analysis of the spatial dimension of listening to music has been marginalised or indeed completely neglected throughout the humanities. In David Morley's book (2000) dealing with media use and territory, for example, the chapter on domestic space makes one passing mention to audio media. The implicit assumption in this text, and in the field as a whole, seems to be that essentially television and film *are* the broadcast media. In this scenario, single-sense media are largely ignored.

When music or audio *is* a central critical concern, the marginalisation of certain aspects is equally apparent. A blatant discrimination, in favour of what might be termed the temporal, against the sonic has proven equally prevalent within the field of music studies. Historically, academia has typically focused on aspects such as the written score, biography and performance over and above notions of social and domestic consumption. Given the patriarchal nature of musicology and so-called 'serious' music analysis, this comes as no surprise. However, more striking has been the failure of the liberal humanities, and particularly popular music studies, to focus on the spatial and domestic dimension, particularly in the light of new technologies and recent cultural shifts in leisure and home-based consumption.

The academic discipline of popular music studies is a relatively new phenomenon. Recent years have witnessed an inevitable diversification in the field, as well as the welcome emergence of interdisciplinarity. Indeed, such is the breadth of recent critical writings that critical readers and collections (e.g. Negus and Hesmondhalgh 2002) can now claim to offer a near-definitive overview of the subject, within the inevitable constraints of space. However, the creative tensions that have existed between musicological ('textual') and sociological ('contextual') approaches have contrived largely to overlook the domestic consumption of music – what I would term the spatial and perspectival dimension.

Musicology tends to overlook consumption in the domestic space because 'home listening' of popular forms is not overly concerned with formal, textual analysis. Sociology pays little attention to this dimension because, although intimately tied in with identity and articulations of gender, sexuality and ethnicity, domestic consumption can be seen as explicitly 'anti-social', albeit without the negative connotations normally applied to that term. As a result, most of the important work carried out by ethnographers has consisted of research into the significance of music upon groups, classes, races and youth subcultures in social spaces (Sara Cohen 1991; Stan Cohen 2002; Willis 1978). Valuable work on space has tended to concentrate on geographical space and social location and identity (Negus and Hesmondhalgh 2002: 205-65; Swiss, Herman and Sloop 1998, *passim*). Where domestic space has been the subject of analysis, many theorists have dealt with this dimension in passing (Attali 1985; Toop 1995). Certainly, some valuable critical contributions have been made (Keightley 1996; Lanza 1995; Eisenburg 1987; Kassabian 2002), and it is my intention to build upon such foundations and attempt to concentrate on certain specific aspects of space and the domestic consumption of popular music – what I have previously termed 'audioculture' (Moy 2000).

Initially I aim to focus on historicising the domestic and aesthetic shifts wrought upon home music consumption by (then) new technologies, and then to concentrate upon what I will term the 'Hi-Fi generation' – broadly speaking, those coming of age with the concurrent development of the home stereo in the UK popular music terrain of the mid-1960s. It is my contention that contemporary consumers of popular music are not members of this generation, despite having access to technologies and musical artefacts far superior to those available in the past. The spatial awareness of today's popular music fans is not the same as those of the past, and their relationship to music (and sound in general) is subsequently different. Music consumption today has less of an 'architectural' dimension, and more of an 'ambient' one. In focusing upon a specific historical period, and its associated anti-social taste-culture, I hope to be able to explore a range of issues relating to class, gender, musical genre, domestic architecture, leisure and lifestyle, and domestic space and perspective.

Historicising Music Consumption in the Domestic Space
Many commentators have offered a historical overview of music developments, whether concentrating on technological innovations, the music industry, economic factors, or studio production (see Cunningham 1996; Millard 1996; Jones 1992; Théberge 1993). All these aspects are indeed important, but how all these historical shifts have acted upon domestic consumption and individual affect has been largely overlooked.

For example, in Millard's book, which concentrates in the main upon the US, the reproduction of a British advertisement from the First World War era indicates the cost of early audio equipment. The cheapest portable gramophone produced by Decca retailed at £7.15.00 (Millard 1996: 71) – the equivalent of several months wages for a serving private. This compared to American equivalents costing as little as $7 in the pre-war period (Millard 1996: 123). Economic factors proved significant for many years to follow, having a huge impact upon availability, location and appropriation in the British domestic space, but we need to take this valuable research into different areas.

Crisell's account (1994) of radio consumption in the early days of the medium casts an interesting light on domestic leisure patterns in the UK in the pre-WW2 period. After its earliest years, when radio sets utilised headphones rather than loudspeakers, audio consumption became a social event in Britain. The cost of owning a radio and affording the licence fee certainly restricted the medium, although by the outbreak of the Second World War in 1939 most of the population had access to a radio set in their own, or a neighbour's, domestic space.

Record players, or gramophones, developed in parallel with radio during this period, although during the depression years of the early-to-mid-1930s, the record industry did lose out to music on radio because of the huge decline in leisure spending in that era of high unemployment. By the 1930s, sound fidelity had been transformed by electrical recording, and radios and record players were combined into the same unit. Although by later standards the quality was still poor, lacking volume, clarity, and dynamic range, both the radio and the gramophone had become central to the domestic space. At this period the sound was monaural, and the equipment to an extent non-portable, being heavy and sometimes reliant upon mains power (Attwood 2002). The players themselves ranged from the functional and utilitarian to the luxurious and beautifully crafted, with many of the finest examples having the status of a piece of fine furniture. Even during this period, the mythologies connecting technology and sound equipment to masculinity and patriarchy were beginning to be well established.

In the post-war period technical innovations and the slow return to prosperity both acted in tandem to transform sound consumption in the domestic space. Innovations such as magnetic tape recording (and recorders), stereophony, the transistor, and the microgroove long-playing album had all made inroads into the UK domestic market by the end of the 1950s. Equally, social shifts in terms of employment patterns, home-ownership, youth income levels and general affluence had a huge impact upon the use of domestic space. Again, Britain lagged behind the US in terms of the pace and extent of domestic changes. Certainly, the notion of the well-equipped 'Batchelor pad', or in-car musical entertainment was no more than a dream to the vast majority of the single population in the UK in the 1950s.

This period saw the development of genuine Hi-Fi sound production and reproduction, with the early attempts of the orchestral field to place the home consumer in the 'best seat in the house' being duplicated within fields such as jazz, vocal and so-called 'light' music. The dominant means of musical dissemination for the Hi-Fi 'aficionado' was the radiogram – a bulky and expensive piece of audio furniture often in walnut veneer. As Bennett (2003: 78) states, during this period the record player's role was often disguised within a cabinet resembling a sideboard. It was thus domesticated, and by extension, feminised. Although providing stereophony, the two speakers were usually around half a metre apart, which resulted in a very restricted stereo field of perspective. Sound was thus mainly monaural, although 'Father's armchair' was most likely placed in the optimum listening position. Before the era when many domestic dwellings had studies (or the mass of the population could afford a house with such a specialised area), even the relatively comfortable would typically divide their communal living into two rooms: the dining room, and the lounge, or sitting / living room. In the early 1950s, the radiogram had pride of place in the latter for the middle classes. In addition, in this era before the wide affordability / availability of double glazing and central heating, the appeal of the chilly study or bedroom as an alternative social or personal space was not significant.

Although television had begun broadcasting in 1936 in the UK, the service closed down for the duration of the war, and it was not until the introduction of commercial broadcasting in 1955 that radio and the radiogram / record player lost its primary position in the living room. By the end of the 1950s television had become the primary source of social entertainment in the domestic space. Concurrent with this domestic shift came developments in music and technology aimed specifically at the young, particularly embodied in the transistor radio, the affordable portable record player, and the musical innovations of rock 'n' roll and beat music. In the US, greater affluence gave many young people the opportunity to adopt the automobile as their primary social / anti-social site of music consumption, but in Britain, financial and geographical constraints militated against the same phenomenon. In Britain, the development of the bedroom as the primary social / anti-social space was more significant, as part of 'the teenage flight from the family TV and living room' (Berland 1993: 35).

In Britain, a host of factors acted to transform the sonic domestic space, particularly for young people, during the late 1950s and the 1960s. Greater affluence, the growth of the 'consumer society' and the easing of hire purchase restrictions all increased the availability of the portable record player (often known generically as the 'Dansette' after one of the most popular commercial brands). Transistor radios, costing around £3–£5 in the early 1960s, were both an intimate music source and a public fashion statement. Although the provision of youth-oriented pop music on British radio was relatively scarce, other outlets such as Radio Luxembourg, the American Forces Network and the pirate broadcasters (from 1964) all served the needs of this huge, 'baby-boomer' market. By the late 1960s, the relatively affluent domestic household might possess a radiogram and a television (in social spaces), one or more transistor radios, a portable record player, and in many cases a reel-to-reel tape recorder.

With the wide adoption of stereophony during the 1960s, the radiogram began to be superseded by the Hi-Fi component system, consisting of a record deck, speakers and an amplifier housed in separate units. In terms of design, this allowed for the old 'feminine' focal point offered by the radiogram to be replaced by the modernistic and stylistically obtrusive (and often louder) stereo system, which provided much better channel separation and spatial perspective. This change encouraged some of the most popular music of the time to fully exploit this new mode of consumption, with production techniques designed to highlight spatial / instrumental separation and cross-channel 'panning' of sounds. However, the secondary audio system, whether radio, record player or tape player, remained monaural in general terms.

New formats such as the cassette player / recorder and the eight-track tape were also often monaural in the early 1970s, although their impact (at least in the case of the cassette) was to be significant, and long lasting – both domestically and within the road vehicle. Car radios began to be fitted as standard on all but the most basic models in the 1970s, to be augmented by a cassette player in the 1980s, and a CD player during the 1990s. At around the same time as the component system superseded the radiogram, headphone sockets began to be widely provided within Hi-Fi systems. As well as offering an internalised musical space, headphones limited the 'leakage' of noise, thus dampening the source of much domestic and inter-generational conflict in the process. Headphones encouraged a further internalisation of music even beyond that offered by the bedroom setting and by genres (such as folk or singer-songwriter music) which seemed almost expressly designed to be consumed in an isolated space. Indeed, it should be recognised that the folk or singer-songwriter genres were equally well known (and derided) by the spatial term 'bed-sit music'.

Performers such as Joni Mitchell, Cat Stevens, Leonard Cohen, Nick Drake and Carole King all utilised musical and stylistic devices that seemed expressly designed to complement an intimate and specific domestic space.

Popular music production had developed various filtering devices, whereby unwanted or extraneous 'oral' noises, such as the fricative clicks and sibilant hisses and whistles which are part of everyday speech, could be minimised or excluded from the vocal recording. However, techniques such as 'close-miking', which overrides the filtering recording process, allows the physical 'grain' of the voice – the mouth, tongue and teeth – to become part of a sensual, even erotic experience, connected listeners ever more precisely with the materiality of sound. For many headphone addicts, this kind of audio experience offered a particularly intense and visceral relationship with both internal sound and their immediate environment. In particular, female voices, with their higher frequency range, and their connotations of 'emotional vulnerability', have often been recorded with the grain of the voice to the fore. Particularly effective examples of this process are found on the ballads of Tori Amos, for example. The opening vocal phrases of *Hey Jupiter* (Amos 1996) show the performer and the recording process working in tandem to communicate an almost unbearably intimate rendition of the song.

This internalising of music consumption was more broadly affected by the development of the personal stereo, which was widely popular by the early 1980s (du Gay *et al* 1996). This new technology was hugely significant in blurring the distinctions between private and public space, placing the consumer simultaneously in an internalised musical environment and an external, social location. For Bennett, the shifts in Hi-Fi design and its domestic role are profoundly gendered:

> The audio system's journey – from this genteel desire to hide in the 1950s post-war home to an almost menacing display of technology in the 1970s and 1980s – is equally the story of a gender war over dominance in the domestic interior (2003: 78).

In recent years the proliferation and wide availability of domestic audio components has continued. As well as the increasing familial atomisation encouraged by contemporary house design and smaller families, audio consumption has become part of a media-saturated and fragmented domestic environment. Although much contemporary housing, particularly the 'executive' variety, is advertised on the basis of the number of bedrooms, this is an inaccurate description of room use. With the birth rate declining, these 'bedrooms' are actually more typically employed for atomised, computer / media-related 'leisure' uses. Another factor to be considered is the increased number of single parent or stepparent households. There has been no significant re-search that investigates how the break-up of the 'nuclear family' has contributed toward the use of sonic space in the domestic context. However, we might conjecture that autonomous space could well have a high priority in less biologically organic households. We can scale down Hakim Bey's work on "Temporary Autonomous Zones" (Bey 2004) from the macro-social terrain, to the micro-intimate within con-temporary house design, leisure patterns and recent family habitation trends.

As my earlier research (2000) indicates, the social appreciation of a single-sense medium (a family all listening to the radio or a piece of music) is now an outdated and unfamiliar occurrence. Indeed, recent evidence suggests that the pop single format – the traditional 'way in' to music appreciation for young people, is rapidly declining in terms of both sales and cultural capital (Branigan 2003: 6). The marginalisa-tion of the single, and indeed CDs in general within large entertain-ment stores such as Virgin and HMV in favour of ring tones, DVD and Play Station software is most evident. It is almost as if the promo-tional mixed media (music television, mobile phones, pop videos) are now themselves the primary source of music, rather than merely ad-vertisements for another single-sense product (recorded music).

More typically, one family member will be watching television on a home cinema, multi-speaker system, whilst another plays computer games whilst listening to two sources of sound / music, whilst another watches music TV – all in separate social spaces (some, in 'bed-rooms'!), within the same household. Although on one level, all of these family members may be consuming truly hi-fidelity sound, they are no longer Hi-Fi enthusiasts, or Stereo'types' with all the connota-tions such descriptions evoke. It is significant that the shelf space given over to traditional Hi-Fi separates in British stores such as Richer Sounds is now slowly being marginalised by that granted to DVD and the 'home cinema' multi-speaker playback system. Whereas stereophony was once enough, now there have to be five or six speak-ers to give true fidelity. So, the Stereo'types' must adapt.

The spatial confinement of the road vehicle, complete with stereo system, has offered an alternative to the atomised domestic space, with whole families encouraged to participate in the same listening experience. However, two factors militate against the car functioning as a truly intimate, single-sense environment. Firstly, the possibilities of 'shutting out' the visual component are much reduced in a mobile environment, thus rendering listening part of a multi-sense experience. Secondly, the most recent development in mobile media is the introduction of the DVD experience, for at least some of those travelling. This innovation once more threatens to marginalise sound in favour of an audio-visual experience. Again, a degree of atomisation, albeit in an intimate space, is the by-product: the viewer supersedes the listener.

Back to 'Ambient' Sonic Architecture

Having historicised the development of spatial sonic architecture, and suggested the divergence of listening modes between the ageing stereotypes and today's youth, I would now like to break with linear argument by again delving back into domestic history. Keightley's fascinating account of the refinement of a gendered domestic space in the US in the decade following the late 1940s provides a template for its extrapolation into the UK domestic space of the late 1960s onwards. As previously indicated, for reasons of simple economics alone, Britain followed in the wake of US Hi-Fi domestic developments by at least a decade.

Keightley's thesis (with parallels to Bennett's work already discussed), distilled from a wide range of sources and disciplines, argues for a gendered dimension within the development of domestic Hi-Fi. Perceptions that the domestic space was becoming increasingly feminised in the post-war period, were countered by middle-class males through the utilisation of volume, mastery over technology, and the architectural dominance over interior space offered by the home stereo system:

> Big, ugly stereos are a bloke thing [...] the audio nerd is almost exclusively male...as is the desire to place a spaceship-like lump of brushed aluminium and black plastic into the heart of a carefully constructed interior (Bennett 2003: 78).

In this scenario, Hi-Fi was seen as a bastion of male 'anti-social' leisure against the re-inscription of open-plan social space in the home that the television, as focal point, encouraged. Males were perceived to feel 'trapped' within this familial 'togetherness' (Keightley 1996: 153). A semiotic analysis of the advertising and articles in the Hi-Fi journals of the time reinforces this thesis, with terms such as 'transported' and 'escape' articulating a symbolic yearning for masculine marginality or liminal status. In a sense, the alternative world offered by Hi-Fi resembles the metaphorical state offered by more physical spaces such as the shed, garage, or games room, or of course the car. The term for the component Hi-Fi system – 'separates' – can be seen as a classic example of double coding in this context, with the male separated both physically and metaphorically. This gendered scenario sees the development of the 'Hi-Fi widow', alienated by technology, volume, the anally retentive nature of collecting and cataloguing, and exclusive individualism. Even the storage of the CD collection can be deconstructed along gender-specific lines. The importance of the masculinised 'trophy racks' for displaying, and holding power over the music catalogue can be judged by the range of designs given over to this artefact in a store such as *IKEA*. Although 'feminine' wood cabinets to 'hide away' the CD collection are also available, they are always far outnumbered by the multifarious racks self-consciously proclaiming their space. As a final observation, it is clear that the development of stereophonic headphones – whose domestic use is often a 'guy thing' – only further exacerbates this gendered bifurcation:

> High fidelity represented a moment of masculine involvement not only in the arrangement of the domestic interior, but also in commodity consumption during a period when women still controlled the majority of retail expenditures (Keightley 1996: 172).

As Keightley concludes, many of the conflicts between the sexes and adults became inter-generational in the following decades, not least over the issues of musical genre and volume. In fact, it could be argued that Britain's comparative lack of affluence and domestic space, compared to the US, automatically grounded the sites of conflict in a different domestic terrain. However, the two countries have both seen a relaxation in the rigid gender-based appropriations of domestic space and domestic duties over the past few decades. It could be argued that the 'feminisation' of male leisure and behavioural patterns (men now shop! men now clean!) has diminished the need for overt and oppositional male spaces in the home. Television consumption is no longer thought of as implicitly feminine, and greater affluence has allowed for the establishment of alternative communal or anti-social spaces in the home, leading to the simultaneous, multi-media patterns of consumption that I outlined above.

Accompanying recent shifts in media technology (and associated shifts in functional domestic space) are changes in the modes of consumption and sonic status. Kassabian builds upon the distinction between "active listening" and "passive hearing" (with its clear connections to Barthes' "mythologists" and "listeners") to talk of the superseding of such binary oppositions within contemporary states of ambience. She argues that "since the mid-to-late 1980s, background music *has become* foreground music" (Kassabian 2002: 134, original emphasis) in the sense that what was formerly background music (or muzak, in its broadest sense) has largely been superseded by less anodyne forms, often disseminated in an ambient, public, 'sourceless', and omnipresent mode. This results in the partial dissolution of the distinctions between public and private space, leading to the concept of 'ubiquitous listening'. This mode of consumption disarticulates sound from its source, "taking place without calling conscious attention to itself as an activity in itself" (Kassabian 2002: 37-8). In opposition to the intimacy offered by genres such as folk or singer-songwriter, the last thirty years have witnessed the growth of the meta-genre of Dance. Much research has concerned itself with the ramifications of this "transcendental signifier" (Reynolds 1998; Rietveld 1998; Garratt 1998). For present purposes, the popularity of dance as both a musical meta-genre and a social activity stands as symbolic of the partial migration of music consumption from the personal to the communal space. Dance genres such as techno, trance and drum 'n' bass most aptly suit a large, usually indoor space. Despite dance not having the explicitly iconic dimension associated with the rock gig, dance venues are still resolutely mixed media. The sonic elements are important, although typically as a component part of the whole. Club-goers are not specifically, or exclusively, 'listeners'.

In the domestic space, young people now typically consume popular music as part of a multi-media text – whether music television or a computer game, or whilst partaking in another activity. In addition, domestic architecture has played its part in this process. In the 1950s the typical British household made great use of absorbent materials and surfaces (heavy curtains, flock wallpaper, thick carpets, large numbers of cloth-covered sofas and armchairs). The trend from the 1960s onwards has been towards a more minimal and modernist use of space and surfaces that is far more sonically reflective ('through lounges', bare walls, glass, metal, wooden or tiled floors). This encourages less containment and more sound leakage, leading on to the inevitable distracted reception as ambient sound reverberates. If we compare the reverberant, and often chaotic sonic environment of many contemporary restaurants, to the more absorbent and calming ambiences of more traditional eating establishments, such shifts become, often painfully clear – at least in conceptual, rather than empirical terms.

Music has become an important component part of the mobile phone. Most recently, downloading musical dial tones based on chart hits has become a huge source of income to the music industry. Again, this renders music part of an audio-visual experience. The popularity of the Walkman has waned over the last few years, threatened by the need of the young to be contactable by mobile phone. However, the growth of text messaging does allow for the two technologies to be combined in one multi-tasking media activity. In addition, the very recent popularity of large memory personal music sources, such as the *I-Pod* and other variants, does maintain audio consumption in the ever-expanding field of media consumption. However, the phenomenon whereby music fans are now dispensing with their CDs in favour of downloading their collections onto a hard drive will only perhaps encourage more distracted reception, with music consumption accompanying another activity. These recent shifts cannot be fully assimilated into the changing aesthetics of sound and consumption for another few years. It is in the chaotic nature of new technologies to often be used in unintended ways, with some achieving rapid adoption, and others failing to establish themselves.

Perhaps naturally, those of us who grew up to believe that music needed to be concentrated upon, and was 'too important' to be background noise do have some problems with these multi-media phenomena. Certainly, it makes my job as a lecturer in predominantly sound-only media a difficult one, because asking a class of eighteen-year-olds to "just listen to this" is to defamiliarise them from their normal mode of consumption. What needs to be recognised is that, firstly, defamiliarisation is a very useful device, both interpretively and pedagogically, and secondly, that it is probably my generation that is the aberrant one.

The shifting nature of music production and mixing must also be considered when exploring the phenomenon of ubiquitous listening. The last twenty years have seen a change in the nature of sound reproduction that has slowly filtered down from the ambient, or experimental 'underground', to infiltrate the commercial 'mainstream' (Prendergast 2000). In empirical terms – if we become critical mythologists – one of the clearest manifestations of this process has been through the increase in 'sub-bass' frequencies. As previously noted, the deeper the frequency, the less likely we are to register its specific architectural origin. Thus, music appears to become ubiquitous, or paradoxically, to originate from within the body itself. Since the introduction of the 'ghetto blaster', in the late-1970s, a common signifier of a superior quality item has been the separate bass speaker. In my household, the ghetto blaster features the 'power drive woofer' as its literal and metaphorical centrepiece. When this function is activated, a red light comes on, the sound mix shifts to foreground sub-bass frequencies, and the woofer itself advertises its role by 'flexing', so not only can this element be felt and heard, but also seen – a multi-media, sensory, ambient experience. This phenomenon can also be literally felt within car-based stereo systems possessing huge sub-bass capability. Again, the aforementioned ubiquity of dance forms has played a significant part in foregrounding sonic elements best experienced at huge volume in a communal space. Genres such as rap, and R 'n' B (and forms now termed 'urban') – loosely contained under the dance umbrella – have always placed great store by the prevalence of bass frequencies. The health implications of these sonic and consumptional shifts, in terms of hearing loss and conditions such as tinnitus are only just becoming evident, but some commentators have talked of such problems in terms of 'epidemic' proportions.

In the contemporary mainstream, if we compare the sonic characteristics of recordings from the likes of Celine Dion, with her historical, generic 'equivalents' (say, Barbra Streisand in the 1960s, or Anita Baker in the 1980s), the increased prominence and emphasis of sub-bass, even on 'middle-of-the-road' tracks such as 'A New Day Has Come' (Nova and Moccio 2002) is significant and deeply symbolic. As I am writing this section, I am listening to two different mixes of this track, which effectively 'flood' my speakers with bass frequencies, to the point at which they 'flap'. There are two points to make: firstly, this is music aimed at a conservative demographic; secondly, if I was to play other, far more challenging or 'radical' music examples from the past (for example punk, metal, or jazz-rock), this system overload would not occur until the amplifier volume was increased.

What does this sonic experiment tell us (apart from the fact that I need a more powerful set of speakers)? It suggests that contemporary music production contributes to an unseen, largely unacknowledged transformation of space. Listening modes have changed, partly because of the nature of sound production, thus effacing the recognition of the very phenomenon that I have outlined. The nature of sound perception, and its contemporary ubiquity, discourages reflexive appreciation. Mythologists will say: "listen to what is happening here, and gauge its social significance"; listeners, however, will metaphorically breathe, be immersed, and move around in an amniotic, ambient sonic environment. After Barthes, however, the one state does not preclude the recognition of the other. Just as train travellers can refocus their visual perception, so active listeners can acknowledge their sonic perception. Kassabian (1999) argues convincingly that the implications of consuming ambient, or 'ubiquitous' sounds are considerable, not least as they impact upon a western value system based on notions of high art and authenticity. Academia has long fought against taking the 'popular' seriously. Although the battle to include popular forms on syllabi has been partly won, the incorporation of 'populist' forms poses a still greater problem. Not only do we need to study the Clash and Kate Bush alongside Brahms and Puccini, but we also need to study muzak and 'unauthored sound'. The nature of sonic perception has changed – perhaps it has become desensitised, but we now need to widen our scope. I am arguing for the necessary (re)birth of the mythologising, active *listener*, at the inevitable expense of the passive *hearer*.

A Life of Longing Behind the Bedroom Door: Adolescent Space and the Makings of Private Identity

Jo Croft

ABSTRACT

This essay takes as its starting point the proposition that adolescence is a time during which a different set of spatial relationships emerge, both between the subject and the house, and between the subject's psyche and body. The discussion of adolescent bedrooms is framed thematically, rather than historically and focuses primarily upon examples found in literary texts produced in the twentieth century, such as Sue Townsend's The Secret Diary of Adrian Mole, Aged 13 ¾, *Martin Amis'* The Rachel Papers, *and Denton Welch's* In Youth is Pleasure. *The author draws upon psychoanalytic theory, particularly the work of Winnicott and Kristeva, in order to consider how and where play figures in the adolescent domestic landscape. Using Susan Stewart's idea of "the house within a house", the final section takes the doll's house as a possible site of excessive interiority and explores the significance of such multiple layers of internal space in relation to adolescence itself.*

Introduction

"The bedroom, in my view, lacks *conclusion*" (Michaux 1992: 149, original emphasis).

Dark, messy, intimate, inaccessible: in our most familiar mythologies about houses, adolescent bedrooms feature as slightly comical but also slightly threatening places, and this tells us something about the ambivalence shaping our broader cultural relationship to adolescence. By looking at adolescent bedrooms in this essay, I want to raise some questions about the ways we use domestic space to invoke, both privately and publicly, an 'inner' psychical element in our lives. There is perhaps something obvious – corny, even – about the attempt to bring together these two different connotations of 'interiority': the 'inwardness' of adolescent subjectivity and the interior space of the bedroom itself. And yet, by focusing upon this tendency to conflate domestic interior space with the interiority of the individual subject, we can perhaps try to rethink some of our assumptions about how the 'inside' of our bodies relates to the 'inside' of our houses.

Private – Keep Out

I begin with the premise that the changed status of the adolescent body somehow ushers in a changed relationship to domestic space. We associate adolescence with a longing to be private, and if there is an adolescent sense of place, it seems to be insistently bound to a highly insecure idea of the 'private subject'. Ideally, the private space that the adolescent seeks to inhabit is furnished with hiding places – doors that can be locked, mirrors that can be looked at in secret, somewhere where the body can be secretly scrutinised. This space, whether it is a bedroom, a bathroom, a wardrobe, a chest or a piece of writing, must somehow shore up, or protect, the fragile boundaries of the adolescent body. But of course not all adolescents actually have a "room of one's own" (Woolf 1929), and adolescence itself is by no means a universal, ahistorical category anyway.[1] In other words, there is a sense that my discussion here relates to the kind of space *sought out* by adolescents, an idealised adolescent room. I am interested, above all, in the adolescent's *longing* for private space, rather than the adolescent's actual possession of their own bedroom, and all of the literary texts that I am going to focus upon in this chapter are shaped, albeit in very different ways, by an insistent yet thwarted desire to find a space that 'fits' their feelings. For instance, in my first two examples – *The Secret Diary of Adrian Mole Aged 13 ¾*, by Sue Townsend (1982), and *The Rachel Papers*, by Martin Amis (1973) – the narrators' bedrooms are explicitly represented as *constituents* of their adolescent identities. In my third example, Denton Welch's 1950 autobiographical novel *In Youth is Pleasure*, we witness a far more complex rendering of adolescent space, where the adolescent protagonist seeks out more and more intensely confining internal spaces – wardrobes and even drawers – in order to express his own ambivalent sensuality. In the last part of the essay I shall consider two texts, *The Silent Twins* by Marjorie Wallace, and *The Lovely Bones* by Alice Sebold, which exemplify thwarted adolescent desire in particularly disturbing ways.

Perhaps most significantly, all of these texts show how adolescence is associated with a sense of dislocation, whereby the relationship between mind and body, or perhaps between inside and outside, is felt to be crisis-bound. Janet Sayers, a psychoanalyst, offers this fascinating example of the adolescent's dislocated self-consciousness in her book, *Boy Crazy: Remembering Adolescence, Therapies and Dreams:*

> A writer friend in his sixties tells me that, beginning when he was 13 and continuing through his teens, he found himself sometimes so horribly conscious of his body he would rush into the next room to get away, only to find, of course, that his body was still with him. He last found himself thus trying to rush away from himself when he was particularly upset on leaving home for college (1998: 45).

The boy here is overwhelmed with a sense of estrangement from his own body, and clearly there is nowhere he feels *at home* – not within his own skin, and not within the walls of his family's house. The urge to "rush away from himself" is thus explicitly expressed in terms which muddle up inside and outside, body and room. Another psycho-analyst, Moses Laufer, offers further poignant examples of adolescent bodily crisis in his paper 'Adolescent Sexuality: A Mind / Body Continuum' (1989). Laufer cites the case history of an adolescent with severe paranoia who feels that "it is as if his body is both the persecutor and his ally" (1989: 286). He also describes how another adolescent "felt as if her body was dead or not her own" (1989: 287). For Laufer, then, the adolescent's sense of their own physicality is profoundly dislocated: a gap has opened up between mind and body, and there seems to be no place that is not haunted by ambivalence:

> Before puberty they could maintain the belief that they could be omnipotent without being sexual. Physical sexual maturity suddenly shattered this illusion and confronted them with the reality of their body as being inadequate and dangerous at the same time (1989: 291).

Play Room

Teenagers, it seems, are both alien to, and contained by the values and routines of everyday family life. And it follows that the rooms inhabited by these borderline subjects also seem to occupy a peculiarly borderline sexual terrain, caught between the parental heterosexual conventions of the 'master bedroom' and the comforting sentiments of the child's bedroom. Sue Townsend's *The Secret Diary of Adrian Mole aged 13 ¾* offers a droll example of this with Adrian Mole's unsuccessful attempt to conceal his 'Noddy' bedroom wallpaper:

I have decided to paint my room black; it is a colour I like. I can't live a moment
longer with Noddy wallpaper. At my age it is positively indecent to wake up to
Big Ears and all of the rest of the Toyland idiots running around the walls. My father says I can use any colour I like as long as I buy the paint and do it myself [...]
I have decided to become a poet [...] Now put on two coats of black paint! Noddy
still showing through! Black paw-marks over landing and stairs. Can't get paint
off hands. Hairs falling out of brush. Fed up with whole thing. Room looks dark
and gloomy. Father hasn't lifted a finger to help. Black paint everywhere (Townsend 1982: 80-1).

Adrian Mole's urgent redecoration represents, in comically literal
terms, how adolescence seeks to establish itself over and against the
patterns of childhood. Townsend, of course, emphasises that Mole's
nihilistic decorating is ineffectual: his bathetic declarations that he
"can't live a moment longer with Noddy Wallpaper" illustrates how
the self-consciously apocalyptic gestures of adolescence still inevitably contain traces of earlier, more optimistic identifications. Adrian
Mole aims to obliterate the sentimentality of Enid Blyton's "Toyland
idiots", and chooses black paint to transform his room into an oppositional version of domestic space. Perhaps most revealingly, though,
Mole's newly asserted "poet" identity is beleaguered by messy and
incomplete boundaries, and his transformation of the room serves instead to accentuate Mole's bodily and domestic chaos ("Black paint
everywhere").

Townsend's satire turns upon a version of adolescent identity inflected with the remnants of a child's vocabulary and grammar. Nevertheless, Adrian Mole's incomplete attempt to banish 'childish
things' still leaves us with a sense that his bedroom can no longer be a
playroom as such. Playing, in other words, does not seem to be part of
a conventional understanding of adolescent space. In Western discourses of childhood, it is the wish to *contain* play that tends to dominate any consideration of children's domestic space. So much is
obvious – we expect children to play, and we also expect that children's play is both potentially disruptive and necessary.[2] But is there
such a thing as adolescent play? I want to suggest that playing does
not simply disappear from adolescent space, but rather that it takes
different forms. Whether it takes place in the bedroom, in the diary, or
in the head, adolescent play seems to turn inwards, away from those
fantasy landscapes conjured in childhood games and stories, and towards a newly configured *inner self*. Adolescence, as I have already
suggested, tends to be characterised by a dislocated, ambivalent
relationship to the subject's own body. It follows, then, that adolescent

tionship to the subject's own body. It follows, then, that adolescent play should be an activity staged around the borders of the adolescent's body itself – such a body, after all is both "dead" and estranged, "inadequate and dangerous", its own "persecutor and ally" (Laufer 1989: 286-91).

D.W. Winnicott's work on playing in his 1971 text *Playing and Reality* seems utterly preoccupied with the idea of *location*. In the chapter 'The Location of Cultural Experience' for example, he explores different ways of approaching the question: "Where is play?" (113). Crucially, he partly answers his own question by placing play firmly on a borderline – emphatically in-between: "Play is in fact neither a matter of inner psychic reality nor a matter of external reality" (113). This then produces a further question for Winnicott: "[If] play is neither inside nor outside, where is it?" (112.). For Winnicott, an answer of sorts lies in the idea of a *"potential space"* (original emphasis):

> The place where cultural experience is located is in the *potential space* between the individual and the environment (originally the object). The same can be said of playing. Cultural experience begins with creative living first manifested in play (118).

The map that Winnicott sketches of this borderline terrain of "cultural experience" is one that equates the in-betweenness of play with a positive notion of potentiality. In turn we might equate this ideal 'potential space' with the daydreaming playground that Bachelard set outs in *The Poetics of Space*:

> [The] house shelters daydreaming, the house protects the dreamer, the house allows one to dream in peace. Thought and experience are not the only things that sanction human values. The values that belong to daydreaming mark humanity in its depths. Daydreaming even has a privilege of autovalorization. It derives direct pleasure from its own being. Therefore, the places in which we have *experienced daydreaming* reconstitute themselves in a new daydream, and it is because our memories of former dwelling-places are relived as daydreams that these dwelling-places of the past remain in us for all time (1994: 6, original emphasis).

Perhaps then, we could say that daydreaming occupies the space of playing for the adolescent. As with Winnicott's "potential space", however, what Bachelard describes seems very much an idealised psychic structure. As a counter to this, maybe, Bachelard much later in his book cites the French poet Henri Michaux from 1952: "Space, but you cannot even conceive the horrible inside-outside that real space is" (1994: 216). Here we are presented with a far more insecure rendering of an 'in-between space'. Michaux's phrase "the horrible inside-outside" could just as well be describing the ambivalence of adolescent space, with its troubled boundaries between body and self. Adolescent bedrooms are places where a number of borderlines coincide, and their occupants are presented with an over-determination of 'in-between' possibilities. No wonder, then, that we sometimes find them such unsettling, unsettled places to be.

Go To Your Room!
So what do we imagine actually happens in adolescent bedrooms? Children's bedrooms seem, rather confusingly, to combine or juxtapose the activities of playing and sleeping. Typically, an 'ideal' bedroom for a young child – with its gendered pastel colours, soft toys and nostalgic images from children's books – bears the imprint of a parental desire for its occupants to be sweet and calm and sleepy. This impulse to exert control over the childhood realm of sleep (an area of children's lives most explicitly bound to the unconscious), is powerfully conveyed in J.M. Barrie's description of Mrs. Darling "tidying up her children's minds" when they are asleep:

> Mrs. Darling first heard of Peter when she was tidying up her children's minds. It is the nightly custom of every good mother after her children are asleep to rummage in their minds and put things straight for next morning, repacking into their proper places the many articles that have wandered during the day [...] When you wake in the morning, the naughtiness and evil passions with which you went to bed have been folded up small and placed at the bottom of your mind; and on top, beautifully aired, are spread out your prettier thoughts, ready for you to put on (Barrie 1911: 12-13).

At times, however, the control exercised by parents over the child's domestic space can mean that a bedroom also comes to represent the very opposite of play: when the command to 'go to your room' is used as an injunction against games that have 'gone too far'. Maurice Sendak's *Where the Wild Things Are* offers a clear demonstration of this function of the bedroom as a "spatial symbol of punishment" or banishment (James *et al* 1998: 39). In Sendak's story, Max "made mischief of one kind [...] and another" (1988: 1-3) and so is sent to his room without any supper. The narrative of this picture book is a familiar one within the canon of children's literature[3] in that it turns upon the idea of the bedroom not only as a place of confinement but also as a site of imaginative transformation: "That very night in Max's room a forest grew and grew and grew until his ceiling hung with vines and the walls became the world all around" (7-12). Vitally, though, such transformations also require that the comfort of domesticity is re-affirmed for the child. After his bedroom adventures Max returns to the wider domestic realm "where he found his supper waiting for him [...] and it was still hot" (35-7).

However, adolescent bedrooms are not so readily associated with this return to a bounded domestic order. Instead, they seem to be held in a peculiar tension with family life – sought out not as places of banishment, but of self-willed exclusion, or perhaps even sanctuary. In other words, adolescent bedrooms mark out a space relatively protected from adult regulation, associated with the assertion of a distinct, individuated identity at odds with a discourse of the integrated nuclear family. However stereotypical, the accessories that furnish adolescent space – posters, loud music, dirty clothes – are read as signs of self-expression. And despite, or perhaps because of, their associations with uncertainty and liminality, it could be argued that adolescent bedrooms can also be places of exploration, and creativity, where identity itself becomes an object of play.

Dressing Room
Martin Amis's 1973 novel of adolescence, *The Rachel Papers*, exemplifies this impulse to *play* with identity. Amis's adolescent protagonist, Charles Highway, draws an explicit and self-conscious link between his feelings and his bedroom:

> *Highway's London*, one of my note-pads, has it that I found the room 'oppressive, sulky with the past, crouching in wan defiance as I turned to look at it' on that September Sunday. My word. I suppose I was just moodier then, or more respectful of my moods, more inclined to think they were worth anything (1973: 15).

Not only does Charles Highway look upon his room as a reflection of his emotional state, he also uses it socially, rather like a stage set, as a means to fabricate and promote a particular version of himself. For example, when he prepares for his new girlfriend's visit, he arranges objects in the room to reflect a more 'desirable' version of himself:

As I dressed I thought about the setting up of the room. I couldn't be as slapdash as I had been with Gloria. It was a hundred to one that I wouldn't get her even into the house, but all the same everything had to be […] just so. I assembled the relevant pads and folders, stroked my chin.

Not knowing her views on music I decided to play it safe; I stacked the records upright in two parallel rows: at the head of the first I put *2001: A Space Odyssey* (can't be wrong); at the second I put a selection of Dylan Thomas's verse, read by the poet himself. Kleenex well away from the bed: having them actually on the bedside chair was tantamount to a poster reading 'The big thing about me is that I wank a devil of a lot.' The coffee table featured a couple of Shakespeare texts and a copy of *Time Out* – an intriguing dichotomy, perhaps, but I was afraid that, no, it wouldn't quite do. The texts were grimy and twisted after a year of A-Level doodling. *The Poetry of Meditation*, in fact a scholarly American work on the Metaphysicals, although from the cover it could have been a collection of beatnik verse: Rachel could interpret as she wished (46).

Amis's parodic portrayal of adolescence is structured almost entirely around the process of editing, whether at the level of re-arranging furniture and objects, or at the level of writing itself. Charles Highway uses his notebooks not only to reflect upon his life but also to anticipate and revise events and relationships. For instance, by ironically asserting that "Rachel could interpret as she wished", the narrator actually draws attention to his prediction, and circumscription, of her interpretations. Charles attempts to write and rewrite his own identity, much like any other text, and crucially, through the bedroom, he reads himself back to himself as an object of desire. It is almost as if he uses his cultural capital (Bourdieu 1984: *passim*) rather than his body to seduce Rachel, and in doing so he eroticises his intellectual props (books, records, magazines) in order to expunge a more literal bodily presence in the room (tissues that betray his masturbation). Throughout the novel his self-scrutiny is saturated with *literariness*, and the space he occupies most insistently and successfully is not his bedroom at all, but his reams and reams of writing. Whereas life outside of his notebooks may be replete with hesitations and failures of communication, within his writing Amis's narrator can sustain a sophisticated, embellished narrative, one that is not riven by conflicting emotional and intellectual demands. As Amis himself later commented in his autobiography, *Experience* (2000), about his own situation when *The Rachel Papers* was published: "My life looked good on paper – where, in fact, almost all of it was being lived" (2000: 33).

Writing Room

Julia Kristeva's short essay, 'The Adolescent Novel' (1990) also emphasises this close association between adolescence and writing. Kristeva insists that the adolescent is "less an age category than an open psychic structure" (8), and crucially she aligns this structure with particular registers in literary production. Writing, she suggests, is associated with "anal mastery [...] within a narcissistic masturbatory gratification", "a stereotyped writing of clichés", or alternatively "the feeling of utilizing, at last and for the first time in his life, a living discourse, one that is not empty, not an 'as if'" (9). Perhaps most significantly Kristeva also stresses that "[through] its solitary economy, writing protects the subject from phobic affects, and if it enables him to re-elaborate his psychic space, it also withdraws that space from reality testing" (10). Here, crucially, Kristeva not only talks about "psychic space" (somehow implying therefore that 'psyches need space'), but she also locates writing itself in the position of a shelter (it "protects") or a screen ("it withdraws"). It is not too a big a leap, then, to draw an analogy between this "solitary economy [of] writing" and adolescent domestic space itself. And if, as Kristeva argues, writing can offer to the adolescent a psychically protected, withdrawn kind of shelter, it follows that adolescents may seek out its physical equivalent within the house. Adolescence, in other words, conjures up a peculiarly overlapping association between domestic space and the space of writing itself. Whether in the form of a bedroom or a journal, adolescent space allows us to express our private selves. By closing doors and hiding away, we show our need for privacy in spatial terms. When we choose to write a secret journal, or a poem, or a letter with no destination, we are also defining the physical boundaries of our private, psychic selves: "The action of the secret passes continually from the hider of things to the hider of self" (Bachelard 1994: 88).

More confusingly, though, when we write secretly, or when we seek out secret spaces within the house, we are also playing with possibility of exposure. Paradoxically, we imagine a possible reader or onlooker for even these most private versions of our selves. In other words, private space is haunted, at its edges, by a ghostly audience, both "persecutor and ally" – sometimes adoring, sometimes threatening, but always there.

Furniture
Bachelard devotes a chapter of his book, 'Drawers, Chests and Wardrobes', to these secret spaces:

> Wardrobes with their shelves, desks with their drawers, and chests with their false bottoms are veritable organs of the secret psychological life [...] They are hybrid objects, subject objects. Like us, through us and for us, they have a quality of intimacy.
>   Does there exist a single dreamer of words who does not respond to the word wardrobe? (1994: 79).

Strikingly, Bachelard draws an association here between the intimate space of the wardrobe and the 'dreamer of words', arguably the literary subject. Like Bachelard's *The Poetics of Space*, Denton Welch's autobiographical novel, *In Youth Is Pleasure*, is replete with images of secret spaces: huts, bedrooms, bathrooms, caves, cloakrooms, wardrobes. Also like Bachelard, Welch interweaves physical and linguistic forms of shelter. Welch's protagonist, Orvil, seeks comfort and pleasure both in the discovery of private hiding places and in literature itself. For instance, the following lines from *In Youth is Pleasure* show how literary and domestic space can converge, as the adolescent seeks both to satisfy his desire and to defend himself from the threatening presence of other people:[4]

> Suddenly, as he gazed thus, blankly, he was overcome with an immense hunger. He passed rapidly through the court to get a book from the writing-room beyond. He knew a book in his hand or on his knee would give him confidence, alone in that throng. It would also add to the pleasure of the food (1950: 39).

Perhaps most remarkably, Welch's novel features a scene where Orvil actually climbs into a wardrobe, as part of an intimate ritual:

> During the next few days, Orvil became strongly influenced by the old fashioned book on physical culture. What had been taken up so idly grew to have great importance for him. Before breakfast every morning he lay on the grey carpet in his bedroom and raised his legs painfully. He delighted in the tightening and hardening and aching of his stomach muscles. He lay face down, his nose buried in the dusty pile, and then raised himself, taking his whole weight on his arms. He twisted his trunk, his neck, his arms, his wrists, his ankles – everything that could be twisted. At the end of the exercises, he went to the wide-open window and took enormous breaths of air, throwing out his arms in a pontifical gesture; then he stripped both eiderdowns off the beds and, wrapping them tightly round him, shut

himself up in the wardrobe. He did this in an attempt to bring about a profuse sweating; this was something the book strongly recommended.

In spite of the violent exercise and the stifling layers of quilt, Orvil never considered that he sweated enough. So one morning he decided not to get into the wardrobe but to shut himself in an even more confined space, the bottom drawer of the dressing-chest. Being small, he found he was able to fit into the drawer, but as soon as he tried to shut it, by pushing against the drawer above, he was overwhelmed with the horror of being a prisoner (1950: 43).

There is a strangely spiralling quality to this passage as Welch's adole-scent protagonist moves from the pages of his "old fashioned book" onto the carpet, and then from the wardrobe into the chest of drawers. Orvil's bodily rituals here are intimately connected to the physical space of the room and its furniture. And so, as Orvil explores his own body – its "tightening and hardening and aching", its twisting and its sweating – he becomes caught up in an erotic relationship with the room and its furniture. Significantly, he seeks out confinement, initially by burying himself in the "dusty pile" of the carpet, and then by shutting himself in the smallest space he can find, wrapped in 'the stifling layers of quilt'. Throughout *In Youth is Pleasure*, Orvil is impelled by an overwhelmingly ambivalent, narcissistic sensuality that, in turn, is shot through with fantasies of imprisonment and punitive physical restraint.

Prison

What might lie behind this adolescent desire to be confined, then? How do we account for an impulse that seems in many ways to go against the grain of adolescent desires: surely, after all, adolescence is most typically associated with a desire to *escape* domestic confinement? And yet, adolescent space is most typically constituted as a withdrawn, potentially phobic realm – a space, in other words, whose excessive inwardness closely resembles that of confinement. Both in his fiction and his journals, the prison is a powerful and recurrent motif for Denton Welch, not least because, after a terrible cycling accident when he was twenty, he himself was often confined to bed (Dela-Noy 1984). Paradoxically, perhaps, his prisons are places of imaginary escape where Orvil, or Welch himself can be consumed by a heightened awareness of literary language:

Orvil sat in the snug bathroom. As usual, he imagined himself locked in there forever. 'What would I do if I were a prisoner locked in a cell no larger than this?' he thought. 'Would I go mad? What would I think about to keep myself sane? My food would be put through the skylight and I'd have nothing to watch all day but that tiny patch of light waxing and waning.'

His set of circumstances changed. He still had a room no larger than a bathroom, but he was rich and free now, if extremely recluse. The walls of his tiny hermitage were entirely encrusted with precious stones, enamel and painting. There would be diamonds, sapphires, rubies, emeralds, topazes, carbuncles, garnets, agates, onyxes, aquamarines, jades, quartzes, pearls, amethysts, zircons, chalcedony, carnelian, turquoise, malachite, amber. Whenever he learned a new name he added it to his list (Welch 1950: 55).

16 September. In Bed. Ten to four p.m.
I seem to have spent a great deal of my childhood in prison – other people's prisons. The Black Tulip prison, the French Revolution prisons, the Spanish Inquisition prisons. And the horror of those prisons was so real to me that I often look back and vaguely remember the straw, the filthy food, the oozing walls and the toads on the floor, as if I were really once in that situation. Whenever I hear about prisons I seem to imagine that I have experienced confinement myself (*The Journals of Denton Welch* 1952: 108-9).

It is no doubt significant that the protagonist of *In Youth is Pleasure* has experienced a childhood and adolescence without any clearly defined familial home. Orvil's mother has been dead for several years, and he has been sent away to boarding school, only meeting up with his father very occasionally in hotels and restaurants. In his hotel room Orvil seems, through his strange routines, to want to conjure up a version of domestic intimacy, albeit in a distorted and exaggerated way. We could argue then, that Orvil *wants* to be confined, because confinement offers precisely the shelter that he lacks. However, I think that *In Youth is Pleasure* also offers a far broader insight into the relationship between adolescence and domestic space. As with the example cited by Janet Sayers of the teenager who rushes "into the next room to get away, only to find, of course, that his body was still with him" (1998: 45), there is a sense in Welch's novel that the borderlines between the adolescent's inside and outside have become blurred or tangled up. More specifically, for Orvil, it is as if his *internal* space has somehow leaked into the *external* domestic space that surrounds him. By wrapping himself in his quilt and climbing into the wardrobe, he seems to want to create further layers of protection against some threatened loss of bodily boundaries. At the same time, though, Orvil also extends or blurs the limits of his body by revelling in its contact with the surfaces around him: he sweats into the quilt, and rubs himself against the carpet. The adolescent's ecstatic and phobic state seems to pull him in two directions, both towards the outside ("the garden beyond") and back towards "some very solitary place":

> Orvil, who could never resist exploring derelict places, felt impelled to get through this hole into the garden beyond. He also fiercely desired some very solitary place; for the frustration and excitement inside him were becoming almost unbearable (1950: 37).

Welch's protagonist uses the wardrobe, and his other hiding places, to access an ever-more internal space capable of accommodating his "almost unbearable" internal feelings. Bachelard describes the wardrobe's intimacy differently. Crucially, he aligns this "veritable organ of the secret psychological life" with the realm of authorship itself. Like Kristeva, Bachelard makes the connection between the desire to write, to become "a daydreamer of words" and the impulse to find shelter. Indeed, for Bachelard, the wardrobe specifically offers "a centre of order that protects the entire house against uncurbed disorder" (1994: 79), and through the protection it affords, the imagination acquires "an entity of depth" (1994: 78). More than anything, perhaps, Bachelard wants to offer his readers an idealised vision of poetic space – those places in the house which encourage us to daydream are deemed, implicitly, to be benign, and "the values that belong to daydreaming mark humanity in its depths" (1994: 6). His project defines itself as a "*positive* study of images of secrecy" containing "studies of the imagination, all of them *positive*" (1994: 78, emphases added). As Welch's writing shows, though, there are other ways in which such secret places are experienced. The adolescent imagination may well acquire *depth* once it finds for itself "some very solitary place", but such secret spaces are almost inevitably furnished by feelings of ambivalence.

Out Of The Doll's House
In this final section I want to consider a form of domestic space which seems to be at a far remove from the teenage bedrooms occupied by the likes of Adrian Mole and Charles Highway: the doll's house. Indeed, the dark messiness of the adolescent bedroom, however contrived, is patently set against the perfectly arranged sentimentality of a doll's house interior. Nevertheless there *is* an association, however negative, between adolescence and the doll's house, not least because the doll's house occupies a space that, potentially, is *excessively inter-*

nal. Therefore, by way of conclusion, I am going to explore the doll's house as a strangely appropriate trope for the adolescent's inner world.

In her book *On Longing: Narratives of the Miniature and the Gigantic* (1993), Susan Stewart describes the doll's house as a "house within a house":

> [It not] only presents the house's articulation of the tension between inner and outer spheres, of exteriority and interiority – it also represents the tension between two modes of interiority. Occupying a space within an enclosed space, the dollhouse's aptest analogy is the locket or the secret recesses of the heart: center within center, within within within. The dollhouse is a materialized secret; what we look for is the dollhouse within the dollhouse and its promise of an infinitely profound interiority (1993: 61).

A poignant example of the destructive possibilities ushered in by the doll's house's multiple layers of interiority is suggested by Marjorie Wallace's biography, *The Silent Twins* (1986). Wallace describes how the adolescent writers, June and Jennifer Gibbons, refused to leave their bedroom, even to have meals or to speak with their family. Much of their self-imposed confinement centred upon a doll's house, which dominated the small space of their shared bedroom. Wallace writes:

> The twins, like the Brontë sisters, were cut off from the world around them, fuelled by adolescent yearning and a desire to overcome their barren surroundings. The twins' fantasy was not the swashbuckling world of Napoleonic battles nor the imperialist-dominated Glass Town; it was a *Clockwork Orange* land of violent suburban America. Their dream city was Malibu, the place where teenagers are perpetually stoned on drugs and alcohol, parents divorce and remarry and divorce again. The 'dolls' took part in gang warfare; they were hijacked on Greyhound buses; they became terrorists involved in assassination plots; they robbed stores and murdered their parents. They were the twentieth-century teenage heroes and heroines – immature, gauche and often funny (1986: 62).

In other words, the form of Kristevan "psychic space" (1990: 10) that June and Jennifer wanted to "elaborate" in their games and in their writing was a violently distorted version of 'normal' teenage life – emphatically American and delinquent, always taking place in an erotically charged, unruly social setting. June and Jennifer were prolific writers, both of diaries and fiction. Interestingly though, until Christmas 1979, when they received red diaries with locks, most of their time in the bedroom was spent playing with their doll's house. June writes "[when] I was sixteen I was still a virgin and played with dolls. We had no friends. Jennifer and I put our whole lives in for the happiness of those little human beings" (Wallace 1986: 43).

Most horrifically, the spiral of inwardness ("within within within") that Stewart associates with the doll's house was experienced as an ever-more intensified "confinement". The twins' retreat from speech and from their family was eventually realised in their appalling, literal confinement in Broadmoor. But paradoxically, this escalation of confinement never produced for them Stewart's desired "infinitely profound interiority", because their private selves were always being wiped out by the shadow of their twinship. The fragile boundaries of their adolescent bodies are perceived to be doubly besieged, not only by their own selfconsciousness, but also by the mirroring presence of another adolescent subject:

> There was always a sense of tension in the air, even when we were all playing with dolls. Jennifer's doll used to be more popular than mine. Me and my little doll, lives apart. I felt sorry for that doll. She suffered just like me, always left out, lonely in our hearts. Rosie and J. ran away from me. I felt like a monster. I felt naked and criticized (quoted in Wallace 1986: 54).

> Nobody suffers the way I do. Not with a sister. With a husband – yes. With a wife – yes. But this sister of mine, a dark shadow, robbing me of sunlight is my one and only torment (quoted in Wallace 1986: 167).

The narratives both Jennifer and June wrote about a dystopian suburban America were initially played out through intricate, morbid scenarios with their family of dolls. The props of conventional childhood play therefore become caught up with the activity of writing, but in this complex over-laying of playing and literary production, a darker terrain than that suggested by Winnicott's "potential space", or even Bachelard's "autovalorization" seems to be conjured. After she was admitted to Broadmoor, Jennifer Gibbons wrote in her diary: "At home my bedroom was a room of blood" (quoted in Wallace 1986: 172). And this "bloody" room has as its axis, a doll's house, of all things.

Alice Sebold's 2002 novel, *The Lovely Bones*, features the doll's house in perhaps the most morbid context of all: the serial killer who rapes and murders the book's adolescent narrator is also a maker of exquisite doll's houses:

> They searched the house perfunctorily and found nothing except both the evidence
> of what they took to be extreme loneliness and a room full of beautiful dollhouses
> on the second floor (2002: 192).

Sebold's narrative is riven with the darkest of internal spaces, or rather spaces *within* spaces, and offers us the most sinister rendering of Susan Stewart's "secret recesses of the heart: center within center, within within within". Perhaps most critically, though, Sebold uses a *literally* disembodied narrative voice, to delve into these layers of interiority, because her narrator, Susie Salmon, tells us her story from a place beyond death. She observes her family, her friends and her murderer from heaven, and yet also somehow lingers as a distinctly adolescent presence on earth. Even her bedroom remains in the house as a kind of shrine, or – perhaps more precisely – as a physical testimony to the unspeakability of her family's grieving:

> Already my private territory had become a no man's land in the middle of our
> house. My mother had not touched it. My bed was still unmade from the hurried
> morning of my death. My flowered hippo lay among the sheets and pillows, and
> so did an outfit I'd discarded before I chose the yellow bell-bottoms (44).

The familiar features of Susie's bedroom, with its "unmade bed" and "discarded clothes" are powerful signifiers of mourning here, because they contain faint traces of her bodily presence. Above all, though, this adolescent space, for all its ordinariness, reminds us of Susie's profound dislocation within her own house. Her adolescent body exists only as a bloody stain on the garage floor, and a collection of bones hidden in an old safe and thrown into a sinkhole by her murderer. Nevertheless, this abject vision of the adolescent body also reminds us (albeit in the most morbid way) of the adolescent bodily dislocations described at the beginning of this essay. Like the adolescents described by Janet Sayers (1998) and Moses Laufer (1989), Sebold's narrator can no longer connect up her mind with her body. Following the trajectory cast by Stewart's (and her murderer's) doll's house ("within within within"), Susie Salmon finds her feelings and her psyche cast adrift. Like Laufer's adolescent patient she experiences her body as "dead or not her own" (1986: 287), and in doing so foregrounds the adolescent's difficulty in negotiating the boundaries between external, physical identity and an inner psychic self.

Conclusion

Michaux's phrase ("the horrible inside-outside") could just as well be describing the ambivalence of adolescent space, with its contested boundaries between body and self. Even for Bachelard, it seems that particular configurations of the borderline can produce both intimacy *and* suffering:

> Outside and inside are both intimate – they are always already to be reversed, to exchange their hostility. If there exists a border-line surface between such an in-side and outside, this surface is painful on both sides (1994: 218).

In this essay I have explored various configurations of the adolescent's borderline position within the house. Daydreaming and play may well be key to how we map the topography of the adolescent bed-room, but if we understand them to be *borderline* mechanisms, then the 'in-betweenness' of this space becomes almost overwhelming. We are, as humans, never perhaps wholly at home in our own skins, and when we explore adolescent space, we are reminded of the fragile seams that keep body and soul together.

Notes

1. Philippe Ariès' *Centuries of Childhood* (1960) is a seminal text in this context.

2. Joe Moran (2002) argues that parental and societal anxieties mean that children's play is increasingly monitored and controlled.

3. See for example C.S. Lewis's *The Lion the Witch and the Wardrobe* (1950), John Burningham's *The Magic Bed* (2003) and many of the poems in Robert Louis Stevenson's *A Child's Garden of Verses* (1966), including 'My Bed is a Boat', and 'The Land of Nod'.

4. It is interesting to note that in Welch's writing, sexual and literary desire is often mediated through a conspicuously sensual relationship to food.

One Widower's Home:
Excavating Some Disturbed Meanings of Domestic Space

Joseph Boughey

ABSTRACT

Taking as its text the widowed author's experience of his own home, this chapter considers grief and loss in relation to meanings of domestic space. The paucity of literature on widowers and their experience of domestic space are set against the historically developed meanings of domesticity. The view of the house as a repository or prop for memory is contrasted with the production of space through the creation of exchange value, compared with the changing meanings of intimate personal space. Bachelard's seminal view of intimate felicitious space dominated by childhood encounter is countered by imagination related to adult experience. Economic value is related to Harvey's recent work on architecture and the use of imagination, compared to Bachelard's incomplete comments on the provision of housing. It is concluded that the idiosyncratic nature of grief and loss renders it difficult to draw general contentions about loss and domestic space. The distinction between the production of space and its experience of space does not necessarily reduce experiences of space to the ephemeral, allowing a possible celebration of domestic intimate space.

Introduction

"Writing", wrote Ronald Fraser in *In Search of a Past*, "is a way of recuperating what has been lost" (1984: 186). In this chapter, I write about some consequences of the loss of my wife Brenda in March 2002, and my relationship with the house in which we lived. Grieving is a complex process of searching and attempted resolution, in which feelings about home are embedded. For this reason, I deal here with a wide range of issues, some of which respond to Gaston Bachelard's view, in *The Poetics of Space*, of intimate felicitous space, and the critique and extensions of his concepts. I also consider the sense in which domestic space can form an archive for autobiographical memory, and the study of memory, imagination and space.

The experience of partner loss can turn a bereaved person inwards, seeking solace and meaning in a private and intimate world; or it can initiate a process of review which turns that person outwards, wondering at, and seeking, wider meanings in their loss and the lives (including those who have 'survived') that have gone. It may include personal isolation, or enlarged engagement with the world (Balk 2004). This study reflects my experience of both types of response. It considers writings in an area that is rarely seen as related to the study of domestic space – death, grief and bereavement – and attempts to relate interpretations from existential phenomenology (Attig 2004) to Bachelard's insights into space, derived from the same philosophical roots.

The review of wider issues is reflected in themes that challenge my very personal view, in the same way as the insights of existential phenomenology can be relativised, if not annihilated, by analyses from a materialist perspective. If phenomenology explains aspects of experience of the world, it is materialism that can explain how the experienced world is constructed, socially and physically. The role of economic value in the construction of domestic space is thus considered, along with corresponding views of that space, against other kinds of value.

The process of explanation is tentative and perhaps incapable of completion, corresponding to a grieving process which is rarely finally 'closed' (Attig 1996). I concur with Rosen's (1998) view of the value, indeed inevitability, of the autobiographical in much writing, even though it may seem to reflect and reveal mere idiosyncrasy. In my case, this is glaringly so: I am a middle-aged, middle-class childless widower, with a strong sense of the past (much in transport history and conservation), and I feel that memories of my wife's past may allow me to recover some meanings of our past and my own. My musings vary between personal details and more 'objective' attempts at explanation, which induce a sense of vulnerability. I should stress my unease at how particular is my loss and my perspectives. Ours is a world in which many middle-aged men do lose partners, but in which the stable maintenance of a comfortable residence is a privilege.

It is acknowledged that the meaning of 'home' is much wider than that of 'house' (Morley 2000), but here I limit domestic space to that within the legal bounds of my house, rather than the suburb in which Brenda and I lived for over forty years of our lives. In a sense, much of the external world that she knew has already changed, and our home is one area in which change has been controlled and spurs memories capable of preservation.

Experiencing Domestic Space

A personal irony in my involvement with domestic space lies in Bachelard's insistence, in the introduction to *The Poetics of Space*: "Space that has been seized upon by the imagination cannot remain indifferent space subject to the measures and estimates of the surveyor" (1994: xxxvi). Before teaching, I was a chartered surveyor, and inspected many residential properties, and later taught aspects of residential property in both property management and environmental management programmes.

My professional work included the surveying and valuing of houses for various purposes, negotiating slum clearance compensation and compulsory acquisitions, managing landlords' interests in various poor-quality investment properties, and later valuing council houses for sale. Exchange value was the dominant consideration here, and the feelings of owners or occupiers, any memories and dreams reflected in their arrangement of domestic space, rarely surfaced. The discovery of building defects might cause distress (beyond its impact on exchange value), with the idea that space fondly regarded was framed by damp walls, leaking roofs or woodworm rather than any psychic connection. In some houses due for demolition, the sentiments invested contrasted with their limited market value; and grief was encountered on occasions when a widowed person still lived in a property handled for probate purposes. Much work involved vacant properties, sometimes set out with longstanding furniture and effects, in ghostly fashion; without the people for whom meanings of this space could be related, such houses were indeed real estate alone.

In teaching, residential properties were viewed as assets to be sold or let, and my task was to discuss what underlay exchange values and how consequent professional work could be furthered profitably. Possibly the base of the value created and appropriated could be someone's wish to make a home from a house, to create and experience intimate domestic space for those they loved, and a place which could form the subject of memory. But exchange value dominated, determining a solely instrumental view of domestic space as something explicitly fostered to create and maintain economic value. I derived a

similar instrumentality from later teaching on environmental management, which viewed buildings' locations and household metabo-
lism as closely related to varied environmental impacts (Bhatti *et al*
1994; Noorman and Uiterkamp 1998; Brown and Bhatti 2003).

My feelings about domestic space partly reflected the instrumental-
ism of professional work; my main concerns in selecting my house in
1992 were its accessibility for public transport and the suitability of
one room as a study. While my feelings have changed and intensified
since my loss, these reflect feelings about Brenda, rather than the
house itself. I have lost one but not the other, and seek to gain new
meanings about a house which was previously just a pleasant and
comfortable shelter.

Loss and Memories
Eakin argues that "[modern] autobiography seems to have emerged
concurrently with – and is perhaps a symbolic manifestation of – people's acquisition of a distinctly personal space in which to live, rooms
of their own" (1992: 100). While he refers to the process of making
formal publishable narrative, this also applies to my lived experience
in its scattered, yet related, fragments, rooted ultimately in our shared
domestic space. This in turn is related both to my experience of
Brenda and to my attempts to recover some notion of her feelings, and
to commune with these.

I have not experienced my loss as a sad event from which I would
'move on' after some temporary unhappiness, but the kind of life-
shattering trauma that led me to review my life and the world in which
it is lived out. Nicholson has expressed this succinctly:

> In trauma we get a direct view of the "end of the world" [...] For in a very imme-
> diate way trauma destroys the individual's sense of a safe world in which to live
> [...] Trauma touches levels from the family to the community to the society to
> humankind to the natural world to the divine (2002: 132).

Nicholson refers to the threat of severe environmental destruction, but
my much more private loss shattered my whole assumptive world,
leaving a very unsafe and uncertain world, one to whose continuation
I responded with apathy at first. What was shattered seemed to be not
just the meanings of our intimate personal space, but the whole question of purpose and identity that made up my life narrative. This made
me reconsider my relationship with the house that framed part of that

narrative for over eight years; considering what she thought of the place, how she shaped much of its interior, and how I now think about that space. Having no children, and no close in-laws, my house now provides major reminders of her life's meaning, often difficult to interpret. My present and developing feelings are as individual as my loss, reflecting Attig's insistence that "[different] objects and places challenge each of us differently when we grieve. Sometimes the same objects and places challenge individuals differently" (1996: 112).

I have spent much of my period of loss seeking to recover and understand parts of my own biography, and hers in the process. This bears out Attig's assertion that "[bereavement] renders incoherent the stories of our lives with those who died and undermines both the self-identity and the sense of meaning and purpose we previously found in those stories" (1996: 149). This rehabilitation of a shattered world, involving the re-imagining of the past, and attempts to imagine an acceptable future capable of integration with that past, is a gradual and fragmented process. In a way, this is similar to some archive-based research – with the discovery of unexpected sources, the need to re-orient perspectives around those discoveries, and the inspiration of new ideas. It reflects the danger that particular accessible sources can dominate accounts and narratives, excluding that which was significant but went unrecorded (Steedman 2001).

Much of my quest, following my wife's death, has been autobiographical, seeking through recording and writing to understand our lives and the space in which they developed. However, I share the frustration that Fraser expressed towards the end of his study: "I've always thought that history served one purpose at least. By discovering the major factors of change one could learn from them. The same ought to be true of an individual's history" (1984: 187). In my own quest I have aspired to re-educate myself about her and about the whole world, but it may be that no personal history can reveal much that is generally applicable about the world. I have attempted to relate my very isolated feelings to the more general forces that shape residential environments, whose explanation threatens to debunk my personal experience of our home. One source of my personal vulnerability has been the knowledge that individual lives are insignificant and that our house represents little beyond the sentiments with which I now cloak it.

While it remains difficult to approach what might be described as our home life, I am trying to retrieve as much as possible of what is lost, because, unknowingly, this was the most precious part of my life. This life was focused on our home, but also on activities that started and ended there. The frame for this can be described: a semi-detached house, built around 1912, in what was then a semi-rural expanding village, whose suburbanisation was only completed in the early 1930s. We acquired the property in the summer of 1992, at a time of crisis in exchange values. It had an unusual history for a family house, with only two owners from the time of completion to the mid-1980s, being occupied for much of the time by a 'spinster' who had been born and grew to old age there. A childless couple had then bought it and modernised it; as with the spinster and her mother, rarely is this kind of household and the meanings with which they endow their domestic space discussed. We renewed some of their attempts at modernisation, and my wife organised redecoration and carpeting, and re-designed the back garden, but otherwise left the house unchanged.

My main concern was for the study, now abandoned and strewn with unsorted books and papers, in which I wrote two books. She it was who endowed the house with meanings, which I took for granted in what was a comfortable space. I now find it difficult to recall fully my own earlier feelings about this, but they changed markedly once I knew that she was terminally ill (and those meanings were threatened), and have continued to change since. To recover the meanings and memories of this space has been to seek a way back towards her, recreating shared meanings and care in retrospect. However, any conscious recording of memory changes that memory, ordering it into a narrative that may present a false unity or resolution (Lowenthal 1985). In that sense, these are delicate memories, subject to fading or irremediable change.

Loss and the Material Imagination
One impact of my loss has been to erase Brenda from my previously imagined future; this would, of course, have included the house and the way in which it would have changed (or we would have moved) as we grew older and our needs and resources changed. I now focus that imagination upon the past (along with imagined futures that might have been), through a past that might illuminate the future; indeed, musings about a possibly recovered past must both lie in the future

and form a component of a satisfactory future. Part of that process involves the reconstruction of our personal histories, of lives re-imagined, imagining how she viewed her environment in order to re-cover some of the love with which she endowed it, imagining the more solid but psychic events and developments that surround the memories that I alone have, with traces (often ambiguous) of those feelings of hers that they indicate. What is imaginary is not always illusory; to apply imagination may be to falsify or to provide a narra-tive unity where none existed, but anything else would simply repro-duce traces, like a series of archived documents that lack meaning in their uninterpreted form.

Imagination can be a source of 'nostalgia' – a term whose original meaning conveyed a pathological longing for home (Chase and Shaw 1989). Sometimes this 'home' lies solely in the past, often a past im-bued with a desire that may mask the realities that were lived or whose potential was not grasped. Nostalgia is so often associated with deceit (sometimes self-deceit) and misrepresentation that its potential is neglected as a source of negotiation with a past, discovering and understanding the grounds for desire and projecting a better future on this basis. In some ways, memory – connection with a past shared with those we have known but who are now gone – is tainted by the dictates of cultural production, and by its use in political discourses to enhance conservative ideologies. This has curtailed any positive bene-fits that might ensue from attempts to resurrect the past (Wright 1985; Samuel 1994).

Attig suggests that any 'relearning' of the world involved in grief must involve the 'relearning' of our orientation to space:

> As we relearn our worlds, we reorient ourselves within lived space and lived time. We do not experience space as a three-dimensional geometrical coordinate system or as a container that is objectively given and filled with physical objects and other persons [...] Space and time are dimensions within which we orient our-selves and assign places to objects and other persons with reference to our cares, concerns, projects, and everyday undertakings. Within the lived space of human care we experience things, places, and persons as near or remote, not more or less distant by some objective measure [...] As we relearn our physical and social sur-roundings, our tasks include recovering or establishing acceptable or comfortable spatial orientation and distance with particular objects, places and persons (1996: 118-19).

The dangers of the impulse to nostalgia must be acknowledged, but memory may recover the intimate meanings of domestic space, possibly for their expression in new or renewed forms of space elsewhere.

Loss and Domestic Space
While variations in experience and orientation make every loss an individual one, Attig suggests that some common elements in partner grief can be anticipated:

> Anyone who loses a spouse must cope with such objects as clothing worn on special occasions […] a house […] gifts from the spouse, and places such as the rooms where the deceased and the surviving spouse were intimate, the town where they first met, the schools and churches they attended, and the sites of the best and worst times of their lives (1996: 27).

For me, our house is indeed a site for some of the best and worst times of our later lives – especially the worst times, for, although Brenda did not die there (as had been anticipated, in the room which is now my study), it was the place from which she was removed twice in emergency. For many, especially those left alone, the excessive reminders of the worst times combined with the poignancy of associations with happier times can make it necessary to relocate, but my reaction has been the opposite. The best times now dominate memories, although this was a place for savouring memories of visits to and from the house. This was much more quiet reflection than joy, and in that respect the house remains as a place for reflection, some of it on the lost sense of contentment, the latter partly created through the process of looking back.

In a sense the house is like a store of images, with much unchanged since she left, even the contents of wardrobes and the arrangement of crockery and kitchen utensils. Her book collection, steadily accumulated, and the dressing table she bought with her first earnings in the early 1960s, spur reminders and perhaps provide psychic comfort. The undisturbed parts are akin to photographs, which nevertheless reflect the inevitability of passing time. As Sontag put it: "Precisely by slicing out this moment and freezing it, all photographs testify to time's relentless melt" (1977: 15). It is not quite the same environment that she knew, but, like an archive, it contains elements that have survived for later discovery and interpretation (Steedman 2001), like a stage set that gives some framework to a play. To determine the associations of the house is a means of putting this archive of memories to use in constructing a new narrative of her and my past, as I build a new story for my life without her. This apart, it remains in part merely a stage set, which might place some limits on the performances that could take place on the stage, but could not determine the life lived out within its borders, or the happy and unhappy experiences therein (Chapman 2004).

Attig's view of 'care' does not refer to the commodity of 'caring', nor a specific relation to interpersonal feelings, but in a broader Heideggerian view of the fundamental relationship between humans and their spatial environments. Whilst there is much to criticise in Heidegger, there is something fruitful in his idea of fundamental dwelling and the process of building. The work of Gaston Bachelard also relates to dwelling.

Bachelard, Time and Intimate Space

In *The Poetics of Space* Bachelard asserted that childhood encounters with (and relations to) domestic space are seminal, and prior to any psychological or psychoanalytical understanding. This is the one time that is prelinguistic, and not susceptible to the clarifications and potential obfuscations involved in language. Poetics thus provides the link between pre-linguistic experience and a language in which this can be expressed: imagination coming prior to intellect. Unlike Freud's view of the significance of the unconscious, Bachelard's emphasis lay upon the power of daydreaming, of the grasping of the material through the process of imagining.

Bachelard viewed a child's first domestic space as its first universe, but limited his commentary on the world evoked by adult domestic space to memories of childhood space. One puzzling lacuna appears to underlie (or possibly undermine) Bachelard's later musings. In 1920, at the age of thirty-six, he was widowed after only six years of marriage, over half of which he had spent away from home. He seems to have then brought up his only daughter, Suzanne, alone. While widowers' experiences vary, questions arise about his life with Mme Bachelard, and their home, and then, the domestic environment that he inhabited with Suzanne. His re-action to his loss seems to have gone unrecorded, but perhaps he was so traumatised that he was unable to discuss or internalise it later. Possibly memories of childhood were safer, part of a world whose disappearance was inevitable with the transition to adulthood, rather than a world that might (and should) have continued with his wife, and was therefore more difficult to contemplate. It seems strange that his much-vaunted daydreaming did not include his lost wife, their brief years together, his daughter's mother (presumably they must have discussed her), perhaps the life that they might have enjoyed together, and the home which they had made, and which he had left.

One unexplored question is whether Bachelard's feelings were not critically shaped also by his widowhood. Loss marks other turning points in the lives of some widowed people, and their work or location or family relationships have developed very differently from those that might have been expected (Leiberman 1996). Bachelard's career was indeed changed, when he pursued academic studies that led him away from engineering towards philosophy.

His perspectives may reflect an excessive (and pessimistic) view of individual human potential as determined by, or strongly constrained by, childhood experience. In such accounts, the influence of experience and orientations in adult life, including the homes that might be occupied, might not be admitted – along with the ability to transcend and change personal, social and economic circumstances and structures.

Bachelard and 'Felicitous Space'

The impact of widowhood might be considered against the loss (through relocation, modification or at least changed use) of the dwelling that provided a child's formative sense of being and its first universe. Bachelard's solitary example of felicitous domestic space may provide something of this:

> I alone, in my memories of another century, can open the deep cupboard that still retains for me alone that unique odor, the odor of raisins drying on a wicker tray. The odor of raisins! It is an odor that is beyond description, one that it takes a lot of imagination to smell (1994: 13).

This expresses a past imagined, rather than one that is coldly recorded and verifiable. The past is embraced with love, not for persons, but for something that Bachelard clearly considered a part of him, "beyond description". But, it is also the sense of an isolated memory – "I alone" – and this implies that this memory of space must link him to his first home and the "leading characters" (14), the shopkeepers who were his parents, other relatives and friends, presumably all gone by the time he was writing. These memories may also have evoked a vanished, socially intimate world. Memory and imagination are combined in this daydream, and he evokes a memory of space, not actual space that could still be experienced. His 'archive' was made from memory and imagination alone, whereas I still occupy my house in a partly undisturbed state, like an archive or museum of artefacts, protected to foster its interpretation for memory.

The space measured by the surveyor in order to estimate its rental or capital value in a capitalist market is thus not the same as the space of imagination, or dwelling, or (although Bachelard does not step outside domestic space) other space that is valued and the subject of care. This would certainly include space associated with, and consciously modified by, one whom is loved but is gone; these meanings are hard to define and they cannot be readily commodified and transferred. The estimation of value, and its role within the capitalist provision of space, involves imagination of a different form, as is discussed below.

Bachelard does not celebrate adult experiences of space, beyond the incorporation of childhood space into adult memory and daydreaming, or the intimacy, with space and with others, that may develop in adulthood. However, he stresses *felicitous space* that is *eulogized space*. (I am tempted to consider my own home to be *elegised* space). For felicitous space, he proposes two values: protective and imaginary. Its value for protection is one that in turn may need protection, "that may be defended against adverse forces, the space we love" (xxxv). This was both physical shelter, against a world that could be dominated and threatened by nature, and also psychic shelter, from which the world outside (presumably including the social world) could be excluded. This protected space would itself need to be protected, from damage and invasion, by anything or anyone that might cross the threshold between the external and internal worlds (Chapman 1999b). Perhaps in a sense that love of space is closely related to the love for those who (supposedly) protect and who may later exist only in memory in later life – as Fraser put it, "[like] people in books whom you can return to time and again" (1984: 186). In turn, memories of them would need to be protected, as would anything that related to their own memories.

The second value was that of images, which he asserted become dominant:

All really inhabited space bears the essence of the notion of home. In the course of
this work, we shall see that the imagination functions in this direction whenever
the human being has found the slightest shelter: we shall see the imagination behind 'walls' of impalpable shadows, comfort itself with the illusion of protection
(5).

His use of 'illusion' here acknowledges that space may not always
protect, but we feel as though it did. Later he puts it this way:

[The] house is not experienced from day to day only, on the thread of a narrative,
or in the telling of our own story. Through dreams, the various dwelling-places in
our lives co-penetrate and retain the treasures of former days [...] We comfort
ourselves by reliving memories of protection. Something closed must retain our
memories, while leaving them their original value as images (5-6).

This view of felicitous space might be related to my own widower's
home. The house is certainly a protected place, and now seems to provide a haven of safety apart from an indifferent or hostile and impersonal world outside. It is a source of images that attract, memories of
love in the past that continues. It embodies physical shelter supplying
comfort and amenities, and also indicates a form of psychic shelter, a
place to which to retreat but from which the external world can be
safely explored. It is a safe corner of the world, in which there are so
many traces of her, in the way she arranged furniture, picked decora-
tions, set out ornaments, even how particular items were placed in the
kitchen. Sitting in the chair in which she mainly sat, now mine, I stare
at photographs of my younger self on the mantelpiece opposite, and
whilst I hardly need to look at these, I leave them in position as a mark
of her love for me, although I have added some of her. They also
evoke a social world of friends in which she left traces, in those of our
friends who remain friends of mine, although in common with many
widowed people, I have found this much changed.

However, there are also photographs of her family members that I
never knew – representing memories that I could never have. So the
house is now a place of an imagined past, not necessarily one that it is
illusory, but one over which memories are uncertain, and provide
doubtful protection. The house held very different meanings for each
of us, and there is now no other household member to develop new
meanings or to trace and (perhaps) revere old ones. Our house now
evokes my memories of her and my feelings about her memories of

the place, the latter the subject of musings. As I do so, I am aware that this feeling of continuing care must be one of care for *my* memories of *her* life, not necessarily for meanings of the house for her that she would revere. For, once she knew she was terminally ill, she embarked upon a process of ridding the house of objects, including furniture, that she no longer felt belonged there, to break the continuity between the settled domestic space of our household and that of the space in which she is now an 'absent presence'.

Economic Value, Domestic Space and Utopia

My current view of the intimate space forming an archive of artefacts and memory is largely a consequence of my loss. However, my earlier view, of the house as an economic asset, the subject of consumption, failed sometimes to cover my more sentimental feelings towards my home. Had I worked on this essay before my loss, I would have written a much more hard-edged critique of intimate domesticity, with its economic and ecological entanglements; I will now highlight some elements of that critique and the extent to which this could invalidate any feelings about intimate space.

In particular, if it is accepted that childhood domestic space determines elements of adult conceptions of intimate space, the question arises as to how space (and presumably accompanying social and economic arrangements) should be shaped in order to provide more authentic experience. A house is a small world that can form a miniature utopia (an idea that can be promoted, for political and economic reasons), and experiences of domestic space may be related to wider utopias.

Bachelard and Utopia

Bachelard offered no direct prescriptions for the future, for more appropriate forms of space that could advance our experience. Yet he suggested the potential revealed by poetic images, to

> give us back areas of being, houses in which the human being's certainty of being is concentrated, and we have the impression that, by living in such images as these, in images that are as stabilizing as these are, we could start a new life, a life that would be our own, that would belong to us in our very depths (33).

This passionate advocacy, evoking much regret, reflects his tendency to polemicise rather than pursue any detailed analysis or rational prescription. He has been regarded as one of several critics of modernism in the design and provision of housing, but only through a form of nostalgia for a provision of residential space that yielded houses (not apartments) with cellars and attics. The provision of such houses – the sort of larger house in rural areas of the France of his youth – reflected economic factors (including formal imagination of their future use and value) at the time of their design and construction. It is unlikely that the kind of connections with 'earth', with a version of nature, such as that celebrated by Heidegger, is in any way historically accurate. Space already provided and inspired by other motives could form a setting, against the kind of psychic impoverishment to which Bachelard points. Nevertheless, he expresses a secondary view that experiencing "areas of being" would enable "new life"; this may point forward rather than back to a past that cannot be revived, only mourned.

For one whose career at the Sorbonne began in German-occupied Paris in 1940, there seems to be a political silence in Bachelard's work, and it is unclear whether he felt his highest ideals could be realised. Economic issues are also somewhat overlooked. After all, economic value expresses the means by which within capitalism the physical space that is psychically experienced is constructed, ordered and protected from invasion; but he does not discuss economic forces.

It would be relatively easy to dismiss much of Bachelard's writings on space as the meanderings of an elderly provincial bourgeois. He does muse upon experiences that were those of a small and privileged minority (as were mine); few people in the world occupy houses with attics and basements, and few in the overcrowded living space of the Paris of his time could share his nostalgia for a rural provincial home.

Questions arise about his childhood home: Who owned this house, or to whom did his family pay rent, and what happened when its lease or tenancy expired? Who built, maintained and furnished it? Who cut and transported the coal that burnt in the fireplaces and provided him with a comfortable home? Who then cleared the ashes from the grate, and upon whose domestic labour did his childhood depend? Was this domestic labour performed by other children, and what sort of life and habitation did the children of domestic labourers enjoy or endure; what daydreaming would this later evoke for them?

Women appear to be absent from his musings, including the departed and absent Mme Bachelard. There has been much criticism of his explicit references to feminine interiors, evoking images of motherhood in domestic space, and celebrating housework (Martin n.d.). Nevertheless, Bachelard grasps something fundamental in *The Poetics of Space*, but its fragility needs to be surrounded by more solid analysis, in a similar manner to my own delicate memories, readily dismissed but still precious. What is missing is any indication as to how the space that he celebrated and loved has been provided in capitalist societies, or indeed how space might be provided in future.

Harvey, Imagination and Domestic Space
Harvey's recent work (2000) makes much of the use of imagination, but one in which formal, rational, imagination dominates. He considers imagi-nation to be closely related to forms of production and consumption, but also to formulate alternatives that partially circumvent the pressures exerted by structures that realise value in capitalism.

To embody this use and potential role of imagination, he uses the figure of the architect, but distinguishes between the architect as a professional designer of space and the sense in which all humans are architects. His reference to the architect who "shapes and preserves long-term social memories and strives to give material form to the longings and desires of individuals and collectivities" (2000: 200) by no means refers to professional architects alone. While much of the structures whereby buildings are commissioned and designed exclude any consideration of collectivities beyond the narrow class of investors, the architect has some scope to subvert these structures.

How could the mundane and transitory space that my wife occupied, which formed the frame for our lives, be related to the exercise of formal imagination, directly controlled and inspired by us? (Or rather, by her, as she made the significant decisions, and this is one reason why I revere the traces of those choices.)

The form of the building and its location remains anonymous, but decoration, internal arrangement and furnishings made it an individual home, along with the relations between its occupiers, so that its history interlinked with our biographies, for which it formed both expression and constraint. Clearly we do not shape our environments beyond the choice of a previously built and located property; the building itself and its suburban location were long fixed, the former in 1912, the latter from the 1930s. Our choice depended upon the availability of finance, in turn dependant upon incomes and capital released from sales of previous houses. As Fine and Leopold (1993) have stressed, for much consumption, the structures of provision are such that we rarely make such choices from some autonomous expression of our needs.

Even if we had acquired a new property, we would not have much influenced its design, and this reflects not just a division of labour between providers, but also one between male designers and builders, and women who are the intended key consumers of domestic space. As Martin has asserted:

> The gendered dynamics of architecture and building are well-defined: men design and build houses, woman decorate them and make them homely. This script still prevails, even though there are many actual women who perform within the male-defined institutions of architecture and building, improvising variations on that script which subtly undermine its authority (2004: 6).

The interior, and those parts of the exterior (such as the garden) under control, offered scope for transformation, and Brenda especially personalised the rear garden, which she redesigned and set out. (For me, this remains the most poignant part of our house to view and work in). This process, of shaping space, had to be achieved, effectively, through consumption, and unremunerated labour.

Economic Value, Commodities and Domestic Space

Consumption does not represent autonomously and freely exercised choices that express people's needs and drives economic development. Willis has pointed to the unfulfilled promise of consumption, which forms a driving force within capitalism: "No commodity ever lives up to its buyer's expectations or desires. That is because in commodity capitalism, use value cannot be fully realized, but rather haunts its fetishized manifestations in the objects we consume" (1991: 6).

This expresses a much less positive aspect of images and imagination than Bachelard, as a means of rendering experience partly illusory, and fostering consumption that will further promote imaginary means of satisfaction. What is also cloaked is the labour involved in the production of specific commodities, which is again hidden by the nature of commodities and the dominance by a commodified world:

> The abstraction of labor, which is the real basis of the fetish quality of commodities, is not something we as consumers can directly grasp, rather it enters our daily life experience as the inability to apprehend fully or even imagine non-fetishized use-values (Willis 1991: 7).

To this might be added the environmental impact of particular forms of commodities: the general inability to determine how much energy and materials go into their production and use, the impact of waste products on the environment, and the co-consumption necessary to realise satisfactions from that product. The impact of particular forms of housing, its location, and the way in which households tend to occupy need also be considered. Yet only at the margins could it be maintained that the provision of domestic space is driven by this (Brown and Bhatti 2003).

If there is a realm in which the writ of commodity capital does not run, perhaps it can be located inside domestic space, wherein imaginative and intimate feelings could constitute a "non-fetishized" (use) value, so that relations cannot be reduced to mere consumption. And yet, when I wander round my home tidying items away, cooking or washing dishes, this notion feels challenged. Those furnishings which were not mass-produced, built for a quick turnover as this season's model, may have been hand-built in some squalid workshop eighty or ninety years ago; the food in the cupboards was produced and processed for rapid sale and probably transported around the globe to satisfy a supermarket's view of lifestyle consumption; even the humble utilities, the supplies of gas, water and electricity, have been commodified, while their use not only contributes to the profits of post-privatisation transnationals, but helps to exacerbate threatened climate change in the process. All this imagination, by one reading, serves as a cloak to mask a hard reality that we are all consumers now, and even our dreams seem to be constructed around commodities and service the production of further commodities. The frame for intimacy, the house, is physically constructed by house-builders, but they also construct it as an imaginative focus, with the dream of domestic intimacy and an idealised family among the selling points (Chapman 1999a).

Beyond and behind the commodification of much of life, some aspects of experience do seem to remain outside consumption. This may be because they are incapable of being traded, too unique or too commonplace. But it may be because they are beyond consumption, beyond price. An example may lie with the way in which continuing involvement with the departed is mildly subversive of corporate capitalism. As Klass and Goss assert, "[consumer] capitalism has had limited success transforming the dead into commodities or tangible assets […] The continuing bonds with the dead remain largely restricted to the private sphere" (1999: 562). They stress that the roots of the detachment perspective lie both with the Protestant attack on mediaeval Catholicism's continuities between the living and dead, and the drive in capitalism towards satisfaction by commodities rather than the celebration of bonds with the departed. My continuing involvement with the very personal meanings of our house and what it indicates of my wife's feelings may reflect this. It has meant engagement in feelings that are non-reproducible and incapable of replacement by substitute commodities – in that sense facing a loss that can never be recovered or compensated.

Conclusions: Lost Space and Utopias
Much could be idealised about my attempts to access the archive of memory that is my personal domestic space. This reflects the tensions between private concerns and public issues, the subjective space of love and the potential for its objective dismissal through professional work and theoretical analysis, between the insights of materialism and of existential phenomenology, between a tiny but precious and fragile corner of the world and the massive forces that shape the whole world.

Grief is a public issue, such is its significance in every life that it touches. And yet there is little in my biographical experience that can be generalised, even though to do so would, potentially, offer helpful insights to many. I have leant heavily, in writing and in later stages of my grieving, on work inspired by Attig, and yet the theoretical basis for this – Heidegger and the whole discourse of postmodernism – is one that I would challenge in other contexts. In relation to space, a larger study would consider the virtues of the 'detachment' approach, demolishing the virtues of our house as an archive of uncertain memories in favour of perspectives that stress the need to develop a new life and new attachments. For me, however, a liveable future must involve the carrying forward of the past, or at least its more positive elements, as part of a continuing re-learning of the meaning of Brenda's love for me.

Phenomenology offers explanations of our experience of the world, including our experience of the loss of those we love, and the need to engage with new life-narratives which can incorporate, in diverse ways, the space which we have occupied and experienced with those we have lost – most notably, domestic space. Bachelard's insights relate to the fundamental underpinnings of this love of specific space, but without reflections upon the precise nature of psychological superstructures and their modification in the face of loss. His nostalgia is not for something that we might have constructed or modified consciously, but only for the world that we first encounter. This fails to consider the means by which experienced space is constructed, or how it might be constructed (and in what social and economic context) so as to enframe more valuable experience. However, to explain the means by which domestic space is provided, and the manner in which this encourages specific types of experiences is not to explain the way in which that space and the history it embodies is actually experienced.

Domesticity is part of the daily life seen by Harvey as a barrier to social transformation:

> [The] struggle to think alternatives – to think and act differently – inevitably runs up against the circumstances of and the consciousness that derives from a localised daily life. Most insidious of all, is the way in which routine, by virtue of its comfort and security, can mask the ways in which the jarring prospects of transformative change must in the long run be confronted. Where, then, is the courage of our minds to come from? (2000: 237).

One response would be to say that the disruptions of bereavement render daily life not so routine. Some indications of disenchantment with a commodified world may derive from experience of domestic space – the modest subversion involved in 'continuing bonds' with the dead rather than a rapid adjustment before a return to 'normal' acquisitiveness and satisfactions is one point of challenge. Another, as Bachelard highlighted, is the desire to provide space that would be truly ours – interpreted away from a conservative nostalgia towards a more radical appropriation and design of space outside the domestic sphere. These remain, however, fragments against a dominant mode of production indifferent to individual experience unless that can be commodified.

If personal space corresponds to the practice of autobiography, then the potential opened up by the development of privacy and personal lives, despite its detractions and misuses, should be acknowledged. What may be celebrated is the personal intimacy, and the personal growth that it can involve, beyond the uses made of this and the way in which personal space is enframed and structured. If this validates personal space, perhaps the meanings generated by that space need not be dismissed as ephemeral.

Nevertheless, in the production of space, or at least its physical and economic frame, the kind of psychic connections that Bachelard endorses have little purchase compared with the driving forces within capitalism. Only if economic value was to correspond to the values that he endorsed could this kind of domestic space be provided and retained.

If we make nothing of our losses, of the lives that have gone before us, we neglect the purpose of their lives and care for us as we continue to care for them. I have written almost nothing about Brenda herself here, but she did have a greater sense of hope than I, despite many vicissitudes, including an early childhood spent in a very cramped and inadequate terraced house very different from my childhood home or our final home. To record a sense of hope, for myself and for other survivors, is to embrace one of her legacies. Attig has paid tribute to continuing love, which

> is desirable both for the dead and the living. Lasting love is good for those who have died in that it furthers some of their interests. It fulfils their desire to make lasting differences while they are here. It fulfils their desires that we live well and hold dear the good in their lives. And it provides a kind of symbolic immortality, an abiding meaning not touched by death (2004: 357).

I realise that part of my quest in regard to our house is to empathise with the meanings and care she bestowed on that area of space, and to enhance her kind of care towards the wider world. Writing about this is part of my process of relearning the world, engaging in some understanding of the grief that continues, and perhaps explaining to others the renewed significance of our domestic space. This chapter demonstrates the difficulty of grappling with my very personal experience and the tendency to feel that the lack of wider significance threatens to disenfranchise the grief that accompanies it; for some, this would be seen as a pathological condition to be rectified (Craib 1994). Many meanings remain elusive and much of the evidence contradictory; the journey to recover old meanings from our home and to go forward towards new ones is a lengthy and inconclusive one.

REFERENCES
(All titles published in London unless otherwise indicated.)

Adams, Florence. 1973. *I Took A Hammer: The Woman's Build-It and Fix-It Handbook*. Chatsworth, California: Major Books.

Alexander, Catherine. 2002. 'The Garden as Occasional Domestic Space' in *Signs: Journal of Women in Culture and Society* 27(3): 857-72.

Alexander, Christopher. 1979. *The Timeless Way of Building*. New York: Oxford University Press.

Allen, Nicholas and Aaron Kelly (eds). 2003. *The Cities of Belfast*. Dublin: Four Courts Press.

Amis, Martin. 1984. *The Rachel Papers* (1973). Harmondsworth: Penguin.

——2000. *Experience*. Jonathan Cape.

Andrews, Elmer. 1997. '"Some Sweet Disorder" - the Poetry of Subversion: Paul Muldoon, Tom Paulin and Medbh McGuckian' in Day and Docherty: 118-42.

Andrews, George Henry. 1853. *Modern Husbandry: A Practical and Scientific Treatise on Agriculture, Illustrating the Most Approved Practices in Draining, Cultivating and Manuring the Land; Breeding, Rearing and Fattening Stock; and the General Management and Economy of the Farm*. Nathaniel Cooke.

Angyeman, Julian and Rachel Spooner. 1997. 'Ethnicity and the Rural Environment' in Cloke and Little: 197-217.

Anzieu, Didier. 1989. *The Skin Ego*. New Haven. Yale University Press.

Ariès, Philippe.1973. *Centuries of Childhood* (1960). Harmondsworth: Penguin.

Attali, Jacques. 1985. *Noise: The Political Economy of Music* (1977; tr. Brian Massumi). Minneapolis: University of Minnesota Press.

Attfield, Judy. 1995. 'Inside Pram Town: A Case Study of Harlow House Interiors, 1951-1961' in Jackson and Moores: 29-300.

Attfield, Judy and Pat Kirkham (eds). 1994. *A View from the Interior: Women and Design*. The Women's Press, 2nd edition.

Attig, Thomas W. 1996. *How We Grieve: Relearning the World*. Oxford: Oxford University Press.

——2004. 'Meanings of Death Seen Through the Lens of Grieving' in *Death Studies* 28: 341-60.

Attwood, David. 2002. *Sound Design: Classic Audio and Hi-Fi Design*. Mitchell Beazley.

Bachelard, Gaston. 1994. *The Poetics of Space* (1958; tr. Maria Jolas). Boston: Beacon Press.

Baden-Powell, Robert. 2004. *Scouting for Boys: A Handbook for Instruction in Good Citizenship* (1908; ed. Elleke Boehmer) Oxford: Oxford University Press.

Bahloul, Joëlle. 1996. *The Architecture of Memory: A Jewish-Muslim Household in Colonial Algeria, 1937-1962* (1992; tr. Catherine du Peloux Ménagé). Cambridge: Cambridge University Press.

Balk, David E. 2004. 'Recovery Following Bereavement: An Examination of the Concept' in *Death Studies* 28: 361-74.

Barber, Stephen. 1995. *Fragments of the European City*. Reaktion.

Barker, Martin. 1989. *Comics: Ideology, Power and the Critics*. Manchester: Manchester University Press.

Barker, Pat. 1984. *Blow Your House Down*. Virago.

Barrie, J.M. 1994. *Peter Pan* (1911). Harmondsworth: Puffin.

Barry, Peter. 2000. *Contemporary British Poetry and the City*. Manchester: Manchester University Press.

Barthes, Roland. 2000. *Camera Lucida:Reflections on Photography* (1980; tr. Richard Howard). Flamingo.

Bell, Michael Mayerfield. 1994. *Childerley: Nature and Morality in a Country Village*. Chicago and London: University of Chicago Press.

Benjamin, Walter. 1999. *The Arcades Project* (trs. Howard Eiland and Kevin McLaughlin). Cambridge, MA: Belknap Press.

Bennett, Oliver. 2003. 'Music to the Dance of Time' in *The Guardian Weekend* (17 May): 78-80.

Bennett, Tony. 1983. 'Texts, Readers, Reading Formations' in *Literature and History* 3(2): 214-27.

Berland, Jody. 1993. 'Sound, Image and Social Space: Music Video and Media Reconstruction' in Frith and Goodwin: 25-44.

Bettelheim, Bruno. 1982. *The Uses of Enchantment: The Meaning and Importance of Fairy Tales*. Penguin.

Bey, Hakim. 2004. *T.A.Z.: The Temporary Autonomous Zone, Ontological Anarchy, Poetic Terrorism*. Autonomedia.

Bhatti, Mark, Jane Brooke and Mike Gibson. 1994. *Housing and the Environment: A New Agenda*. Coventry: Chartered Institute of Housing.

Bhatti, Mark and Andrew Church. 2004. 'Home: The Culture of Nature and Meanings of Gardens in Late Modernity' in *Housing Studies* 19(1): 37-51.

Billig, Michael. 1995. *Banal Nationalism*. London and New York: Sage.

Bird, Jon. 1995. 'Dolce Domum' in Lingwood: 110-25.

Boime, Albert. 1972. 'The Comic Stripped and Ash Canned: A Review Essay' in *The Art Journal* 32(1): 21-30.

Borden, Iain *et al* (eds). 1996. *Strangely Familiar: Narratives of Architecture in the City*. London and New York: Routledge.

Bourdieu, Pierre. 1990. *The Logic of Practice* (1980; tr. R. Nice). Stanford: Stanford University Press.

——1984. *Distinction: A Social Critique of the Judgment of Taste* (tr. R. Nice). Routledge and Kegan Paul.

Boyce Davies, Carole. 1994. *Black Women, Writing and Identity*. Routledge.

Boym, Svetlana. 2001. *The Future of Nostalgia*. New York: Basic Books.

Brand, Stewart. 1994. *How Buildings Learn: What Happens After They're Built*. Viking.

Branigan, Tania. 2003. 'Pop Charts Head For Obscurity' in *The Guardian* (19 May): 6.

Brett, C.E.B. 2001. 'Victorian and Edwardian Belfast: Preserving the Architectural Legacy of the Inner City' in Neill and Schwedler (eds): 85-99.

Brett, David. 1991. 'Historicism and Modernity: New Building in Belfast' in *Circa* 56: 30-33.

Brown, Tim and Mark Bhatti. 2003. 'Whatever Happened to "Housing and the Environment"?' in *Housing Studies* 18(4): 505-15.

Brunsdon, Charlotte. 2003. 'Lifestyling Britain: The 8-9 Slot on British Television' in *International Journal of Cultural Studies* 6(1): 5-23.

Brunskill, Ronald William. 1992. *Traditional Buildings of Britain: An Introduction to Vernacular Architecture*. Gollancz.

Burnett, John. 1986 *A Social History of Housing 1815-1985*. Methuen.

Burningham, John. 2003. *The Magic Bed*. Jonathan Cape.

Caffyn, Lucy. 1986. *Workers' Housing in West Yorkshire, 1750-1920*. HMSO.

Cameron, Dan. 1993. 'Partial View: Transgressive Identity in Willie Doherty's Photographic Installations' in *Willie Doherty*. Dublin: Douglas Hyde Gallery: s.p.

Carpenter, Humphrey. 1985. *Secret Gardens: A Study of the Golden Age of Children's Literature*. Allen & Unwin.

Carson, Ciarán. 1987. *The Irish for No*. Newcastle-upon-Tyne: Bloodaxe Books.

——1989. *Belfast Confetti*. Meath: Gallery Press.

——1997. *The Star Factory*. Granta.

Caunce, Stephen. A. 2003. 'Houses as Museums: The Case of the Yorkshire Wool Textile Industry' in *Transactions of the RHS* 13: 329-43.

Chamberlain, Mary. 1975. *Fenwomen: A Portrait of Women in an English Village*. Quartet Books.

Chapman, Tony. 1999a. 'Stage Sets for Ideal Lives: Images of Home in Contemporary Show Homes' in Chapman and Hockey (1999): 44-58.

——1999b. 'Spoiled Home Identities: The Experience of Burglary' in Chapman and Hockey (1999): 133-46.

Chapman, Tony and Jenny Hockey (eds.). 1999. *Ideal Homes? Social Change and Domestic Life*. Routledge.

Chase, Malcolm and Shaw, Christopher. 1989. 'The Dimensions of Nostalgia' in Shaw and Chase: 1-17.

Chevalier, Sophie. 2002. 'The Cultural Construction of Space in France and Great Britain', *Signs: Journal of Women in Culture and Society*. 27(31): 847-856.

Childs, Peter and Mike Storry (eds). 1995. *Encyclopaedia of Contemporary British Culture*. Routledge.

Cieraad, Irene (ed). 1999. *At Home: An Anthropology of Domestic Space*. New York: Syracuse University Press.

Clarke, A.B. 1904. 'Cottages for Rural Labourers' in *The Journal of the Royal Agricultural Society of England* 55: 125-47.

Cloke, Paul and Jo Little (eds). 1997. *Contested Countryside Cultures: Otherness, Marginalisation and Rurality*. London and New York: Routledge.

Cohen, Sara. 1991. *Rock Culture in Liverpool: Popular Music in the Making*. Oxford: Clarendon Press.

Cohen, Stan. 2002. *Folk Devils and Moral Panics* (1973). Routledge.

Connor, Valerie *et al* (eds). 2002. *Something Else: Irish Contemporary Art*. Turku: Turku Art Museum.

Corcoran, Neil (ed.). 1992. *The Chosen Ground: Essays on the Contemporary Poetry of Northern Ireland*. Bridgend: Seren Books.

Corrin, Lisa G. *et al* (eds). 2001. *Rachel Whiteread*. Serpentine Gallery of Modern Art.

Crenshaw, Kate. 1994. 'Mapping the Margins: Intersectionality, Identity Politics, and Violence against Women of Color' in Fineman and Mykitiuk: 93-118.

Crisell, Andrew. 1994. *Understanding Radio*. Routledge.

Cunningham, Mark. 1996. *Good Vibrations: A History of Record Production*. Castle.

Dant, Tim.1999. *Material Culture in the Social World*. Buckingham: Open University Press.

Davidoff, Leonore *et al*. 1999. *The Family Story: Blood, Contract and Intimacy 1830-1960*. Longman.

Davidson, Harriet. 1991. '"In the Wake of Home": Adrianne Rich's Politics and Poetics of Location' in Easthope and Thompson: 166-77.

Davis, Fred. 1979. *Yearning for Yesterday: A Sociology of Nostalgia*. New York: Free Press.

Day, Gary and Brian Docherty (eds). 1997. *British Poetry from the 1950s to the 1990s: Politics and Art*. Basingstoke: Macmillan.

Deane, Seamus. 1996. *Reading in the Dark*. Vintage.

de Certeau, Michel. 1984. *The Practice of Everyday Life* (1980; tr. Steven F. Rendall). Berkeley CA: University of California Press.

de Certeau, Michel, Luce Giard and Pierre Mayol. 1998. *The Practice of Everyday Life, Volume 2: Living and Cooking* (1994; tr. Timothy J. Tomasik). Minneapolis: University of Minnesota Press.

de-la Noy, Michael. 1984. *Denton Welch: The Making of a Writer*. Viking.

Derounian, James Garo. 1993. *Another Country: Real Life Beyond Rose Cottage*. NCVO.

Dickens, Charles. 1976. *Great Expectations* (1861). Pan.

Dickson, Albert (ed.). 1985. *Art and Literature* (tr. James Strachey, Penguin Freud Library 14). Harmondsworth: Penguin.

DiMarco, Danette. 1998. 'Exposing Nude Art: Carol Ann Duffy's Response to Robert Browning' in *Mosaic: A Journal for the Interdisciplinary Study of Literature* 31(3): 25-39.

Docherty, Thomas. 1991. 'Ana-; or, Postmodernism, Landscape, Seamus Heaney' in Easthope and Thompson: 68-80.

Doherty, Claire (ed.). 1998. *Claustrophobia*. Birmingham: Icon Gallery.

Doherty, Willie. 1990. *Willie Doherty: Unknown Depths*. Derry: Orchard Gallery.

——1999. *Dark Stains*. San Sebastian: Koldo Mitxelena.

——2002. *False Memory*. Dublin: Irish Museum of Modern Art.

Dreyfus, Herbert L. and Harrison Hall (eds.). 1992. *Heidegger: A Critical Reader*. Oxford: Blackwell.

Douglas, Mary. 1993. 'The Idea of Home: A Kind of Space' in Arien: 261-81.

Duffy, Carol Ann. 1985. *Standing Female Nude*. Anvil.

——1987. *Selling Manhattan*. Anvil.

——1990. *The Other Country*. Anvil.

——1993. *Mean Time*. Anvil.

——1999. *The World's Wife*. Picador.

——2002. *Feminine Gospels*. Picador.

Duffy, Rita. 1997. 'Territory' in *Banquet*. Derry: Ormeau Baths Gallery. S.p.

du Gay, Paul (ed). 1996. *Doing Cultural Studies: A History of the Sony Walkman*. Sage / Open University Press.

Duncan, Nancy (ed.). 1996. *Bodyspace: Destabilizing Geographies of Gender and Sexuality*. Routledge.

——1996a. 'Renegotiating Gender and Sexuality in Public and Private Spaces' in Duncan (1996): 127-45.

Dunleavy, Patrick. 1981. *The Politics of Mass Housing in Britain 1945-1975*. Oxford: Clarendon Press.

Dunne, Aidan. 2001. 'A Broken Surface: Victor Sloan's Photographic Work' in Sloan: 23-147.

Eakin, Paul John. 1992. *Touching the World: Reference in Autobiography*. Princeton: Princeton University Press.

Easthope, Anthony and John O. Thompson (eds). 1991. *Contemporary Poetry Meets Modern Theory*. Hemel Hempstead: Harvester Wheatsheaf.

Ehrenreich, Barbara. 2002. *Nickel and Dimed: Undercover in Low Wage USA*. Granta.

Eisenburg, Evan. 1986. *The Recording Angel: Explorations in Phonography*. Pan.

Ellis, John. 2000. *Seeing Things*. I.B. Tauris.

Erävaara, Taina. 2002. 'Willie Doherty' (tr. Michael Garner) in Connor *et al*: 73.

Faubion, James D. (ed.). 1998. *Aesthetics, Method and Epistemology* (Essential Works of Foucault, Volume Two). Penguin.

Fennell, Desmond. 1991. *Whatever Yor Say, Say Nothing: Why Seamus Heaney is No.1*. Dublin: ELO Publications.

Fine, Ben and Ellen Leopold. 1993. *The World of Consumption*. Routledge.

Fineman, Martha A. and Roxanne Mykitiuk (eds). 1994. *The Public Nature of Private Violence*. Routledge.

Fletcher, J. and A.E. Benjamin (eds). 1990. *Abjection, Melancholia and Love: The Work of Julia Kristeva*. Routledge.

Foucault, Michel. 1986. 'Of Other Spaces' in *Diacritics* 16 (Spring): 22-7.

——1998. 'Different Spaces' (1967) in Faubion: 175-85.

Fraser, Ronald. 1984. *In Search of a Past*. Verso.

Freeman, Mark. 2003. *Social Investigation and Rural England, 1870-1914*. Woodbridge, Suffolk: RHS & Boydell.

Freud, Sigmund. 1985. 'The "Uncanny"' (1919) in Dickson: 335-76.

Frith, Simon and Andrew Goodwin (eds). 1993. *Sound and Vision: The Music Video Reader*. Routledge.

Gaffikin, Frank, Michael Morrissey and Ken Sterrett. 2001. 'Remaking the City: The Role of Culture in Belfast' in Neill and Schwedler: 141-62.

Garber, Marjorie. 2001. *Sex and Real Estate: Why We Love Houses*. New York: Anchor.

Garcia, Jo and Sara Maitland (eds). 1983. *Walking on the Water: Women Talk about Spirituality*. Virago.

Garratt, Sheryl. 1998. *Adventures in Wonderland: A Decade of Club Culture*. Headline.

Gelber, Steven. 1997. 'Do-It-Yourself: Constructing, Repairing and Maintaining Domestic Masculinity' in *American Quarterly* 49(1): 66-112.

Giles, David Clifford. 2002. 'Keeping the Public in Their Place: Audience Participation in Lifestyle Television Programming' in *Discourse and Society* 13(5): 603-28.

Gill, Richard. 1972. *Happy Rural Seat: The English Country House and the Literary Imagination*. New Haven and London: Yale University Press.

Gillis, John R. 1996. *A World of Their Own Making: Myth, Ritual and the Quest for Family Values*. Cambridge, Mass.: Harvard University Press.

Goddard, Henry. 1849. 'On the Construction of a Pair of Cottages for Agricultural Labourers: First Prize Essay' in *Journal of the Royal Agricultural Society of England* 10: 230-46.

Goldstein, Carolyn M. 1998. *Do It Yourself: Home Improvement in Twentieth-Century America*. New York: Princeton Architectural Press.

Graham, Brian. 1998. 'Contested Images of Place among Protestants in Northern Ireland' in *Political Geography* 17(2): 129-44.

Graham, Colin. 2001. *Deconstructing Ireland: Identity, Theory, Culture*. Edinburgh: Edinburgh University Press.

——2001a. 'Metropoli' in *Source Magazine* 26: 7-16.

——2003. 'Belfast in Photographs' in Allen and Kelly: 152-67.

Graham, Colin and Kirkland, Richard (eds). 1999. *Ireland and Cultural Theory: The Mechanics of Authenticity*. Basingstoke: Macmillan.

Grahame, Kenneth. 1999. *The Wind in the Willows* (1908). Oxford: Oxford World's Classics.

Green, David. 1996. 'Thwarted Vision: New Works by Willie Doherty' in *Portfolio* 24: 55-57.

Green, Peter. 1959. *Kenneth Grahame, 1859-193: A Study of his Life, Work and Times*. John Murray.

Gregson, Ian. 2000. *Poetry and Postmodernism: Dialogue and Estrangement*. Basingstoke: Macmillan.

Grier, Katherine C. 1988. *Culture and Comfort: Parlor Making and Middle-Class Identity, 1850-1930*. Washington DC: Smithsonian Institution Press.

Groarke, Vona. 1999. *Other People's Houses*. Meath: Gallery Press.

Gullestad, Marianne. 1995. 'Home Decoration and Popular Culture: Constructing Homes, Genders and Classes in Norway' in Jackson and Moores: 321-35.

Halley, Peter. 1997. 'The Everyday Today: Experience and Ideology' in Harris and Berke: 191-4.

Hanson, Clare. 2000. 'During Mother's Absence: The Fiction of Michèle Roberts' in Werlock: 229-47.

Hardy, Thomas. 1985. *Jude the Obscure*. (1896). Harmondsworth: Penguin.

Harris, Steven and Deborah Berke (eds). 1997. *Architecture of the Everyday*. New York: Princeton Architectural Press.

Harvey, David. *The Condition of Postmodernity: An Enquiry into the Origins of Cultural Change*. Oxford: Basil Blackwell. 1989.

——2000. *Spaces of Hope*. Edinburgh: Edinburgh University Press.

Heaney, Seamus. 1966. *Death of a Naturalist*. Faber.

——1975. *North*. Faber and Faber.

——1980. *Preoccupations: Selected Prose 1968-1978*. Faber.

——1991. *Seeing Things*. Faber.

——1996. *The Spirit Level*. Faber.

Hederman, Mark Patrick. 1985. 'Poetry and the Fifth Province' in *The Crane Bag* 9 (1): 110-119.

Heidegger, Martin. 1993. *Basic Writings*. (rev. edn; ed. D.F. Krell). London and New York: Routledge.

Hillen, Seán. 1999. *Irelantis*. Dublin: Irelantis.

Hillis Miller, J. 1995. *Topographies*. Stanford: Stanford University Press.

Hockey, Jenny, Jeanne Katz and Neil Small (eds). 2001. *Grief, Mourning and Death Ritual*. Buckingham: Open University Press.

Hodge, Joanna. 1995. *Heidegger and Ethics*. London and New York: Routledge.

Holder, Julian. 1998. 'Meyer Vaisman' in Doherty: 84-86.

hooks, bell. 1990. *Yearning: Race, Gender and Cultural Politics*. Boston: South End Press.

Horner, Bruce and Thomas Swiss (eds). 1999. *Key Terms in Popular Music and Culture*. Oxford: Basil Blackwell.

Horton, Patricia. 2001. '"The Half-Sure Legislator": Romantic Legacies in the Writing of Derek Mahon and Tom Paulin' in *Irish University Review* 31(2): 404-19.

Hoskins, W.G. 1955. *The Making of the English Landscape*. Hodder and Stoughton.

Hourihane, Ann Marie. 2000. *She Moves Through the Boom*. Dublin: Sitric Books.

Hughes, Eamonn. 1999. '"Could anyone write it?": Place in Tom Paulin's Poetry' in Graham and Kirkland: 162-92.

Hunt, Pauline. 1995. 'Gender and the Construction of Home Life' in Jackson and Moores: 301-13.

Jackson, Stevi and Shaun Moores (eds). 1995. *The Politics of Domestic Consumption*. Hemel Hempstead: Harvester Wheatsheaf.

James, A., Jencks, C. and Prout, A. 1998. *Theorizing Childhood*. Cambridge: Polity Press.

James, Henry. 1994. *The Turn of the Screw* (1898). Penguin.

Jamieson, Lynn. 1998. *Intimacy: Personal Relationships in Modern Societies*. Cambridge: Polity Press.

Jerome, Jerome K. 1984. *Three Men in a Boat*. (1889). Harmondsworth: Penguin.

Johnstone, Robert. 1990. *Belfast: Portraits of a City*. Barrie and Jenkins.

Jones, Steve. 1992. *Rock Formation: Music, Technology and Mass Communication*. Sage.

Kanneh, Kadiatu. 1998. *African Identities*. Routledge.

Kassabian, Anahid. 1999. 'Popular' in Horner and Swiss: 113-23.

——2002. 'Ubiquitous Listening' in Negus and Hesmondhalgh: 131-42.

Kealey McRae, Jill F. 1994. 'A Woman's Story: *E Pluribus Unum*', in Lieblich and Josselson: 195-229.

Kearney, Richard. 1988. *Transitions: Narratives in Modern Irish Culture*. Manchester: Manchester University Press.

——1997. *Postnationalist Ireland*. London and New York: Routledge.

Kearney, Richard and Mark Patrick Hederman (eds). 1982. *The Crane Bag Book of Irish Studies*. Dublin: Blackwater Press.

Keightley, Keir. 1996. '"Turn it down!"' she shrieked: Gender, Domestic Space and High Fidelity, 1948-59' in *Popular Music* 15(2): 149-77.

King, Anthony. 1990. *Global Cities: Post Imperialism and the Internationalization of London*. Routledge.

Kinnahan, Linda A. 2000. '"Now I am *Alien*": Immigration and the Discourse of Nation in the Poetry of Carol Ann Duffy' in Rees-Jones and Mark: 208-26.

Kirby, Peadar, Luke Gibbons and Michael Cronin (eds). 2002. *Reinventing Ireland: Culture, Society and the Global Economy*. Pluto Press.

Klass, Dennis and Robert Goss. 1999. 'Spiritual Bonds to the Dead in Cross-cultural and Historical Perspective: Comparative Religion and Modern Grief' in *Death Studies* 23: 547-67.

Klein, Melanie. 1986. 'Notes on Some Schizoid Mechanisms' (1946) in Mitchell: 176-200.

Kristeva, Julia. 1990. 'The Adolescent Novel' in Fletcher and Benjamin: 8-23.

Kubert, Joe. 1998. *Fax from Sarajevo, A Story of Survival*. Milwaukie: Dark Horse Books.

Kundera, Milan. 1995. *Testaments Betrayed* (1993; tr. Linda Asher). Faber and Faber.

La Breque, Eric.1993. 'In Search of the Graphic Novel' in *Print* 47: 21-35.

Langhamer, Claire. 2005. 'The Meanings of Home in Postwar Britain' in *Journal of Contemporary History* 40(2): 341-62.

Lanza, Joseph. 1995. *Elevator Music*. Quartet.

Laufer, Moses. 1989. 'Adolescent Sexuality: A Mind / Body Continuum' in *The Psychoanalytic Study of the Child* 44: 281-94.

Lawrence, Roderick J. 1987. *Housing, Dwellings and Homes: Design Theory, Research and Practice*. Chichester: John Wiley and Sons.

Lawson, Bryan. 2001. *The Language of Space*. Oxford: Architectural Press.

Le Corbusier 1946. *Towards a New Architecture* (1923; tr. F. Etchells). The Architectural Press.

Lefebvre, Henri. 1984. *Everyday Life in the Modern World* (1968; tr. S. Rabinovitch). New Brunswick: Transaction.

Levy, Gideon. 2003. 'The Lowest Points in Israel' in Segal and Weizman: 167-72.

Lewis, C.S. 1969. *The Lion, the Witch and the Wardrobe* (1950). Harmondsworth: Penguin.

Lieberman, Morton. 1996. *Doors Open, Doors Close: Widows Grieving and Growing*. New York: Grosset / Putnam.

Lieblich, Amia and Ruthellen Josselson (eds). 1994. *Exploring Identity and Gender: The Narrative Study of Lives*. London and New Dehli: Sage.

Lingwood, James (ed.). 1995. *Rachel Whiteread: House*. Phaidon Press.

——1995a. 'Introduction' in Lingwood (1995): 6-11.

Lively, Penelope. 2001. *A House Unlocked*. Viking.

Longley, Edna. 1994. *The Living Stream: Literature and Revisionism in Ireland*. Newcastle-upon-Tyne: Bloodaxe.

Longley, Michael. 1998. *Selected Poems*. Jonathan Cape.

Lorés, Maite. 1999. 'The Streets Were Dark with Something More Than Night: Film Noir Elements in the Work of Willie Doherty' in Doherty: 110-17.

Lowenthal, David. 1985. *The Past is a Foreign Country*. Cambridge: Cambridge University Press.

Luckhurst, Roger. 1996. '"Impossible Mourning" in Toni Morrison's *Beloved* and Michèle Roberts's *Daughters of the House*' in *Critique* 37(4): 243-60.

Lury, Celia. 1996. *Consumer Culture*. Cambridge: Polity Press.

Lyotard, Jean-François. 1991. *The Inhuman: Reflections on Time*. (1988; tr. Geoffrey Bennington and Rachel Bowlby) Cambridge: Polity Press.

McAllister, Andrew. 1988. 'Interview with Carol Ann Duffy' in *Bête Noire* 6: 69-77.

McCloud, Scott. 1994. *Understanding Comics*. New York: Harper Collins.

McDonaugh, Paul. 1991. Review of *The Irish for No* (1987) and *Belfast Confetti* (1989) by Ciaran Carson in *Éire-Ireland: An Interdisciplinary Journal of Irish Studies* 26(1): 120-26.

McEldowney, Malachy, Ken Sterrett and Frank Gaffikin. 2001. 'Architectural Ambivalence: The Built Environment and Cultural Identity in Belfast' in Neill and Schwedler: 100-17.

McGonagle, Declan. 1987. 'Troubled Land'. *Troubled Land: The Social Landscape of Northern Ireland*. Grey Editions. s.p.

McGuckian, Medbh. 1988. *On Ballycastle Beach*. Oxford: Oxford University Press.

Mack, Arien (ed.). 1993. *Home: A Place in the World*. New York: New York University Press.

Maclean, Gerald, Donna Landry and Joseph P. Ward (eds). 1999. *The Country and the City Revisited: England and the Politics of Culture, 1550-1850*. Cambridge: Cambridge University Press.

McLeer, Brigid. 1998. 'Collapsing Here' in *Circa* 86: 17-22.

MacNeice, Louis. 1988. *Selected Poems* (ed. Michael Longley). Faber.

Mandelstam, Nadezhda. 1971. *Hope Against Hope: A Memoir* (tr. M. Hayward). Collins.

Marc, Olivier. 1977. *Psychology of the House* (tr. Jessie Wood). Thames and Hudson.

Marshall, Catherine. 2003. *The Unblinking Eye: Lens-based Work from the IMMA Collection*. Dublin: Irish Museum of Modern Art.

Massey, Doreen. 1994. *Space, Place and Gender*. Cambridge: Polity Press.

——1995. 'Space-Time and the Politics of Location' in Lingwood (1995): 34-49.

——1996. 'The Trees will Outlast us All' in Borden *et al*: 74-76.

Mezei, Kathy and Chiara Briganti. 2002. 'Reading the House: A Literary Perspective' in *Signs: Journal of Women in Culture and Society* 27(3): 837-46.

Michaux, Henri. 1992. *Spaced, Displaced* (1985) (tr. D. and H. Constantine). Newcastle Upon Tyne: Bloodaxe.

Michelis, Angelica and Antony Rowland. 2003. *The Poetry of Carol Ann Duffy: 'Choosing Tough Words'*. Manchester: Manchester University Press.

——2003a. '"Me not know what these people mean": Gender and National Identity in Carol Ann Duffy's Poetry' in Michelis and Rowland: 77-98.

Millard, Andre. 1996. *America On Record: a History of Recorded Sound*. Cambridge: Cambridge University Press.

Mitchell, Juliet (ed.). 1986. *The Selected Melanie Klein*. Harmondsworth: Peregrine.

Moran, Joe. 2002. 'Childhood and Nostalgia in Contemporary Culture' in *The European Journal of Cultural Studies* 5(2): 155-73.

Morley, David. 2000. *Home Territories: Media, Mobility and Identity*. Routledge.

Morrison, Toni. 1989. *Beloved*. Picador.

——1993. *Jazz*. Picador.

——1998. *Paradise*. Chatto & Windus.

Moseley, Rachel. 2000. 'Makeover Takeover on British Television' in *Screen* 41(3): 299-315.

Mostafavi, Mohsen and David Leatherbarrow. 1993. *On Weathering: The Life of Buildings in Time*. Cambridge, MA: MIT Press.

Moy, Ron. 2000. *An Analysis of the Position and Status of Sound Ratio in Contemporary Society*. Lewiston, N.Y.: Edwin Mellen Press.

Murtagh, Brendan. 2002. *The Politics of Territory: Policy and Segregation in Northern Ireland*. Basingstoke: Palgrave.

Muthesius, Stefan. 1982. *The English Terraced House*. New Haven, CT: Yale University Press.

Myerson, Julie. 2004. *Home: The Story of Everyone Who Ever Lived in Our House*. Flamingo.

Nakazawa, Keiji. 1972-73. *Hadashi no Gen*. Tokyo, Project Gen (tr. by Project Gen and republished 1989 as *Barefoot Gen: A Cartoon Story of Hiroshima* by Penguin Books).

Negus, Keith and Hesmondhalgh, Desmond. 2002. *Popular Music Studies*. Arnold.

Neill, William J. V. 2001. 'The Urban Planning Context in Belfast: A City Between War and Peace' in Neill and Schwedler: 42-53.

Neill, William J.V. and Hanns-Uve Schwedler (eds). 2001. *Urban Planning and Cultural Inclusion: Lessons from Belfast and Berlin*. Basingstoke: Palgrave.

NESC (National Economic and Social Council Report No. 105). 1999. *Opportunities, Challenges and Capacities for Choice*. Dublin: Stationery Office.

Neville-Grenville, Ralph. 1973. 'Cottages' in *The Journal of the Bath and West of England Society for the Encouragement of Agriculture* (3rd series) 5: 196-8.

Newman, Oscar. 1972. *Defensible Space: People and Design in the Violent City*. Architectural Press.

Nicholson, Sherry W. 2002. *The Love of Nature and the End of the World*. Massachusetts: MIT Press.

Noorman, Klaas Jan and Ton Schoot Uiterkamp. 1998. *Green Households?: Domestic Consumers, Environment and Sustainability*. Earthscan Publications.

Nora, Pierre (ed.). 1996. *Realms of Memory: Rethinking the French Past, Volume 1: Conflicts and Divisions*. (tr. A. Goldhammer, ed. L. D. Kritzman). New York: Columbia University Press.

——1996a. 'General Introduction: Between Memory and History' in Nora (1996): 1-20.

Normile, John (ed.) 1945. *New Ideas for Remodelling your Home*. Special issue of *Better Homes & Gardens*. Des Moines, USA: Meredith Corp.

Nye, Andrea. 1994. *Philosophia*. Routledge.

O'Donoghue, Bernard. 1992. 'Involved Imaginings: Tom Paulin' in Corcoran: 171-88.

Oliver, Paul. 1987. *Dwellings: The House Across the World*. Austin: University of Texas Press.

Ortner, Sherry B. 1974. 'Is Female to Male as Nature is to Culture?' in Rosaldo and Lamphere: 67-87.

O'Toole, Fintan. 1997. *The Ex-Isle of Erin*. Dublin: New Island Books.

——1997a. *The Lie of the Land: Irish Identities*. New Island Books.

——1999. 'Introducing *Irelantis*', *Irelantis*. Dublin: Irelantis: s.p.

——2003. *After the Ball*. Dublin: New Island Books.

Owen, Ursula (ed.). 1983. *Fathers: Reflections by Daughters*. Virago.

Patterson, Glenn. 2003. *Number 5*. Hamish Hamilton.

Paul, Samuel. 1954. *The Complete Book of Home Modernizing*. New York: Stuttman & Co.

Paulin, Tom. 1980. *The Strange Museum*. Faber.

——1983. *Liberty Tree*. Faber.

——1984. *Ireland and the English Crisis*. Newcastle: Bloodaxe.

——1985. *The Riot Act: A Version of Sophocles' Antigone*. Faber.

——1987. *Fivemiletown*. Faber.

——1992. *Minotaur: Poetry and the Nation State*. Faber.

——1994. *Walking a Line*. Faber.

——1998. *The Daystar of Liberty: William Hazlitt's Radical Style*. Faber.

——1999. *The Wind Dog*. Faber.

——2002. *The Invasion Handbook*. Faber.

——2004. 'Shades Off, No Sheds' in *Times Literary Supplement* (30 January 2004): 5.

Pearce, Susan M. (ed.). 1994. *Interpreting Objects and Collections*. London and New York: Routledge.

——1994a. 'Objects as Meaning; or Narrating the Past' in Pearce (1994): 19-29.

Pennartz, Paul J.J. 1999. 'Home: The Experience of Atmosphere' in Cieraad (1999): 95-106.

Perec, Georges. 1997. *Species of Space and Other Pieces* (1974; tr. John Sturrock). Penguin.

Perryman, Mark. 1994. *Altered States: Postmodernism, Politics, Culture*. Lawrence and Wishart.

Phelan, Vincent B. 1949. *Handy Manual of House Care and Repair*. Washington: US Government Print Off.

Philo, Chris. 1992. 'Neglected Rural Geographies' in *The Journal of Rural Studies* 8(3): 193-207.

Prendergast, Mark. 2000. *The Ambient Century*. Bloomsbury.

Radford, Jean (ed.). 1986. *The Progress of Romance: The Politics of Popular Fiction*. Routledge and Kegan Paul.

Rajchman, John. 1998. *Constructions*. Massachusetts: MIT Press.

Raleigh Yow, Valerie. 1994. *Recording Oral History: A Practical Guide for Social Scientists*. London and New Dehli: Sage.

Ravetz, Alison. 1994. 'A Place of Their Own' in Attfield and Kirkham: 187-205.

Reed, Christopher (ed.). 1996. *Not at Home: The Suppression of Domesticity in Modern Art and Architecture*. Thames and Hudson.

Rees-Jones, Deryn. 1999. *Carol Ann Duffy*. Devon: Northcote.

Rees-Jones, Deryn and Alison Mark (eds). 2000. *Women's Poetry: Reading, Writing, Practice*. Basingstoke: Macmillan.

Reynolds, Simon. 1998. *Energy Flash*. Picador.

Rietveld, Hillegonda. 1998. *This Is Our House: House Music, Cultural Spaces and Technologies*. Aldershot: Ashgate / Arena.

Roberts, Michèle. 1983. 'The Woman who Wanted to be a Hero' in Garcia and Maitland: 50-65.

——1983a. 'Questions and Answers' in Wandor: 62-8.

——1983b. 'Outside My Father's House' in Owen: 105-12.

——1986. 'Write, She Said' in Radford: 221-36.

——1993. *Daughters of the House*. Virago.

——1994. 'Post-Script' in Roe: 169-75.

Roe, Sue *et al*. 1994. *The Semi-Transparent Envelope: Women Writing - Feminism and Fiction*. Marion Boyars.

Romines, Ann. 1992. *The Home Plot: Women Writing and Domestic Ritual*. Amherst: University of Massachusetts Press.

Rosaldo, Michelle Z. and Louise Lamphere (eds). 1974. *Woman, Culture and Society*. Stanford: Stanford University Press.

Rose, Jacqueline. 1984. *The Case of Peter Pan, or, The Impossibility of Children's Fiction*. Basingstoke: Macmillan.

Rosen, Harold. 1998. *Speaking from Memory: The Study of Autobiographical Discourse*. Trentham Books, Stoke-on-Trent.

Rybczynski, Witold. 1986. *Home: A Short History of an Idea*. Pocket Books.

Sabin, Roger. 1993. *Adult Comics: An Introduction*. Routledge.

Sacco, Joe. 2003. *Palestine* (1993). Jonathan Cape.

Sage, Lorna. 1992. *The House of Fiction: Postwar Women Novelists*. Basingstoke: Macmillan.

Said, Edward W. 2003. 'Foreword' (2001) in Sacco: i-v.

Said, Edward W. and Mohr, Jean. 1993. *After the Dark Sky: Palestinian Lives*. Vintage.

Samuel, Raphael. 1994. *Theatres of Memory, Volume 1: Past and Present in Contemporary Culture*. Verso.

Sara, Dorothy. 1955. *The New American Home Fix-It Book*. New York: Books Inc.

Sayers, Janet. 1998. *Boy Crazy: Remembering Adolescence, Therapies and Dreams*. Routledge.

Sceats, Sarah. 1996. 'Eating the Evidence: Women, Power and Food' in Sceats and Cunningham: 117-27.

Sceats, Sarah and Gail Cunningham (eds). 1996. *Image and Power: Women in Fiction in the Twentieth Century*. Longman.

Schlieker, Andrea. 2001. 'Pause for Thought: The Public Sculptures of Rachel Whiteread' in Corrin *et al*. 59-65.

Schwartz Cowan, Ruth. 1989. *More Work for Mother: The Ironies of Household Technology from the Hearth to the Microwave*. Free Association Books.

Seawright, Paul. 2000. *Paul Seawright*. Salamanca: Ediciones Universidad Salamanca. 83-105.

Sebold, Alice. 2003. *The Lovely Bones*. Picador.

Segal, Rafi and Eyal Weizman (eds). 2003. *A Civilian Occupation: The Politics of Israeli Architecture*. Tel Aviv / London, New York: Babel / Verso.

Sendak, Maurice. 1988. *Where the Wild Things Are* (1963). Bodley Head.

Sharrock, David. 1995. 'A Door into the Dark' in *The Guardian* (12 October 1995): 62-4.

Shaw, Christopher and Malcolm Chase (eds). 1989. *The Imagined Past: History and Nostalgia*. Manchester: Manchester University Press.

Short, John R. 1982. *Housing in Britain: The Post-War Experience*. Methuen.

Sinclair, Iain. 1998. *Lights Out for the Territory: Nine Excursions in the Secret History of London*. Granta.

Small, Neil. 2001. 'Theories of Grief: A Critical Review' in Hockey, Katz and Small: 19-48.

Smyth, Gerry. 1998. *Decolonisation and Criticism: The Construction of Irish Literature*. Pluto Press.

——2001. *Space and the Irish Cultural Imagination*. Basingstoke: Macmillan.

Sontag, Susan. 1977. *On Photography*. Allen Lane.

Spiegelman, Art. 1986. *Maus - A Survivor's Tale: Volume I - My Father Bleeds History*. Penguin.

——1992. *Maus - A Survivor's Tale: Volume II - And Here My Troubles Began* (1991). Penguin.

Spufford, Francis. 2002. *The Child that Books Built.* Faber and Faber.

Steedman, Carolyn. 1986. *Landscape for a Good Woman: A Story of Two Lives.* Virago.

——1995. *Strange Dislocations: Childhood and the Idea of Human Interiority, 1780-1930.* Virago.

——2001. *Dust.* Manchester: Manchester University Press.

Stevenson, R.L. 1966. *A Child's Garden of Verses.* (1913). Oxford University Press.

——1998. *Treasure Island* (1883). Oxford: Oxford World's Classics.

Stewart, Susan. 1999. *On Longing: Narratives of the Miniature, the Gigantic, the Souvenir, the Collection* (1993). Durham: Duke University Press.

Stone, Lawrence. 1977. *Family, Sex and Marriage in England 1500-1700.* New York: Harper and Row.

Swiss, Thomas, John Sloop and Andrew Herman (eds). 1998. *Mapping the Beat: Popular Music and Contemporary Theory.* Oxford: Blackwell.

Taylor, Charles. 1989. *Sources of the Self: The Making of Modern Identity.* Cambridge: Cambridge University Press.

——1992. 'Heidegger, Language, and Ecology' in Dreyfus and Hall: 247-69.

Taylor, Lisa. 2002. 'From Ways of Life to Lifestyle: The Ordinarization of British Gardening Lifestyle Television' in *European Journal of Communication* 17(4): 479-93.

Théberge, Paul. 1997. *Any Sound You Can Imagine: Making Music / Consuming Technology.* Middletown CT: Wesleyan University Press.

Thompson, Flora. 1979. *Lark Rise to Candleford: A Trilogy* (1939, 1941, 1943). Harmondsworth: Penguin.

Thompson, Michael. 1979. *Rubbish Theory.* Oxford: Oxford University Press.

Tobin, Gráinne. 2002. *Banjaxed.* Kilcar: Summer Palace Press.

Toop, David. 1995. *Ocean of Sound: Aether Talk, Ambient Sound And Imaginary Worlds.* Serpent's Tail.

Tosh, John. 1999. *A Man's Place: Masculinity and the Middle-Class Home in Victorian England.* Yale University Press.

Townsend, Sue. 1982. *The Secret Diary of Adrian Mole aged 13 ¾.* Methuen.

Turner, Victor. 1969. *The Ritual Process: Structure and Anti-Structure.* New York: Aldine de Gruyter.

Vidler, Anthony. 1992. *The Architectural Uncanny: Essays in the Modern Unhomely.* Cambridge, MA: MIT Press.

Yow, Valerie. 1994. *Recording Oral History: Practical Guide for Social Scientists.* Sage.

Viner, Katherine. 1999. 'Metre Maid' in *The Guardian* (25 September 1999).

Walker, Lynne. 2002. 'Home Making: An Architectural Perspective' in *Signs: Journal of Women in Culture and Society* 27(3): 823-36.

Wallace, Marjorie. 1996. *The Silent Twins* (1986). Vintage.

Walter, Tony. 1994. *The Revival of Death.* Routledge.

——1999. *On Bereavement: The Culture of Grief.* Buckingham: Open University Press.

Wandor, Michelene (ed.). 1983. *On Gender and Writing.* Pandora.

Ware, Chris. 2001. *Jimmy Corrigan: The Smartest Kid on Earth.* Jonathan Cape.

Welch, Denton. 1950. *In Youth is Pleasure.* Vision Press.

——1984. *The Journals of Denton Welch* (1952; ed. Michael De-la-Noy). Allison and Busby.

Welsh, Irvine. 2002. *Glue*. Vintage.

Werlock, Abby H.P. (ed.). 2000. *British Women Writing Fiction*. Tuscaloosa: University of Alabama Press.

Wheeler, Wendy. 1994. 'Nostalgia isn't Nasty: The Postmodernising Parliamentary Democracy' in Perryman: 90-112.

Whitaker, T.K. 1958. *Economic Development*. Dublin: The Stationery Office.

Whiteread, Rachel. 2001. 'A Conversation with Rachel Whiteread, March 2001', in Corrin *et al*: s.p.

Wicks, Susan. 2000. 'Home Fires' in Rees-Jones and Mark: 18-23.

Williams, Raymond. 1979. *Culture and Society 1780-1950* (1958). Penguin.

Willis, Paul. 1978. *Profane Culture*. Routledge.

Willis, Susan. 1991. *A Primer for Daily Life*. Routledge.

Winnicott, D.W. 1999. *Playing and Reality* (1971). Routledge.

Woolf, Virginia. 1993. *A Room of One's Own and Three Guineas*, (1929; ed. M. Barnett). Harmondsworth: Penguin.

Wright, Patrick. 1985. *On Living in an Old Country*. Verso.

Wullschläger, Jackie. 2001. *Inventing Wonderland: The Lives of Lewis Carroll, Edward Lear, J.M. Barrie, Kenneth Grahame and A.A. Milne*. Methuen.

Yates, Frances. 1984. *The Art of Memory* (1966). Ark.

Yorke, Liz. 1999. *Impertinent Voices: Subversive Strategies in Contemporary Women's Poetry*. London and New York: Routledge.

Young, Michael and Peter Willmott. 1962. *Family and Kinship in East London* (1957). Harmondsworth: Penguin.

Zipes, Jack. 1991. *Fairy Tales and the Art of Subversion*. Routledge.

Other Sources

Adams, Jeff. 2000. Interview with Joe Sacco (author of *Palestine*), 11 September 2000 (unpublished).

Amenábar, Alejandro (dir.). 2001. *The Others*.

Amos, Tori. 1996. *Hey Jupiter*. East West.

Aust, Rebecca and Jon Simmons. 14th March 2002. *Rural Crime: England and Wales*. On line as http:www.homeoffice.gov.uk/rds/pdfs2/hosb102.pdf (consulted 20.01.2004).

BBC *Changing Rooms* Factsheet. On line at http:www.bbc.co.uk/homes/design_inspiration/factsheets/715.shtml (consulted 30.03.2005).

Bentham, Jane. 2002. Selections from an interview with Carol Ann Duffy in *Young Writer Magazine* 20 (January). On line at http:www.mystworld.com/youngwriter/authors/carolannduffy/ (consulted 21.09.2004).

Changing Rooms (Bazal for BBC, 1996-2005).

Clayton, Jack (dir.). 1961. *The Innocents*.

Davies, John. On line at http:www.johndavies.uk.com/metropoli.htm (consulted 11.10.2004).

Dion. Celine. 2002. *A New Day Has Come* Radio Remix. Sony.

——*A New Day Has Come* Album Edit. Sony.

Friedkin, William (dir.). 1973. *The Exorcist.*

Hitchcock, Alfred (dir.). 1960. *Psycho.*

Hooper, Tobe (dir.). 1974. *The Texas Chainsaw Massacre.*

Martin, Sylvia. *The House That Lizzie and Sylvia Built.* On line at http:www.skk.uit.no/WW99/papers/Martin_Sylvia.pdf (consulted 16.04.2004).

Myrick, Daniel and Eduardo Sanchez (dirs). 1999. *The Blair Witch Project.*

Mirza, Munira. 'All the table's a stage'. On line at http:www.spiked-online.co.uk (consulted 30.03.2001).

Natsume, Fusanosuke. 2002. 'The Structure of Manga Expression'. Paper presented at the symposium *Manga and Art: Visual Culture in Contemporary Japan* (London College of Fashion, London W1, 1 February 2002; organised by Chelsea College of Art and the Japan Foundation).

Peckinpaw, Sam (dir.). 1971. *Straw Dogs.*

Pool, William Henry, Grocer's Account Books. 1872-1950. Chipstable, Somerset, (MERL Reading, P POOL AC1/3; P POOL AC1/4; P POOL AC1/5; P POOL AC1/6).

Said, Edward W. 1998. *In Search of Palestine.* BBC TV, screened in the UK on 17 May 1998 at 20.00hrs on BBC 2.

Shyamalan, M. Night (dir.). 1999. *The Sixth Sense.*

Sloan, Victor. 2001. *Victor Sloan: Selected Works, 1980-2000.* Text by Aidan Dunne and Gerry Burns. Derry: Ormeau Baths Gallery / Orchard Gallery.

Social Trends 32. 2002. The Stationery Office.

Social Trends 35: 2005 edition. On line at http:www.statistics.gov.uk (consulted 30.03.2005).

http:www.sbu.ac.uk/~stafflag/carolannduffy.html (consulted 21.09.2004).

INDEX